JUNG
AND THE
LOST GOSPELS

Cover art by *Ann Kilgore*

Illustrations by *Jan Saether*

STEPHAN A. HOELLER

JUNG
AND THE
LOST GOSPELS

INSIGHTS INTO THE DEAD SEA SCROLLS
AND THE NAG HAMMADI LIBRARY

A publication supported by
THE KERN FOUNDATION

Quest Books
Theosophical Publishing House

Wheaton, Illinois ♦ Chennai (Madras), India

Fifth Printing 2002

The Theosophical Publishing House
306 West Geneva Road
Wheaton, Illinois 60187

A publication of the Theosophical Publishing House,
a department of the Theosophical Society in America.

Library of Congress Cataloging-in-Publication Data:

Hoeller, Stephan A.
    Jung and the lost Gospels : insights into the Dead Sea
scrolls and the Nag Hammadi library / Stephan A. Hoeller.
    —1st ed. p.   cm.
    Includes bibliographical references.
    ISBN 0-8356-0652-X
    ISBN 0-8356-0646-5 (pbk.)
    1. Jung, C. G. (Carl Gustav), 1875-1961—Contributions in
occultism.   2. Jung, C. G. (Carl Gustav), 1875-1961—
Contributions in gnosticism.   3. Dead Sea scrolls—
Criticism, interpretation, etc.   4. Nag Hammadi codices—
Criticism, interpretation, etc.   5. Occultism.   6. Gnosticism.
I Title.
BF1999.H623   1989
296.1'55—dc20   89-40174
                                                      CIP

Printed in the United States of America

Once again to Kristofer, dear friend and helper;
and to Sidney and Jean Lanier, with grateful thanks

Contents

Foreword
June Singer

When the canon of the Bible was closed, those who determined what should constitute the Holy Writ and stand as a bulwark against heathenism and heresy had their reasons for excluding some writings while including others. Surely there were questions of authenticity and quality, but there was also an urgency to establish a standard by which all other religious expressions could be measured in the future. Both Judaism and Christianity had suffered the necessity of clarifying and strengthening their doctrines so that their adherents would have a firm basis for withstanding the opposition they faced from the pagan world and from Rome. These formulations necessarily left little room for individual interpretation or variance from the newly established norms.

Among Jews and also among the early Christians, there were those dissidents whose points of view differed from that proclaimed in the Bible concerning what constitutes the spiritual life and, in Christianity, what was the true nature and teaching of the Anointed One sent by God to proclaim His message to humankind. Their writings, contemporary with the biblical books, were considered dangerous or spurious by the reigning religious authorities, and the writers of those extra-canonical works were branded as heretics—which indeed they were if heresy means taking a position in opposition to the orthodoxy of the times. The writings nevertheless became touchstones for communities whose members sought freedom of thought and of worship, relief from the imposition of authority, and an opportunity to experience

ix

God directly without mediation by a churchly hierarchy. Much of the content of these works had to do with eschatology, the portents of the Last Days when God would rain down destruction upon His people because of their having capitulated to the forces of evil in the world. Also expressed in these works was a hope for eventual redemption, depicted among Jews as the coming of a Messianic Age and in Christianity as the Second Coming of Jesus Christ. Over the years many of these works were lost, some were preserved and continued to be read as more or less esoteric literature, and some were secreted in caves and other unlikely places awaiting another time when the world might be more ready to attend to their messages.

Until 1945, only a few fragments of the lost gospels were available for reading by the public. Here and there some scholars and seekers learned of the existence of certain of the writings and studied them. Among these was the great Swiss psychiatrist C. G. Jung. It was in 1945, you will remember, when the United States, in the cause of peace, dropped atomic bombs upon Hiroshima and Nagasaki. Curiously enough, within a year or two of that date, were discovered the two most important finds of this lost sacred literature in modern history. One was the Dead Sea Scrolls, the work of the men of the ascetic Jewish community of Essenes at Qumran, near Jerusalem; the other was the Nag Hammadi library, a collection of papyrus books written by members of a Gnostic sect within two or three hundred years after the time of Jesus and found in a jar in a cave in upper Egypt. From the time of their discovery until now, the new-found treasures have kept teams of scholars occupied in piecing them together, deciphering them, and attempting to understand them.

Indispensable as the work of these learned men and women has been, their scholarship is only the vital opening act to a drama of cosmic proportions. These scholars' contribution in their first act was to understand the words and then the context from which they were written before any interpretation could be undertaken. The second act would have to concern apprehending the personal psychological significance of this material for people today, and the third would consist of understanding this mythic material in terms of its wider, even global, significance. Scholars and translators working on the Dead Sea Scrolls and the Nag Hammadi books have been pursuing their endeavor with the requisite dedication to objectivity. Consequently one rarely detects in their work any indication of the degree to which they themselves are or are not in sympathy with the particular perspectives that characterize these texts.

If one were to describe these documents in a single word, that word would be *heterodox*, in the sense of differing from, or contrary to, an established religious point of view. These works are radical departures from the normative Judaism or orthodox Christianity of their times. The early Church Fathers had no difficulty declaring the Gnostic Gospels heretical. Scholars today who undertake the study of religious texts in the ancient Semitic or Coptic languages as a rule come from fields such as biblical theology and criticism. The academic rigor of the translators and editors who worked with these writings allowed for little overt expression of personal opinion, much less for a passionate response. As a Jungian analyst, I cannot help wondering what those exegetes really think, in their private thoughts, of these works that so dramatically challenge the accepted doctrines of their day, as well as our own.

It was C. G. Jung who discovered for himself and became enraptured by the literature of the Jewish and Christian Gnostics, whose writings included the Lost Gospels. The word "enraptured" can be used advisedly, for Jung did not come to these materials as a scholar who relied on the researches and support of predecessors and colleagues. He encountered the personifications of the myths directly, through the medium of the unconscious—as an eruption of mysterious ideas and images of unknown origin carrying messages about the nature and workings of the human psyche. The story of how the Gnostic material revealed itself to Jung is found in his autobiographical work *Memories, Dreams, Reflections*. Only after meeting with Gnostic ideas, in the form of dreams or fantasies or active imagination, was Jung inspired to look to myth and literature for amplifications of what he had experienced. Here he detected astonishing parallels to his own findings in material that was only just emerging from the translations of the Nag Hammadi Library, as well as from other Gnostic texts in Jewish and Christian sources.

As a psychiatrist, Jung was interested in why people think as they think and believe what they believe. He sought for clues in mythology, especially for that which gives rise to religious and spiritual traditions. He understood the spiritual thrust in men and women as expressive of the human psyche and its yearning toward the Source of Being. When he became interested in pursuing the study of the ancient Gnostic texts, it was to support and amplify his own experience as well as that of certain of his patients whose orientations were toward the life of the spirit. Jung did not pretend to be neutral about this material. He used it freely when it illuminated such issues as the necessity of reclaiming an interior view of oneself and the world in which we live. He understood and reframed much of the Gnostic mythology in psychological terms, recognizing in the manifold characters of Gnostic mythology the same archetypal images that reside in the human psyche everywhere, driving people to love, fear, hate, covet, and all else they would not do of their own conscious free will. Yet Jung, for all his awareness of what Gnosticism means and for all his fascination with its symbolic manifestations, stopped short of identifying himself openly as a Gnostic. First and last, he thought of himself as a psychiatrist and a healer of souls. He explored in great depth the *ideas* about God and about the gods as they appear in the human psyche. He insisted that he did not feel comfortable in saying who or what God is—although in one memorable and often quoted interview he revealed, "I do not need to believe in God; I know." But this is stated with a twinkle in his eye, as if to say to the interviewers that if they do not know what he means by this, he will not tell them.

Now the time has come for one who is openly a Gnostic to speak out of his own conviction and commitment. Dr. Stephan A. Hoeller's exposition of historical Gnosticism and its contemporary implications brings this ancient discipline out of the past and into immediate confrontation with the crucial issues we face today. He finds in the psychology of Jung an appreciation of the spirit of Gnosticism as well as some answers to the most vital question: What has Gnosticism to do with the predicaments in which our world finds itself today? Hoeller addresses the fundamental concerns of the Gnostic who goes in search of self-knowledge: Where have we come from? How did we get to this place? What is our purpose here? Where are we going? Human beings have been asking these questions since the dawning of conscious awareness. Based on his own personal experience of Gnosis and his studies in comparative religion and philosophy, Hoeller serves as a spiritual teacher, throwing light on the meaning and significance of these questions.

The first part of the book graphically portrays that other earlier time when the traditions of Church and State had lost their luminosity. In Judea, the once inspired teachings of the kings and prophets had become rigidified and limiting: legalism obscured the noble intentions of the commandments; minutiae hid the sense of the grandeur of the divine; and political considerations overly occupied the religious leaders. The small band of Essenes withdrew from what they saw as a corrupt society and founded their own ascetic community in the Judean desert. Some suggest that when the Temple in Jerusalem was destroyed in 70 A.D. the Essenes took the Temple treasures, including some precious scrolls, into the desert for safekeeping until the time should come when the world would be ready to receive them. Similarly, in the early days of Christianity, the presence and the teachings of Jesus and the apostles inspired their followers. These men and women were ready to undergo any privation or martyrdom for the sake of their eternal souls. But when Christianity had to bolster its defense against the threat of Rome, the faith became an institution with all the credos, rules, and strictures that institutionalism implies. There were those who left the Church to seek spiritual freedom and a direct personal experience of the holy. These Gnostics took with them, or created in their self-imposed exiles, the secret knowledge that came to them from within, from what they understood to be an immanent God. In a way that enables us to compare those times to our own, Hoeller tells us how this came to pass, and he relates the fragmentation of those times to our own sense of spiritual fragmentation. The quest of those early seekers for wholeness is shown to be not different from our own desire to understand how so much evil can exist in the phenomenal world and how we may take a position with respect to it.

The major part of Dr. Hoeller's book relates and interprets the strange and marvelous mythology of the Gnostics. He presents the myths in their demonic terror and angelic glory, so that we are carried by them into the farther reaches of our own imagination. Then, taking his inspiration from Jung, Hoeller brings insights from contemporary depth psychology to interpret each of these legends. Through this process, he makes it clear that mythology is truly the language of the soul—and not only of the ancient soul but of our own.

The Epilogue is surprising and startling. Hoeller reminds us that the bomb fell on Hiroshima in the very year that the lost gospels were discovered. This synchronicity is doubly striking, for in 1945, as in the time of the original writing of the lost gospels, predictions and prognostications of world-wide catastrophe filled the air. During the past forty years or more since that time, portents for the future have been looking even more grave. In the old days people believed that God would destroy the world because of the evil acts of human beings. Today we do not need God for that; we humans have become capable of bringing total destruction down upon ourselves.

As we move ever more swiftly toward the End of Days, Hoeller seeks and finds in the writings of the Gnostics some hints as to what we may do to avert the final catastrophe. But he also does something not many have the courage to do—to consider what if: *What if we do not manage to avoid nuclear disaster or the systematic destruction of earth's atmosphere?* What then? Is this material world all that exists? Or, is there something other? These are questions we cannot avoid unless we cling desperately to our ignorance and unconsciousness. Stephan Hoeller addresses the issues directly. His reflections give us much to ponder.

Preface

The plan of writing this book was first conceived when following the 1985 Good Friday service of the Los Angeles Gnostic community, a distinguished visitor, Dr. James Robinson, the moving spirit behind the translation of the Nag Hammadi Gnostic scriptures, remarked to me: "We scholars have completed our work, it is time now for a Gnostic to write about the Gnostic scriptures."

Since I was a boy I have been powerfully attracted to Gnosticism and by the time I reached adulthood I had become a committed practitioner of this ancient faith. My Gnostic dedications have also led me to modern variations on the age-old theme of the Gnosis contained in Theosophy, mystical Christianity, and the psychology of C. G. Jung. The favorable response elicited by my book, *The Gnostic Jung and the Seven Sermons to the Dead* (1982), further served to convince me that our Western culture was at last ready to take a second, more sympathetic look at the tradition that has brought me so much meaning and illumination throughout my life. And so it came to pass that the present work was written.

Conversations and correspondence with several experts in Gnostic and related studies have led me to expand the scope of my work by including in it an evaluation of certain aspects of the Dead Sea Scrolls of Qumran. Professors Gilles Quispel, Gershom G. Scholem, and Kurt Rudolph have all impressed upon me the vital connection joining the Essene and the Gnostic transmissions, and my own studies have led me to expand upon their suggestions. Naturally flowing from such

xvii

considerations there arose my view that Jewish Essenes and Christian Gnostics were both exponents of the same stream of spirituality and that the discovery of their long-lost scriptures augurs well for the revival of a similar spirituality today.

Contact with and study of the work of translators has brought me another important insight, namely, that knowledge of Coptic and other arcane tongues does not always coincide with a sympathetic understanding of the spirit of the documents translated. As Jungian psychologist Ean Begg has pointed out in his *Myth and Today's Consciousness*, there frequently exists a psychological gulf separating the translators from the texts they are elucidating. Thus, the word *Metropator*, a Gnostic name for the Deity, which makes good psychological and Gnostic sense when rendered as "Mother/Father," was translated instead as "maternal grandfather" by one scholar. Another translator was wont to reply to his assistant, who protested that the translation of a particular passage did not make sense, "This is a Gnostic text, it is not supposed to make any sense." Such incidents made me appreciate Dr. Robinson's statement that it is time that a Gnostic interpret the Gnostic scriptures.

Above all, my work was informed and guided by the thought of the greatest of modern Gnostics, C. G. Jung. His sympathetic insight into the myths, symbols, and metaphors of the Gnostics, whom by his own admission he regarded as his long-lost friends, continues as the brightest beacon of our day, capable of illuminating the Gnostic gospels and their precursors, the Dead Sea Scrolls. Following Jung's lead, I have endeavored to elucidate the Lost Gospels to a major extent in psychological terms, albeit using the term "psychological" in a wider sense than many would understand it. This is a book about Gnosis, that is, about the true individuation of the human psyche. I hope that it will be a small contribution toward the goal to which both Jung and the ancient Gnostics were dedicated, namely, the redemption of the spirit from the darkness of limitation and ignorance.

S.A.H.

Acknowledgments

The author wishes to express his appreciation to the following: the Academy of Creative Education and the Lawrence Rockefeller Foundation, whose generous financial assistance made the writing possible; Mr. Roger Weir for encouragement and advice; Mrs. Roseanna Gartenmann for her devoted work in typing and correcting the manuscript; Mr. Jan Saether for generously executing and donating the illustrations in this book; Dr. James M. Robinson for his kind gift of H. M. Schenke's German translations of several of the Nag Hammadi scriptures, greatly facilitating my translation of the passages of the four gospels from the same collection (included in chapters 11, 12, and 13); Dr. June Singer for her insightful foreword and her encouraging comments; Mrs. Shirley J. Nicholson for initially prompting me to undertake the writing of this work, and also for her excellent work as editor.

Grateful acknowledgment is made to *Gnosis* magazine and author Dennis Stillings for permission to quote from the article "Invasion of the Archetypes" that appeared in the Winter 1989 issue.

Prologue

How the West Was Lost:
Loss and Recovery of
Psychological Spirituality

The thought of C. G. Jung is currently receiving an increasing amount of sympathetic interest in Western culture. A synthesis of human knowledge seldom before achieved by anyone discloses itself to those who seriously investigate the work bequeathed to us by this remarkable man. Beginning as a physician concerned with the welfare of the mind, he discovered in his patients and in his own soul the great truth of the reality of the psyche, and he explored its phenomenology at a depth to which others did not dare venture. His systematic observation of the workings of the deepest strata of the human mind in turn enabled him to cast his glance with singular insight into the great forces within human culture—myth, religion, art, philosophy, and literature.

In the course of these observations Jung came to discover that all truly powerful symbols and mythologems experienced and expressed by humanity arise from a common deep substratum of the mind, which he called the collective unconscious, with which every person continues to be connected in the course of his or her spiritual life. Jung's discovery of the collective unconscious (today increasingly called the "objective psyche"), has made it possible to approach experiences and ideas that hitherto have been conceived as religious or metaphysical, in a new way: his discoveries have provided a mediating hypothesis between the traditional belief in metaphysical reality and modern psychology.

1

In a certain sense Jung's discoveries are not truly new but are ancient knowledge; however, his approach to them is new and differs from the traditional position, which holds that spiritual truths are revealed manifestations of a different kind of reality from beyond the human psyche. In contrast with the positions held by most advocates of the mainstream religious traditions, Jung's orientation may be fairly characterized as being *intrapsychic*, that is, based on what is interior to the human psyche. Thus Jung seldom speaks of God as a person; rather, he affirms that he is not concerned with a metaphysical God at all, but with the image of God as it is perceived within the human soul.

This attitude continues to trouble persons who are attached to the time-worn metaphysical formulations of the mainstream traditions, but their tribulations are often not as justified as they might think. When they object to the possibility of God, angels, demons, or the Virgin Mary being "merely in our psyches," they fail to apprehend the breadth, scope, and majesty Jung attributes to the human soul. Jung commented on such criticisms as follows:

> For this is how Western man, whose soul is evidently "of little worth" speaks and thinks. If much were in his soul he would speak of it with reverence. But since he does not do so we can conclude that there is nothing of value in it. Not that this is necessarily so always and everywhere, but only with people who put nothing into their souls and have "all God outside."[1]

Only those who have allowed their psyches to be devalued by the extraversion of mind that invaded the religious mainstream of the West from a certain time onward in history, will consider the soul an unworthy vehicle for the transcendental archetypes and symbols. Jung was also heard to say, when responding to someone who accused him of deifying the soul, that he had done no such thing, but that the Creator himself had deified it already!

Students of history remember that there certainly was a time when the dignity and majesty of the soul were recognized by the leading exponents of spirituality in Western culture. During the first three centuries of the Christian era there flourished in the Mediterranean area several schools of spirituality that held the creative and revelatory potential of the soul in very high regard indeed. It is interesting to note in this connection that Jung never claimed credit for the discovery of the concept of the archetypes, but readily admitted that he had discovered this idea in the religious philosophical teachings of the Hellenistic world:

> . . . there are present in every psyche forms which are unconscious but nonetheless active—living dispositions, ideas in the Platonic sense, that perform and continually influence our thoughts and feelings and actions. The term "archetype" occurs as early as Philo Judaeus, with reference to the *Imago Dei* (God-image) in man. It can also be found in Irenaeus, who says [while quoting a Gnostic source—S.A.H.], "The creator of the world did not fashion these things directly from himself but copied them from archetypes outside himself." In the *Corpus Hermeticum*, God is called . . . "archetypal light" . . . for our purposes this term . . . tells us that . . . we are dealing with archaic or—I would say—primordial types, that is, with universal images that have existed since remotest times.[2]

Unfortunately, the internalist position of early Alexandrian wisdom was replaced by an institutionalized externalism, where God and other transcendentally toned archetypal images were once again conceived as being "all outside." What might be called the *psychological spirituality* of the first few centuries of the Christian era went underground, and the compensating internalist movements still subsisting within the framework of Christianity were declared heretical. Thus came about a transmission of alternative reality that maintained its psychological or internalist emphasis in opposition to the externalist mainstream. As we shall demonstrate in the following chapters, this transmission did not spring fully grown from the Hellenistic milieu but had its roots in a preexisting alternative movement in Judaism, the last surviving branch of which, just prior to the coming of Christianity, was the school of the Essenes. The Jewish Essene then gave way to the Christian Gnostic, whose spiritual progeny were the monastic Christian mystics within the Church and the alchemists, ceremonial magicians, Cathars, Rosicrucians, Kabbalists, and in modern times Theosophists and related movements of alternative spirituality.

The alternative stream never ceased, but its external manifestations were spasmodic and never gathered enough strength to seriously challenge the (self-declared) orthodoxies of the mainstream. The emphasis of spiritual interiority thus remained as a muted tradition, frequently repressed and at times ignored by the dominant religions and by the culture at large. The growing edge (some might call it the fringe) of the culture, consisting of artists, visionaries, and unconventional and alienated thinkers never stopped being attracted to the alternative stream, and in a few instances significant inroads were made by certain manifestations of it. One of the major examples of such an eruption of the alternative spirituality into the main body of the culture was certainly the phenomenon of the Renaissance, as historian Frances Yates appears to have proven to the satisfaction of many in her several impressive works on this subject.*

Jung believed that the endorsement of the Aristotelian position in philosophy on the part of Thomas Aquinas, and subsequently by Western Christendom, had contributed greatly to the uprooting of spiritual interiority.

---

*Frances A. Yates, *Giordano Bruno and the Hermetic Tradition* (Chicago: University of Chicago Press, 1964); *The Rosicrucian Enlightenment* (London: Routledge & Kegan Paul Ltd., 1972); *The Art of Memory* (Chicago: University of Chicago Press, 1966); *Theatre of the World* (Chicago: University of Chicago Press, 1969); *The Occult Philosophy* (London: Routledge & Kegan Paul Ltd., 1969).

He repeatedly stated that the sense of the reality of the psyche vanished in proportion to the adopting by Western religion and culture of the Aristotelian slogan: "Nothing in the intellect except through the senses." On this point Jung agrees with Paul Tillich, who was wont to say that the Aristotelian orientation of theology after Aquinas was the single greatest factor that made atheism possible. When people cease to experience God, they are forced to believe in him, implied Tillich—and belief is a commodity subject to loss. The inner sense of God is a quality of the deeper psyche and not of reason. With the ascendancy of reason over the psychological awareness of archetypal truth, the way for rationalism and ultimately for materialism and atheism became wide open. Thus, says Jung, and agrees Tillich, the West was lost.

When the West was lost to spiritual interiority, all that remained was belief, or the religious euphemism for it, faith. Jung, like the modern Gnostic he was, mercilessly castigated the prevailing religious emphasis on faith over interior experience. It is generally agreed, he wrote, that "faith includes a *sacrificium intellectus* (sacrifice of the intellect)," and he adds in brackets, "provided that there is an intellect to sacrifice." At the same time, he continues, it is usually overlooked that faith also requires "a sacrifice of feeling." This, he says, is the reason why "the faithful remain children instead of becoming as children, and they do not gain life because they have not lost it." What Jung understands by "sacrifice of feeling" he explains as follows: "Faith tries to retain a primitive mental condition on purely sentimental grounds. It is unwilling to give up the primitive, child-like relationship to hypostasized figures; it wants to go on enjoying the security and confidence of a world still presided over by powerful, responsible, kindly parents."[3]

Mature spirituality, it would seem, requires more than faith, especially when faith is comprised of belief grounded in fear. For the child, faith in the structures of existence is sufficient, because the child is contained in them. For the adult, the perception of order and meaning has to be achieved afresh in the face of great challenges. Increased awareness and actual experience of life's vicissitudes conflict with the faith that was appropriate to the condition of the child. If there should be a new assurance of meaning, even of security, it must come about as an achievement, as the arising of a new kind of certainty wrested from acute insecurity and alienation. Such a mature spiritual state requires a certain kind of inward knowledge rooted in experience. This is what in ancient times was known under the Greek term *Gnosis.*

Unfortunately, though contemporary Western culture has outgrown the phase of development that is akin to that of the child, it has not put away childish things. We in the West still treat inward apperceptions as if they were merely by-products of objective facts and no more. (Even certain contemporary fads, endorsed by the "New Age," such as the shibboleths of left and right brain, reflect this extraverted one-sidedness.) In this way, said Jung, the divine "degenerates into an external object of worship" and "is robbed of its mysterious relation to the inner man."[4]

The question arises, and is being asked by critics of the alternative spiritual currents, whether the attitude of inwardness does not open the door to an unlimited subjectivism of the kind often encountered among the less discriminating devotees of fringe spirituality. It is also feared that preoccupation with the denizens and forces of one's interior landscape may disrupt the orderly pattern of society. Jung has replied to such questions and doubts in the following words:

> The prominence of the subjective factor does not imply a personal subjectivism, despite the readiness of the extraverted attitude to dismiss the subjective factor as "nothing but subjective."[5]

In fact, says Jung, the subjective is not as subjective as we think, for the deeper we reach into the psychic currents of inner life, the more we leave behind the merely personal and touch those elements of experience that are timeless, unaffected by personalistic factors, and thus in a certain sense truly objective. Imagination is not arbitrary, as many would envision it; on the contrary, it is based on the laws of unconscious apperception, which do not change.

In essence, the Gnosis of old postulates, and Jung also affirms, that the ideas which form the content of every religion are not primarily the product of an externally originating revelation, but of a subjective revelation from within the human psyche. In *Answer to Job* he says simply: "Religious statements are psychic confessions based on unconscious, i.e. transcendental processes." Do these "psychic confessions" correspond with metaphysical postulates? Jung does not say, and probably he neither knew nor cared. To the mind of the believer the objects of faith are metaphysical realities. To the Gnostic, and thus to Jung, the phenomena of experience deserve priority over metaphysical speculation. In Jung's view it is more important to recognize the subjective root, in the mind, of our ideas about the Divine than to accept metaphysical and theological statements. It has been said that theologians know a great deal *about* God but very little *of* God. This is a condition that can be rectified only by the kind of direct experience advocated by mystics and Gnostics in every age.

What bestows meaning on life is not the kind of condition that was described by William James as "faith in somebody else's faith." Rather, what is needed in this regard is a particular act of perception that grips and taxes our entire being because of its direct impact and numinous quality. Whenever this kind of perception is absent, the inadequate vision of the human being turns against him. In every soul there is a hunger for that kind of direct vision that bestows wholeness and true meaning. Unless we know how to deal creatively with this hunger, it projects itself outward, independently of our will, even against our will, usually upon an unsuitable object.

Aldous Huxley described political ideologies as "substitute mysticism," and a similar definition could be given to the numerous projections of humanity evoking fanatical, unbalanced, and monomaniacal attitudes and allegiances. Where the real is not present, the unreal intrudes itself as a substitute, and the results are inevitably disastrous. Jung writes about this: "Not even the medieval epidemics of bubonic plague or smallpox killed as many people as certain differences of opinion in 1914 or certain political 'ideals' in Russia."[6] Only consciousness, engendered by Gnosis, can prevent the living out of false projections and the consequent violence and cruelty.

The age of faith is past or, to say the least, is passing. The portentous question facing us today is: What will take its place? Unless we claim the gift of prophecy we cannot answer this question with any certainty. What we can say is this: We *know* what *ought* to take its place; namely, an age where the interior, or psychological, spirituality unwisely discarded long ago may be able to come into its own once more. Fr. John Dourley writes of this task from a Jungian and Christian point of view:

> One interesting and lively option . . . would be the re-appropriation and assimilation of those movements of the spirit which Christianity, in the interest of its own survival, has historically been forced to declare heretical. With this in mind, Jung's thought challenges orthodox truths it has hitherto felt obliged to reject. This is what must be done, in Jung's view, if Christianity is to come into possession of a conception of humanity and human spirituality that is more appropriate to the psychological process of becoming whole.[7]

Jung knew that the one and only tradition associated with Christianity that regarded the human psyche as the container of the divine-human encounter was that of the Gnostics of the first three centuries of our era. For this reason he called for a renewed appreciation of this ancient tradition, and particularly for a return to the Gnostic sense of God as an inner directing and transforming presence. Literalism and historicism, so Jung felt, have trivialized Western spirituality long enough, and the time has come to reverse the process that was initiated by the church fathers who drove the Gnosis underground after the third century. In the face of persistent opposition to Gnosticism, and its disparagement as "dualistic," "world hating," and "immoral," Jung asserted that

> Disparagement and vilification of Gnosticism are an anachronism. Its obvious psychological symbolism could serve many people today as a bridge to a more living appreciation of Christian tradition.[8]

The task thus is clear: What must take place, if we accept Jung's judgment, is a restoration of certain approaches to spirituality that contain the necessary compensation for the extraverted, literalist, and one-sided orientation of Western religion. In an age of desacralization, trivializing liturgical reforms, and liberation theologies, Jung points the way toward a *restoration theology and psychology* designed to reappropriate the discarded wisdom of the psychological spirituality known to the Gnostics, mystics, and alchemists throughout the centuries. The stone that the builders rejected can and indeed must return to the structure of our culture if a condition of wholeness is ever to arise therein.

A drive toward wholeness, operating as a unifying process bringing together the many disparate components of the soul of both individual and culture, is one of the great, crucial realities underlying the collective and individual movement of history. The process of individuation, or becoming whole, brings with it the experience of the divine and the perception of transcendence in the symbolic dimension of life. Our culture thus must take heed: Psychological fragmentation can ultimately only lead to dissolution, while potential integration promises the renewal of life, of meaning, of love and creativity.

The so-called Lost Gospels—whereby with some imaginative license we mean to describe the Gnostic gospels from Nag Hammadi and their forerunners, the Scrolls from the caves of Qumran—are our principal collections of documents relating to the discarded and repressed shadow of Western spirituality, and indeed of Western culture. The present work endeavors to illuminate the context and content of these scriptures in relation to the task of restoration and reappropriation pioneered by the efforts of Carl Gustav Jung. It is no exaggeration to say that our culture cries out today for wholeness, balance, and the consequent signs of sanity. Understandably but regrettably, the need for wholeness felt by so many is still understood predominantly in terms of the entrenched extraversion that Jung deplored so much. Many speak and write of world peace and the envisioned "one world" without recognizing that such ideals can never be realized on the external plane until enough individuals have come to wholeness within themselves. The late J. Krishnamurti rightly said: "The world problem is the individual problem." And we might add that the individual problem must be faced within the individual.

Now as before no *deus ex machina*, no externally precipitated saving deity will extricate us from our predicament. Our spiritual enfeeblement is *not* due to a fall from grace on the part of Adam and Eve in paradise as some would have us believe, and our regeneration will not come about by accepting a personal savior in history. Nor has the fall of our culture come about by the eclipse of a benign matriarchy and its replacement by a malign patriarchy, which condition we are told might be remedied by a restored matriarchy presided over by a rehabilitated chthonic Goddess. We will not be saved by a risen Redeemer any more than by a resurrected earth Mother, but only by the reconciliation of the gods and goddesses within us. The West was lost because of an unwarranted outward turn of consciousness; it may be regained by a reestablishment of balance attendant upon a reclaiming of inward realities.

It is the present writer's conviction that the Lost Gospels could play a vital role in the reclaiming of the lost wholeness of the West. When illumined by the insight of Jung, these documents and the tradition they represent can serve to supply the missing element for the alchemical opus of our personal and our collective individuation. In the following pages, the writer has endeavored to put before his readers a body of myth and symbol, augmented by historical fact and psychological insight, in the hope that by these means some of the Gnosis long lost to our culture might be found again. None of us could help being deprived of this Gnosis, but we can only blame ourselves if we fail to recover it now.

PART I
The Other Tradition

Gnostic Alchemical Serpent

1

A Tale of Two Heresies:
Nag Hammadi and Qumran

There is a belief almost universally held which declares that when humanity is in its greatest hour of need spiritual help comes forth from transcendental quarters. Well-known among the testimonies given regarding this belief is the one attributed to Sri Krishna in the portion of the great Hindu epic the *Mahabharata*, which has become known and beloved as the *Bhagavad Gita*:

> When goodness grows weak,
> When Evil waxes mighty,
> I make for myself a vehicle.
> In every age I return
> To deliver the holy,
> To destroy the fault of the evildoer,
> To establish true goodness.[1]

Similarly, in the sacred lore of Tibet, as recounted by the late Dr. W. Y. Evans-Wentz in his work, *The Tibetan Book of the Great Liberation*, Padma-Sambhava, the mysterious magician-guru who introduced Buddhism to Tibet, is reputed to have hidden numerous documents of wisdom in various secret places in the Himalayas, there to be discovered in subsequent historical epochs when the need for them would be the greatest.

It has been rightly said that the night is always darkest before the dawn. The macrocosm of human history and the microcosm of the psychology of the individual both

15

testify to this truism. When the alienation of our mind from its life-giving sources is the greatest, when the despair of the dark night of the soul descends upon us with the full force of its apalling weight, then the dawn of redeeming and healing enlightenment breaks on the eastern horizon of the soul. Depth-psychological insight declares that the greatest and most enduring enlightenment of the soul comes only after the full experience of darkness and despair. C. G. Jung was wont to attribute this phenomenon to the principle enunciated by the Pre-Socratic philosopher Heraclitus, known as *enantiodromia*, where the deepest point of saturation with darkness gives birth to a rapidly expanding point of light. History and psychohistory both bring to our attention a principle of synchronistic response whereby the forces of being that strive for union, wholeness, and ultimate meaning spring into effective manifestation at the time of the greatest need. The great German mystical poet Johann Ch. F. Hölderlin gave proper expression to this principle when he wrote: "Near is God, and difficult is He to apprehend, but where the danger is great, there the saving power ever draws near."

These considerations are eminently relevant to the strange tale of the discoveries of two of the most outstanding finds within the history of biblical and religious archaeology, namely, the Nag Hammadi library of Gnostic scriptures and the Dead Sea Scrolls of Qumran. In 1945, when the physical and psychological ruins of World War II were still painfully evident in Europe, Africa, and Asia; at the very time when the hecatombs of Auschwitz, Dachau, and Bergen-Belsen were about to be matched and superseded by the death camps of Stalin's Gulag Archipelago; when it seemed to many that the world would never recover from the greatest calamity of human history—at this very moment of deepest darkness and despair of the world soul, an Egyptian peasant, riding his camel while searching for fertilizer, came upon a number of ancient documents that possess the potential of aiding the West in the recovery of a substantial portion of its lost soul. At the very time when the sage C. G. Jung wrote and spoke about modern man in search of a soul, a long forgotten, or rather repressed, component of the soul of Judeo-Christian religiosity and of Western culture in general emerged from the soil at the base of the mountain range Jabal al-Tarif near the river Nile in Upper Egypt. In a storage jar made of claylike material the Egyptian peasant and his companion found a collection of ancient manuscripts, consisting of 1,153 pages bound into twelve leather-bound primitive books (known as codices), containing fifty-two separate writings (called tractates). The writings, as subsequent investigation revealed, were copies by third and fourth century Egyptian scribes from works that originated for the most part in the Apostolic Age, when the memory of the enigmatic Rabbi Jehoshva, known as Jesus, still lived powerfully in the minds of numerous persons who were present during his brief but portentous lifetime.

Only a little over two years later, in the summer of 1947 in Palestine, an Arab goatherd was searching for one of the goats of his flock. The goatherd was young and agile and with his athletic prowess climbed about on the limestone cliffs overlooking the Dead Sea. While engaged in these exercises he espied a small hole leading into a cave in the mountain. Being afraid of evil spirits, the young man first fled from the cave and returned the next day with a companion. The two young men descended into the cave where they found a number of clay jars covered by bowl-like lids. Most of the jars were empty, but one contained a large bundle composed of a piece of leather wrapped in rags. They took the mysterious package home and upon unwrapping it found that it contained a scroll, or roll of parchment, which, when unrolled, stretched from one end of their tent to the other. The same discovery was made concerning two more bundles found in the same jar. The two youths had in their possession three scrolls filled with writing of a nature they did not comprehend. A few days later they sold the three scrolls to a dealer who traded for the most part in illegal

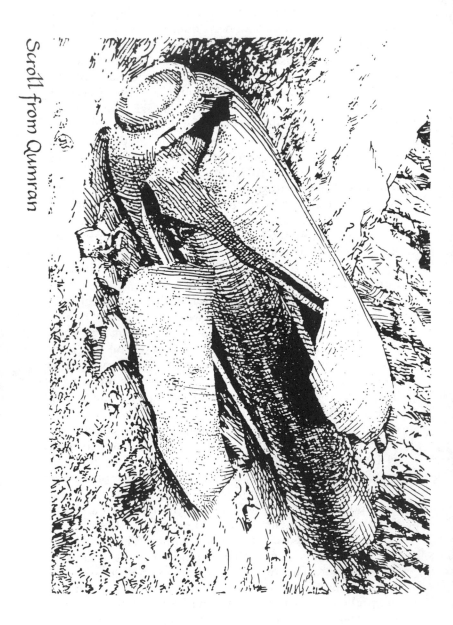

Scroll from Qumran

merchandise in the town of Bethlehem. The pilgrimage of what became known as the Dead Sea Scrolls had begun.

The first three scrolls thus discovered on the shore of the Dead Sea were soon deciphered and named the Isaiah Scroll, the Habakukk Scroll, and the Manual of Discipline. They were followed by a large number of additional scrolls found by successive waves of expeditions sponsored by a number of governments and academic institutions. The worldwide publicity that followed revealed that the scrolls were the writings of a heterodox community of Jews, called Essenes, who resided at the site of the discovery from about 130 B.C. to A.D. 70 (with an intermission of about thirty years prior to the year 4 B.C.) and whose strange doctrines and practices as well as their chronological proximity to the beginnings of the Christian dispensation were bound to cause widespread interest.

At first the two finds impressed the observers with their dissimilarity. The earlier discovery contained writings in the Sahidic dialect of Coptic, a popular language of Hellenistic and Roman Egypt; the latter find consisted of works written for the most part in Hebrew and Aramaic, the Semitic tongues used in contemporary Palestine. The authors and scribes of the Nag Hammadi library were Christians of the Gnostic persuasion; the persons involved in the authorship and copying of the Dead Sea Scrolls were Jews of the Essene sect. Even the outer format of the writings showed a radical divergence in appearance: The Egyptian Coptic writings are the earliest example of the format of bookbinding known as the *codex*, whereas the Palestinian documents are in the form of long scrolls. To make the divergence complete, the Jewish sectarian writers used parchment, and the Christian Gnostic writers wrote on papyrus, a derivative of the papyrus reed from whence the modern word "paper" originates.

The differences dividing the two discoveries were dramatized in the radically different turns that their respective fates took subsequent to their initial reappearance.

The Coptic Gnostic library was not to see the light of widespread public attention for many decades to come. The first complete translation into the English language did not appear for thirty-two years after the discovery. Wranglings among scholars, politicians, and antiquities dealers, as well as much obtuseness and indifference on the part of many of the individuals involved, has made most persons awaiting the publication of the Nag Hammadi find well-nigh despair over its prospects. The more imaginative of the would-be readers might even have remembered that the ancient Gnostics, like true magicians in the Egyptian mode, were given to the practice of attaching awesome curses and binding guardian spirits to their concealed holy books. In fact, one of the gospels of the Nag Hammadi collection, *The Gospel of the Egyptians*, was found to contain a magical admonition of just such an ominous nature:

> Thou shalt write down what I tell thee, and of which I shall remind thee for the sake of those who come after you and be worthy (of such). And thou wilt make this book repose upon the mountain, and thou wilt call up the guardian, (in this wise): "O Come, Thou Dreadful One!"

To this statement might be added another, appearing in *The Apocryphon of John*, near the text's end where Jesus addresses John by pronouncing what has become known as the "Jesus curse":

> "For truly I have given these things to thee to record them, and they shall be deposited in a safe place." Then he spoke thus to me (John), "Cursed is everyone who shall impart any of this in return for a gift, or for food, or for drink, or for clothing, or for anything of a like kind."

Whatever the effect of such curses, it appears that after the passing of a quarter of a century, various individuals as well as at least one international public agency (UNESCO) began to overcome the forces opposing the publication of the Nag Hammadi scriptures. It is to be noted also that the only portion of the Gnostic find to leave the turbulent and hostile climate of Nasser's Egypt of the 1950s and thus to become accessible to scholars without restriction was purchased by the Jung Institute of Zurich and presented as the "Jung Codex" to C. G. Jung on his eightieth birthday. On November 15, 1953, at a convocation of leaders of the Swiss government, as well as numerous academic and professional authorities who had gathered to honor him, the octogenarian Jung held in his hands this document that after some 1,200 years heralded the possible rebirth of the Gnosis to which the Swiss sage gave so much of his work and devotion. It is most tempting indeed to imagine that now at last the Nag Hammadi find made its connection with a truly worthy heir of the tradition within which it had its origin. The principle that Jung called synchronicity has once again worked its uncanny magic: the barriers began to be lowered, the obstacles slowly diminished, and the long-lost heritage of Jung's "old friends," the Gnostics, became accessible to all who would appreciate it. The opportunities delayed had not passed; indeed, new psychological and social developments arose in the 1960s and 1970s that created a climate of receptivity in regard to much unconventional spirituality, including that of the Gnostics. The message of Nag Hammadi was finally on the march.

The fate of the scrolls from the shore of the Dead Sea was of a different nature. As in the instance of the Coptic Gnostic papyrus books in Egypt, so here the discoverers knew nothing of the real nature of their find. As the result of the intervention of the Syrian Orthodox Metropolitan of Jerusalem, as well as the mounting interest of a number of scholars, including the redoubtable Professor E. L. Sukenik of Hebrew University, some eighteen months after the initial discovery the news broke upon the outside world. At first the news was greeted with incredulity. Surely, so many thought, there must be some fraud or mistake. The soil of Palestine, unlike that of Egypt, was regarded as a most unlikely repository for parchment and papyrus; the climate of the Judean mountains was regarded as too humid for the preservation of such perishable materials. The nineteenth century and early twentieth century saw an appalling neglect of biblical archeological research in this area, and there appears to exist evidence indicating that some valuable finds were disregarded as fraudulent merely on the basis of the dogma declaring that the caves in the region were far too damp to permit the survival of delicate ancient documents.

By 1949 the scholarly climate had changed, however, and many authorities were prepared to admit that the three scrolls found by the Arab goatherd were genuine. Nor were political conditions identical with those prevailing prior to the two world wars. In lieu of the torpid regime of the Ottomans and the subsequent colonial administration, two "people of the book," the Jews of the newly born republic of Israel and the Arabs of the Hashemite kingdom of Jordan, were exercising sovereignty over the lands of the Bible. Of these, the Jordanian government was the more directly concerned, owing to the fact that the Qumran region was located within its territory. Some time after the initial dust from the discovery had settled, the Jordanian government was instrumental in creating an international team of scholars to edit the available scrolls, the number of which was steadily increasing as the result of new finds by various expeditions. Significantly—and perhaps regrettably—the team, headed by Roland De Vaux, a Roman Catholic priest, was composed almost exclusively of men of religion. The lone individual who came to describe himself as the "nonreligious person" on the team was the British scholar John Marco Allegro, whose contribution must be regarded as crucial to our considerations.

Not only were most of the scholars on the team clergymen, but they were also all Christian clergymen. There was not a single Jew among them (a condition that was more than compensated for in later years when the Israeli government obtained a monopoly on the scrolls). The notion that the researchers were far from objective in their attitude toward the contents of the find soon began to receive some publicity. In 1955 the late and noted American literary figure Edmund Wilson wrote a series of articles on the scrolls for the *New Yorker* magazine. Wilson stated in these articles that the materials contained in the scrolls frightened church leaders who feared that the documents might reveal information that would detract from the unique claims of Christianity. The similarity of much of the Essene doctrine and history to the later Christian New Testament could have justly alarmed the guardians of church orthodoxy. In more than one way, the Essenes of the Qumran community appeared as a group of Proto-Christians. Did they not baptize like John and later the apostles? Were they not opposed to the Temple priesthood in Jerusalem, the legitimacy of which they viewed as abrogated? And, most importantly, did they not speak of one of their own leaders, a "teacher of righteousness," whose life and death show supremely uncomfortable similarities to those of Jesus of Nazareth?

The role that the apprehensiveness of orthodox Christian minds may have played in obscuring the message of the scrolls will remain a matter of conjecture. Still, there are at least some facts to consider. The early Dead Sea Scrolls were divided for purposes of research among eight members of the international team. It is generally agreed that the theologically most sensitive material, containing the history and practices of the Essene community, was given to a Polish Roman Catholic priest from France, Josef Milik. Today, thirty years later, the majority of this material remains unpublished in the hands of Milik. It has also become known that Father Milik has since quietly left the priesthood. Could it be that the content of the documents destroyed his faith, but that his commitment is still strong enough not to wish to make public his conclusions? Looking at the entire body of the Dead Sea Scrolls, only 20 percent of the documents has been published, the remaining 80 percent being still in the hands of scholars. One can certainly sympathize with the lone maverick scholar,

John M. Allegro, who, in a lecture in 1985 in Ann Arbor, Michigan, declared: "Why are my dear colleagues sitting on the stuff? It has driven me mad. . . . It's a scandal. The public has got to be made aware, then maybe people will start asking (the scholars) questions."[2]

The caves of the Qumran mountain range continued to yield additional materials. The Antiquities Department of the Jordanian government (which came to appoint John M. Allegro as its chief agent in this project) continued to sponsor and support expeditions, one of which yielded the famous copper scroll that was transported to England and, in 1955 and 1956 under Allegro's supervision, opened and deciphered. The copper scroll and other more recently discovered documents began to reveal a picture of the Essene community of Qumran which indicated that the saintly Jewish heretics were involved in much more than the hitherto known spiritual pursuits. The copper scroll, for instance, seemed to indicate that they were the custodians of the buried treasure of the Temple of Jerusalem, destroyed and looted by the Roman legions in A.D. 70.

As the plot thickened in regard to the content of the scrolls, the ever-turbulent developments of the politics of the Middle East added a new keynote to the story of Qumran. After 1961 in the wake of the so-called Three-Day War, the sites of the find were annexed by the State of Israel. The British and American influences in the project were now displaced by the politico-religious zeal of the Israelis. The late general-statesman-archeologist Yigael Yadin became the leading explorer and guardian of the newly discovered writings. Dozens of additional caves were explored, most of which contained various materials hidden there by the Jewish sectarians in the last two centuries B.C. and the first century A.D. Not only the caves, but also the site of some ancient ruins in the region yielded additional documents. The Israeli influence did not prove a great improvement in regard to the publication of the vast amount of available material. A division arose between the Israeli custodians, on the one hand, and the Jordanian Dead Sea Scrolls Fund (headed by Allegro as trustee), on the other. The Essene library, which in its original state is estimated to have consisted of more than 600 scrolls, slowly faded from public view. By the 1960s the attention of the public and scholars alike had begun to move away from the subject of the scrolls. The mist that for a large part of every year broods over the briny waters of the Dead Sea reenveloped the Essene treasure that it had concealed for two millennia. Although removed from their place of concealment in the bleak and parched wilderness, the Dead Sea Scrolls still have not yielded the secrets they guarded for so long. The mystery remains.*

The depth-psychologically oriented observer of these events might perceive certain mythic patterns woven into the story and fate of the two discoveries that may shed additional light on their meaning. In a particularly dark period of the history of the Western psyche two significant discoveries were made. Both were the result of chance rather than a deliberate, purposeful intent. The agonizing psychic need of the culture was thus met by a synchronistic response from the innermost center of reality. The hopelessness and spiritual bankruptcy of the West in the wake of the Second World War and at the outset of the atomic age brought forth two remarkable sources of a vital but hitherto missing ingredient of its collective soul. Long ago the guardians of Western spirituality unwisely banished an important expression of their tradition from the daylight of religious life. The Essene and Gnostic alternative tradition became the equivalent of the psychological shadow to the Judeo-Christian mainstream religiosity. Yet, the human psyche cannot forgo the effective presence of its shadow for too long. The time always comes when the hitherto rejected and consequently missing portion of our selfhood mightily calls attention

---

*Regarding the lack of the publication of certain materials from the Qumran find, the author relied primarily on published statements as well as information imparted verbally by the late John M. Allegro.

to itself. The stone that the builders rejected surfaces once more in order to be incorporated into the structure, indeed, more often to become the cornerstone of the same.

According to Jungian and related depth-psychological thought, spiritual and religious concerns are ultimately founded upon a universal human drive toward wholeness. The disparate components of our nature eventually undergo a process of progressive unification (called by Jung "individuation"), which has wholeness as its objective. It would appear that with the coming of the post-World War II era the time for a certain advanced phase of the individuation of Western culture had come. Faced with the appalling evidence of human evil manifest in the war and in totalitarian tyrannies and shocked by the prospect of global death and destruction resulting from nuclear warfare, Western culture reached a psychological impasse wherein its repressed shadow could play a healing and redeeming role. The time was finally ripe for the admission of the rejected spirituality of the Gnostics and the Essenes.

The arising of such an opportunity for the healing of Western spirituality (and with it of Western culture) should not be taken to mean that difficulties and resistances to such a process of healing would not be encountered. All persons familiar with the practice of depth psychology know that the content of the psyche will yield its true meaning only after prolonged exposure to the light of consciousness, coupled with an informed effort to illuminate this content with the amplifying light of appropriate symbols. One can wrest a revelation from the depth of the psychic mystery, but one can never be certain that the revelation will not undergo a process of obscuration and distortion. The religious content of the psyche is particularly subject to such pitfalls. When writing about the need to illuminate psychologically the symbolic statements of religion, Jung gave expression to his concern regarding the ever-present tendency toward unconsciousness and obscurantism in this highly charged area of endeavor:

I have to ask myself also, in all seriousness, whether it might not be far more dangerous if Christian symbols were made inaccessible to thoughtful understanding by being banished to a *sphere of sacrosanct unintelligibility.* [Italics ours—S.A.H.] They can easily become so remote from us that their irrationality turns into preposterous nonsense.[3]

In the foregoing we have noted the existence of certain evidence indicating that conscious as well as unconscious efforts have been made to banish the heritage of Nag Hammadi and Qumran to just such a "sphere of sacrosanct unintelligibility." Scholars indoctrinated by the monolithic worldview of the Old and New Testaments have encountered great psychological resistances in their own minds when confronted with the challenge of discoveries that, when brought into the light of thoughtful understanding, may reveal themselves as an *Other Testament* differing radically from and often contradicting the two accepted testaments.

The challenge of consciousness is always to let go of the lesser in order to be able to include the greater. Similarly, the challenge of the Gnostic and Essene documents is to give up an incomplete and one-sided religious consciousness in the interest of a greater, more inclusive one. It would seem that this option is quite forcefully demanded of us by the imperative of the growth and healing of the human psyche both at the individual and the collective levels of its expression. The alternative would be a repetition of the fatal mistakes made by religious authorities and their followers in the past—the very mistakes, in fact, that have led to the lamentable lack of wholeness of the mainstream spirituality of the West. In view of the evident need of the culture in the midst of its present crisis, such an alternative appears to be unacceptable.

Another testament has come to us in this latter portion of the twentieth century. Like all testaments it is a *witness* (which is the term from which *testament* is derived). The Other, or Alternative, Testament bears witness to the existence of a worldview that is at once different from and complementary to the one adopted by the West in the form of mainstream Judaism and Christianity. It is a heretical testament, a heritage that deviates radically from much that was accepted as normative and regular in religion and culture for some 1,600 years. Although its full extent and content have not yet emerged into plain view, its available documents suffice to permit us an adequate perspective concerning its character and potential impact. Such, in brief, are the recognitions that ought to motivate us in our search for both the manifest content and the implicit meaning of the Other Testament, beginning with its expression that can chronologically lay claim first to our attention, namely, the heritage of the Essenes.

2

Saintly Rebels:
The People of the Scrolls

The Dead Sea Scrolls were discovered at a place known today as Qumran (pronounced koomrahn), an Arabic name without any certain meaning. It is an ancient site, probably one of the "cities of the wilderness" mentioned in the Book of Joshua. Allegro believes that the mysterious people of the Scrolls purposely came to locate their community upon an earlier Israelite settlement of biblical prominence known once as the city of *Secacah*. A few miles to the north of the present Qumran is the ancient site of Jericho and of the fords where Joshua, son of Nun, led the people of Israel across the river Jordan, repeating after a fashion the miraculous crossing of the Red Sea initiated by Moses. As the Red Sea had parted for Moses, so the Jordan stopped in its flow for Joshua in order to permit the crossing of the Jews—at least so all believers held.[1] The region at and around Qumran was hallowed by a sacred past. It was a place where miracles happened, where the God of Israel intervened in the course of nature to show His favor to the children of His covenant.

Curiously enough, beneficent divine miracles are not the only events whereby this region is remembered. The plain clearly visible from Qumran is the very one where, under a dreadful hail of fire and brimstone, the unhappy populace of Sodom and Gomorrah found their last, sad resting place. Even more significantly, the Rift Valley in the immediate vicinity of Qumran was traditionally

The caves of Qumran

believed to contain the Abyss of Judgement wherein the rebel angels with their chief, *Azazel*, were cast by God in order to languish until the day of the final judgment. Such apocryphal books as those of Enoch and Jubilees (both of which were favorite reading of the Essenes of Qumran) outline an entire dark myth dealing with Azazel and his angelic host, who intermarried with humans and became the forebears of a race mighty in knowledge and magical skills. These beings, at times called Watchers and *Rephaim* (related to the Hebrew verb *rapha*, to heal), were regarded by at least some of the People of the Scrolls as the spiritual ancestors of their own tradition, which was popularly called *Essene*, related to healers and physicians.[2] Sometime after the Essenes, the Gnostics of Nag Hammadi also viewed themselves as spiritual kin of both the rebellious inhabitants of Sodom and Gomorrah and, at least by implication, of the *Rephaim* as well. It may not be too audacious to imply that the very locale of the discovery of the Dead Sea Scrolls, and with it the headquarters of the most famous Essene community known, gives clear indications of a rebellious tradition opposed to orthodox establishments of doctrine and devoted to secret knowledge and practices.

Turning from the place to the people themselves, we must note that the Dead Sea Scrolls were by no means the first evidence of the existence of the Essenes. The Roman writer Pliny the Elder, the historian Josephus, as well as the Jewish philosopher Philo of Alexandria have left us much testimony concerning those whom they called Essenes. The Greek word *Essenoi* is of uncertain derivation, but it is related by scholars to the Hebrew *Asah* (he acted), *Hazah* (he saw visions), as well as to the Aramaic *Hasaya* (pious) and *Asa* (he healed). The modern Talmudic Hebrew word *Hasid* (pious) may also be reckoned among the cognate words. We may thus speculate that they were people of action, visionaries, persons distinguished by extraordinary piety, and above all, individuals preoccupied with healing, for which reason (especially in Egypt) they were also frequently called *Therapeutae*, meaning physicians or healers. While the early descriptions stressed asceticism and piety, the find of the Scrolls brought into increasing view their rebelliousness and heterodoxy.

For centuries the world of scholars viewed the Essenes as a numerically small (Pliny gave their number as around 4,000), quietist, and pacifist movement, desperately concerned with purity in all forms—celibate, ascetic, given to dietary eccentricities, and utterly unworldly and otherworldly in outlook and practice. Along with these notions went also the acceptance of the hyperorthodoxy and strict legalism imputed to the Essenes, who thus were made out to be merely an extremely orthodox and ascetic group of Jews whose doctrines and actions were in conformity with mainstream Judaism as known throughout history. The picture emerging from the Scrolls is, to say the least, very different from this earlier view of the Essene character.

After the discovery of the Scrolls a good deal of learned discussion was carried on in scholarly quarters about whether the authors of the documents were Essenes or whether they might have been what were called Zealots. As is known, in the years A.D. 66-70 a great revolt took place in Israel that swept through the country and that in A.D. 70 led to the final destruction of the Temple of Jerusalem and the subsequent abolishing of the Jewish homeland, which was not to be reestablished until the middle of the twentieth century. The instigators of this disastrous uprising were the Zealots, who came to look upon the Roman occupying forces as the embodiment of cosmic evil and upon themselves as the army of light destined to rid Israel and the world of the demonic host embodied in the power of imperial Rome. The Scrolls (at least in part) propound a warlike mythos very similar to that espoused by the Zealots. In one, the Sons of Light, led by a princely Messiah and easily identifiable as the Essenes themselves, would assume a leading role in the struggle against the Children of Darkness, who in turn are led by the prince of darkness, Belial, or the devil. This thoroughly dualistic document clearly established the People of the Scrolls as being far removed from the pacifist image attributed to them earlier. It also reminded many of the later Gnostic and Manichaean myths of the struggle of the knowers against the host of evil, led by the *archon* (ruler) of darkness. The first indications of a Gnostic or at least Proto-Gnostic tradition within Hellenistic Judaism thus made their appearance. No less an authority than the universally respected scholar R. Bultmann was prompted by the evidence of the Scrolls to write: "*a pre-Christian Judaism of Gnostic character* which hitherto could only be inferred from later sources *is now attested to by the newly discovered Dead Sea Scrolls.*[3] (Italics ours)

It has been said by one of the most insightful translators of the Scrolls, Theodor H. Gaster (in his work *The Dead Sea Scriptures in English Translation*), that the Scrolls are essentially mystical documents and that the experiences spoken of in the document called the Scroll of Hymns are genuine mystical experiences. The "wondrous mysteries" of God revealed to the authors of the Scrolls according to their testimony remind one of similar mysteries and mystical experiences alluded to and documented in various Gnostic scriptures, notably *The Treatise of the Eighth and the Ninth* as well as others of the Nag Hammadi collection. It is more than likely that the Essenic authors of the Scrolls, not unlike the Gnostic authors of the Nag Hammadi codices, were partakers of visions and revelations of an esoteric nature and that the content of the Scrolls could be viewed as possessing an inner, hidden meaning or code. (The Essenes were in fact inclined to employ codes, as the discovery of the so-called *Taxo-Asaph* disguise by way of the use of the *Atbash* cipher proves.)*

---

*For details regarding this code and cipher, see Chapter 3 of the present work, as well as Hugh Schonfield, *The Essene Odyssey* (Shaftsbury, England: Element Books, 1984).

As C. G. Jung repeatedly pointed out, the Gnostic documents, including those of Nag Hammadi, were not based
on dogmatic or philosophical considerations but contained primary revelations from the deepest strata of
the human psyche. Similarly, the latest research seems
to reveal that at least a large portion of the Dead Sea
Scrolls also originates in such direct, firsthand mystical
experiences partaken of by the Essene mystics of the
Qumran community. The Gnostics of the later period
did not feel it necessary to disguise in code and cipher
the visionary nature of their inspiration. An excellent
example of such a Gnostic description of mystic vision
is to be found in a scripture referred to earlier, *The Treatise
of the Eight and the Ninth:*

> How shall I describe the All? I see another *Nous* [spiritual
> soul—S.A.H.] who moves the soul. I see one who speaks
> to me through a holy sleep. Thou givest me strength. I see
> myself! I am willing to discourse! I am overcome with a
> trembling! I have found the origin of the Power above all
> powers, which has no origin! I see a wellspring bubbling
> up with life! . . . I have seen what discourse cannot reveal,
> for the entire Eighth, O my son, with the souls therein
> and the angels are singing in silence. But I, the Nous,
> understand.[4]

While admitting that "wondrous mysteries" have been
revealed to them, the writers of the Dead Sea Scrolls
utilize metaphors and imagery from nature to indicate
their own mystical and secret experiences. Thus we read
in the *Thanksgiving Hymns* of the Scrolls:

> But Thou, O my God, hast put into my mouth as showers
> of early rain for all who thirst and a spring of living
> waters. . . . Suddenly they shall gush forth from the secret
> hiding places. . . .[5]

In the same collection of hymns (possibly written by the
mysterious Teacher of Righteousness himself), the image
of a variety of trees is used to denote the Essenes themselves. These "trees" are nourished by the living waters
that gush forth from the secret places of God's secret

wisdom, and among them prominently mentioned is
the myrtle, the name for which in Aramaic, *assaya*, is
virtually identical with the word for healing, from which
one of the popular names of the Essenes derives. Linguistic
ciphers and other metaphors are thus used by the People
of the Scrolls to both reveal and conceal their esoteric
character.

Let us then address ourselves to the question: "Who
and what were in reality these Essenes, these People of
the Scrolls?" Their outer history is fairly quickly recounted. About a century and a half prior to the birth
of Jesus, a non-Jewish king named Antiochus Epiphanes
decided to impose a pagan form of religion on the land
of the Jews. Under the leadership of Judas Maccabaeus
a revolution broke out, which by the year 142 B.C. came
to establish the religious and political freedom of the
Jewish people. Among the followers of the revolutionary
leaders were many "pious ones," i.e., Hasidim or Essenes,
who adhered to an alternative form of mystical spirituality
and whose spiritual traditions went back a long time in
Jewish history. The aftermath of the revolution of the
Maccabees, however, created a permanent rift between
these pious mystics and the religious-political establishment in Jerusalem. The Hasmonean royal family established by the revolution had done a deed that the Essenes
considered unforgivable: The kings drove from their sacred
seat of the high priesthood of the Temple the members
of the tribe of *Zadok*, who had held this office for some
eight centuries, ever since the reign of King Solomon.
The new high priests became none other than the kings
of the new dynasty themselves. This was the state of
affairs that the Essenes could not accept. They packed
up their belongings and removed themselves from the
jurisdiction of the newly installed politician-high priests
by moving into the mysterious area of Qumran, there to
practice their special form of religious purity, conduct
secret rites, converse with angels and demons, and plot the
overthrow of the establishment of those whom they ever
after called "the wicked priests."

From this time on the Essenes of Qumran became
openly declared heretics. Their teacher, a messianic figure
whose personal name they never mentioned and to whom
their literature always refers as the "Teacher of Righteousness," was slain by the royal and priestly tyranny around
the year 100 B.C. This cruel act, which, as we shall see,
shows many startling similarities with the execution of
Jesus a century and some years later, embittered the
People of the Scrolls even further. From then on they
engaged in grand apocalyptic tasks of mythmaking and
prophesied the dawning of a new age wherein the sons
of light would fight a great war with the sons of darkness,
which would lead to the establishment of a new kingdom
of light and righteousness under the inspiration of the
pious Essenes themselves. For decade upon decade the
holy heretics brooded in their rock-hewn dwellings and
labyrinthine caverns and prepared for the coming of the
new age of light. It was within this period of sad and irate
introspection that they wrote and copied their numerous
heterodox scriptures, many of which became known nearly
two millennia later as the Dead Sea Scrolls.

The Hasmonean kings were finally brought to their
downfall by the power of Rome in alliance with the non-
Jewish dynasty of Herod. The "evil priests" no longer
ruled in Jerusalem, their place having been taken by a
foreign king supervised by a Roman governor. While the
chief antagonists of the Essenes were eliminated, conditions in the lands of Judea were still not to their liking.
Many probably drifted back to the towns and hamlets of
their ancestral land, some even found refuge in Jerusalem,
the hated seat of the usurping establishments of throne
and altar. Yet others traveled to distant regions, notably
the land of mystery and magic called Egypt, where the
equally heretical Jew Philo of Alexandria was to call
them *Therapeutae,* or healers. But the majority in all
likelihood continued to hold out in the mountains and
caves of Qumran, awaiting the new age of a Messiah who
would establish the long-awaited kingdom of light that
had eluded the expectations of the pious ones. By the

year A.D. 1 when an obscure infant was allegedly born in Bethlehem, whose brief career seemed to be patterned so closely on that of their Teacher of Righteousness, the People of the Scrolls were inwardly ready for at least certain elements of the new covenant which was proclaimed some years later by the followers of the mysterious Rabbi Yehoshva, better known by his Latin name, Jesus.

It is here that the content of the Scrolls sheds much new and valuable light on the Essene impact on the shaping of Christianity, and beyond that, on the shaping of a certain creative heterodox variety of Christianity, known as Gnosticism. The Scrolls from Qumran confirmed most of the already available information about the Essenes, but added much invaluable material in the form of teachings concerning the messianic warrior prince expected by the People of the Scrolls. This is how John Allegro characterizes the expected Essene Messiah of the Scrolls:

> This charismatic leader of the future, born of the lineage of the famous King David, would establish a new world order where the will of God reigned supreme. Such a blessed state could only come about after wars and bloody revolution in which the "Anointed" ... would personally lead the forces of Light in their apocalyptic struggle against the powers of Darkness under the arch-fiend Belial, the Devil. . . . All in all, the first eager perusals of the new material supported the idea that in Essenism we might expect to find clues to the conception of Christian ideas.[6]

The Dead Sea Scrolls revealed thus that the Messiah expected by the Essenes conformed much more closely to the image of Jesus than the vague intimations and prophetic expectations of the orthodox Judaism of the first century. Not only is there a great similarity between the Essene Messiah and the Christ figure of the Jewish heresy called Christianity, but also there is every reason to suspect that the Essene variety of Judaism might have served as the matrix of an even more unorthodox Christian heresy known as Gnosticism.

There is no other variety of Judaism besides that of the Essenes that is so closely related to the entire body of New Testament religiosity, including the Gnostic portions thereof. Essene and Christian were both practicing if not a form of communism, at least a communitarianism. Both were persecuted and therefore resentful of the religious establishment at Jerusalem. Both baptized their initiates; both practiced a sacramental ritual meal. In addition to these important similarities, both were greatly attached to the writings of the prophets and expected a cataclysm and a glorious inception of a messianically ruled new age.

The relationship of the People of the Scrolls to the New Testament, and beyond it to the Gnostic gospels, is undeniable. In addition to this there are certain other questions nonetheless portentous for being unanswered. If the traditional chronology of the lifetime of Jesus and of the subsequent spread of the Christian communities is accepted, then it appears almost imperative that some sort of an already existing organizational structure must have been utilized by the early Christians to build their church. The time between the commonly supposed date of the crucifixion of Jesus and the writing of the earliest of the Pauline letters is much too short to allow for the development of a highly complex network of organized communities with well-developed methods of communication, funding, and a structure of authority that presents itself to the reader of the Epistles of Paul. There was only one organization in existence that could have served as the foundation for this rapidly developing structure, and it was the order of the Essenes. Centered on its monastic headquarters by the Dead Sea, but extending all over Judaea and in all likelihood into Egypt, Rome, and Asia Minor, the Essene organization served as a ready-made matrix upon which the new Christian association of communities could be built. If, as we are suggesting, the Essenes were the ones who swelled the number of converts to the new Christian covenant in the first and formative years of the Church, then the miraculous rapid

growth and organization of the Christian network becomes much more plausible. In this case we must also
admit, as Allegro has done, concerning the Essenes:

> ... their doctrines, and particularly their messianic expecta-
> tions, were very much closer to those of their Christian
> mentors than anything that appears on the surface in
> the Scrolls.[7]

A Messiah who failed to transform not only the world
but even the fate of his own countrymen in his igno-
miniously terminated three-year public ministry would
not have inspired spectacular mass conversions to his
gospel. If the same Messiah had been foretold by the
prophetic traditions of the People of the Scrolls, or if
enough of these people believed that such was the case,
then the Essene-Christian connection received full
justification. As Hugh Schonfield pointed out:

> We have to allow now what was previously so clearly
> evident to no more than a relatively few scholars, that
> the Messianic concepts to which Jesus and others of his
> time were responsive were far from being confined to
> biblical sources. They were being shaped by writings
> and teachings emanating largely from the Essenes and
> widely regarded as inspired. Until it became possible in
> recent times to be fully aware of this, and to have access
> to much of their literature, the true story of Christian
> beginnings could not be ascertained.[8]

Let us then in conclusion summarize those features
of the People of the Scrolls that have a direct bearing on
the connections, not only historical but also what might
be called psychological, that join the Essene transmission
with the new covenant of Christianity, and more particularly within that covenant with the early Gnostic variant
of Christianity. It is to be hoped that such a summary
will present the reader with a deeper understanding of
the genius of the People of the Scrolls and of the culmination of this genius in an approach to the Christian message
that found its most complete literary expression in the

Nag Hammadi collection of Gnostic scriptures discovered but a few short months before the Scrolls of Qumran.

1. *The Qumran community was located on a site that eminently lends itself as a backdrop to the growth and development of a heresy of a generally Gnostic character.* The choice of the location of the community joined the Essenes of Qumran on the one hand with the messianic figure of Joshua, son of Nun, and on the other, with the demons and supernatural "watchers" connected with the Abyss of Judgement located in the Rift Valley. All of this could be taken as a documentation of the Essene myths that is at once messianic and angelic-demonic.

2. *The influence of the Essene Teacher of Righteousness created a predisposition among the Essenes toward dualism a rejection of the existing world order and the identification of the world as evil*—all positions that later became associated with the Gnostics. Admittedly this predisposition originated in the political conditions of the Jewish kingdom; however, in the minds of the Essenes of Qumran the originally mundane issues soon became transformed into cosmic and metaphysical calamities and predicaments. The rule of the Hasmonean "evil" priest-kings became the forerunner of the dominion of the archons and the Demiurge of the Gnostics. The sons of light were the early embodiment of the pneumatic Gnostics, and the sons of darkness were similarly the prototypes of the minions of the dark rulers of the lower world recognized by the Gnostics.

3. *The inspiration derived by the authors of the Scrolls did not originate primarily in Jewish dogma and law but in vivid, emotionally charged personal experiences of a mystical nature.* Some of these experiences are freely admitted in the Scrolls; others are disguised by way of metaphors and codes based on such ever-popular ciphers as the transposition of letters and the like. The latest scholarship also agrees—largely as the result of the insights of Jung— that the origin of the writings of the Gnostics is to be sought in direct, personal experience of the mysteries of being rather than in pure syncretism, philosophic speculation, and the like.

4. *The specific variety of messianism developed by the Essenes in conjunction with their attachment to the tragic figure of their mysterious Teacher of Righteousness, prepared the way not only for the messianic career of Jesus, but also for the mystical and cosmic messiahship embodied in the figure of the Gnostic Christ who speaks to us and is extolled in the Nag Hammadi Gnostic gospels.* This circumstance may have been greatly reinforced by the likely possibility that a large number of the earliest converts to Christianity were Essenes.

This final point of our summary brings us quite directly and logically to the consideration of the figure of Jesus and to the ways in which this figure may be related to the most intriguing though elusive character within the Essenic drama: the Teacher of Righteousness. Assuredly it is in the relationship of these two immensely important figures that we may find the most important indications of how the "pre-Christian Judaism of Gnostic character" (*gnostisierendes Judentum*) recognized by Bultmann came to serve as the principal fountain and origin of Gnosticism.[9] It is in the relationship of the Essene Messiah to the Christian Jesus, and beyond him to the Gnostic Christ, that the link may be discovered which joins the Dead Sea Scrolls of Essene origin with the collection of Gnostic gospels found in Nag Hammadi.

3

Essene Messiah and Gnostic Christ:
From Prototype to Archetype

In the Gospel of Matthew (16:13) we find a description of Jesus questioning his disciples concerning their view of him. The disciples reply first by describing the opinions expressed by various people concerning the identity of Jesus: "Some say that thou art John the Baptist, some Elias, and others, Jeremias, or one of the prophets." According to this version of the story, (there is a quite different one to be found in the Gospel of Thomas from Nag Hammadi), the apostle Peter gives the correct answer and is commended by Jesus by being told that flesh and blood have not revealed this answer to him, but that it came from the Father in heaven.

As in the days described by Matthew, the characterizations of Jesus differ sharply one from the other throughout history. It is very difficult to determine what the concept of the early Christians was concerning their executed founder. It is virtually certain that their concepts varied and that no uniform belief about Jesus was present in the early Christian communities. Turning to the Gnostic Christians we find that their Jesus was an enigma, a well-nigh insoluble mystery. Sometimes they represented him as a man, sometimes as the divine Anthropos, the wisdom-man who had come to rescue the sparks of light that had fallen into darkness. At times he had a body and a human voice wherewith he uttered many wise sayings, at other times he had a phantom-body that only seemed

like any other. Like the trickster-god of the American
Indians or the Fool of the Tarot deck, he was everywhere
and everything; he was in a body and without it; he was
in the world and outside of it. In the Gnostic *Odes of
Solomon* he is made to say the words that still seem true
today: "I seem to them like a stranger because I am from
another race."[1]

Such was the image of Jesus for the first three centuries:
All-inclusive, mysterious, ubiquitous—like his emulator
Paul, he was all things to all men. In the catacombs we
still find a very universal, very Gnostic Jesus. He is depicted as a form of Bacchus holding a staff with grapes
and surrounded by vines. He is a shepherd carrying a
lamb on his shoulders. He is the mysterious *Ichtos*, the
fish, for which analogy no biblical justification can be
found, as one might conjecture in the case of the Good
Shepherd and the grape plant, both metaphors which he
is said to have applied to himself.

Beginning in the third, fourth, and fifth centuries, this
mythos of unceasing, overflowing creativity becomes
confined to dogmatic formulations. At the Council of
Chalcedon, in A.D. 451 the church fathers declare it a
dogma, or article of belief, that Jesus was the union of
the two substances of divinity and humanity, that he was
"perfect God of the substance of the Father" and "perfect
man of the substance of the Virgin Mary his mother."
The leaders of the Church here tried to rationally define
what previously was discerned as a nonrational realization, and their attempt as a matter of inevitable necessity
ended in failure.

From this time on the figure of Jesus undergoes first a
gradual and then an ever more rapid devolution, or
deterioration. In the dazzling mosaics of the Byzantine
empire, as presently visible in Ravenna and Con-
stantinople, Jesus is still present as a superhuman being
of cosmic dimensions; he is still the all-ruling *pantocrator*
with orb and scepter, the representative of a transcendental
dominion over earthly life. At the same time one cannot
escape the conclusion when contemplating these

representations that somehow the creative unity has departed, the chalice of the eucharist no longer can be said to overflow with creative power as it did in the early centuries. Something is still there, but something also has been lost. Then come the long, dark Middle Ages with the still nonhuman figure of Jesus, austere, regal, sometimes agonizing on the cross, but capable of repeating—although with less conviction—the Gnostic statement: "I am from another race."

Next we arrive at the Renaissance, where in accordance with the atmosphere of humanism Jesus becomes thoroughly human in appearance. He becomes the perfect man, the model of anatomical perfection of the human body: a classical hero-god with vaguely messianic overtones. The perfect God has given way to the perfect man; the divine king has now become the perfectly proportioned human body. The dictate of the Council of Chalcedon has been fulfilled: He who was declared both perfect God and perfect man now has been experienced under both aspects, but the unity between the two has been broken irrevocably.

After the Renaissance there comes what might be justly called the period of the Great Decline, at least as far as the image of Jesus is concerned. This period begins with the Reformation and ends in the soulless materialism of the nineteenth and twentieth centuries. Luther detests the pagan beauty of the Renaissance Christ. In his desperate attempt to oppose the so-called paganism of Renaissance Rome he manages to degrade and downgrade the Christ figure still further. He boasts that Jesus dirtied his diapers like other human infants (thereby giving Freudian psychologists of a later era a fine excuse to invade the field of religion with one of their favorite obsessions, i.e., the issue of toilet training). Luther wants to make Jesus real and relevant, but instead of this he merely initiates the great historical development that will make him banal and irrelevant.

The other great reformers, particularly the stern and guilt-ridden John Calvin and his fanatical disciple

John Knox, leave Jesus more and more out of their calcu-
lations and worship a Christianized form of the Old
Testament Godhead instead. It is this vengeful and cruel
archetype that becomes the God of the Puritans and
eventually the Lord of the industrial revolution, of the
wool merchants of Manchester and the Yankee traders
of New England. Under the influence of the industrialized
Jehovah image, the concept of the Old Testament Israel
is replaced by the chosen people of the successful, the
industrious, the rich. Calvinist predestination comes to
declare that the Puritan God loves the rich more than
the poor and that wealth and success are signs of divine
favor.

And where in all this is Jesus? He is still present, but
he has been dethroned. The seventeenth and eighteenth
centuries use him as a sentimental object of maudlin
devotion and little more. He becomes a sentimental com-
forter, a friend on whose shoulder the bereaved may cry
and the downtrodden hope but never quite find complete
consolation. What a far cry is this pale, sentimentalized
image from the fierce defender of the outcasts of society
who appears in the New Testament! And also, how far
removed from the majestic, transcendental universal
king of the Byzantine mosaics, not to mention the
mysterious, ubiquitous well of the living waters that once
flowed from the Gnostic figure of Christ in the first few
centuries A.D.

The bottom of the abyss, the nethermost circle of the
inferno of history, follows. Rationalism becomes the
deity of the eighteenth and nineteenth centuries. The cult
of reason begun by Voltaire and the encyclopedists makes
heads roll under the guillotine in a less than reasonable
manner, while revolutionary rationalists enthrone a
Parisian prostitute on the altar of the republic, pro-
claiming her the Goddess of Reason. God is dead, long
live reason! Reason triumphant thus rides her chariot
into the nineteenth century, but her apostles are no
longer the genteel, aristocratic *philosophes* of the eighteenth
century. Darwin, Haeckel, and their fellows thrust the

sword of reason into the process of life and discover no God and no savior there, only blind force and the survival of the fittest. Rationalism also looks at Jesus and uses its wiles to assert that as a figure of historical fact he can hardly be said to exist. Renan, Legge, and countless others, including Albert Schweitzer, declare that the quest for the historical Jesus leads nowhere. "Jesus is a myth," so cry the positivists, implying thereby that lacking in clearly recognizable historicity he is a mere unreality, an invention without either substance or merit. The chorus of materialists, from science, philosophy, and art to Marxist politics, joins in with fierce glee.

God is dead, religion is the opiate of the people, and Jesus does not exist. Or does he? Comparative mythologists appear on the scene who are not so sure. Behind the vague and uncertain historical data surrounding the figure of the founder of Christianity they begin to discover a powerful mythic reality no less impressive for being at least in part remote from physical history. The historical Jesus gives way to the Jesus of myth. Scholarship discovers that the image of the crucified Nazarene is intimately connected with a large number of savior gods of antiquity: Osiris, Horus, Tammuz, Mithra, Orpheus, and many others. Upon the heels of the mythologists appear the representatives of modern depth psychology, among them C. G. Jung.

Unlike the rationalists, positivists, and the followers of Freud, Jung comes to hold the symbolic and mythic content of religion in great reverence. Not for him the sneering and debunking of Jesus, nor of any great figure of the spirit. In his teachings concerning the collective unconscious, or objective psyche, he brings forward the notion that religious symbols arise from a common human source in the depth of the mind. The physical reality of a historical Jesus is far less important to Jung than the psychic reality of the Christ figure as discernible within the functioning of the human soul. The symbols and myths on which various religious faiths are based reveal the powers of interior transformation and redemption that heal and unify the fragmented and tormented minds and hearts of people. Working from such premises, Jung views the Christian myth with its central redemptive figure of Christ as a great and well-nigh unique gift to humanity. The psychological and spiritual value of the Christ symbol as a unifying and healing expression of that intrapsychic principle, which he calls the Self, appears as a never-varying recognition in Jung's utterances and writings. He admits that Osiris, the Son of Man in the Book of Enoch, the Buddha, Confucius, Lao-Tse, and Pythagoras all played a psychological role similar to the one of Jesus, but he holds that Jesus mobilized more powerful transformative projections than these other figures.[2]

By recognizing Jesus as the greatest and latest symbolic representative of the archetype of the Self, Jung has given us an invaluable tool to be utilized in the study of Christian origins and indeed within all concerns and disciplines that address themselves to the religious problems of Western culture. Jung's recognitions may also be taken as signs of hope indicating that the era of negative and confused attitudes regarding this most significant archetype of our culture may be coming to an end.

Of course, confusing voices and opinions are still plentiful. The world of entertainment presented us in the 1970s with such products as *Godspell*, wherein Jesus appeared as an unreal and whimsical clown, and *Jesus Christ Superstar*, where he was seen as an abrasively unpleasant social critic. In the world of popular scholarship we have a few new Jesuses as well. One is the psychedelic-phallic symbolic figure emerging from the controversial work of John M. Allegro, of the Dead Sea Scrolls fame, entitled *The Sacred Mushroom and the Cross*[3]; another is the erotic magician conjured up by the noted scholar Morton Smith in his book *Jesus the Magician*.[4] The German author Johannes Lehmann, in his book *Jesus-Report: Protokoll einer Verfälschung* (which created a great sensation in Europe in the 1970s), represents Jesus as a somewhat confused Essenian Rabbi unjustly killed and buried in a cabbage patch.[5]

Perhaps the most influential of all the popular books on the story of Jesus was certainly Hugh J. Schonfield's *The Passover Plot*, in which Jesus engages in a plot to establish his messiahship by deliberately fulfilling the prophecies made concerning the Messiah in Jewish holy writ. The plot or coup misfires in the end and Jesus perishes, to the sad astonishment of his followers.[6] Merely as a matter of amusement we may give mention to a curious book by the Australian journalist Donovan Joyce entitled *The Jesus Scroll*. Here Jesus becomes a Zealot warrior, who survives to extreme old age and finally dies a hero's death at the last stand of the Jewish patriots in Masada. (Incidentally, the document written by Jesus himself just before his death, allegedly viewed by the author for a brief time, is purloined by the KGB and reposes in the vaults of the Kremlin where it serves as an instrument of blackmail against the Vatican.) All of this merely proves that the public in this post-Christian (or semi-Christian) era is quite hungry for alternative versions of the story of the founder of the Christian faith, irrespective of the credentials of authors and the kind of sensationalism manifest in their books.*

The confusion and ambivalence surrounding the figure of Jesus stand a good chance of being substantially reduced as the result of some developments of an entirely different nature; namely, the increasing awareness of scholars and laypersons alike concerning the content

---

*The above list of unconventional theories and books about Jesus is by no means complete. Speculation continues about the tomb of a personage by the name of Jo-asaph at Shrinagar in the Kashmir, identified by some as the tomb of Jesus. The turgid sensationalism of *Holy Blood, Holy Grail* by Michael Baigent, Richard Leigh, and Henry Lincoln, fantasizing about a surviving Jesus married to Mary Magdalene and procreating numerous offspring scattered over France, may serve to convince us further of the hunger for information about Jesus.

of the Dead Sea Scrolls. As noted earlier, the Essenes of Qumran were the chief carriers of the messianic impulse in Hellenistic Judaism. Their own Teacher of Righteousness described in the Scrolls shows so many similarities with the Christian Messiah that the suggestion has been repeatedly put forward that the two might, in fact, be one and the same. While such statements are little more than exaggerations, the similarities joining the two figures are nevertheless impressive. In addition to the Teacher of Righteousness, the People of the Scrolls also awaited a coming princely and priestly duo of messiahs, who together would reestablish the new dispensation of true godliness and righteousness. Indeed it may be said that when it came to messianic expectations and speculations the Essenes were by no means lacking in prodigious talent and accomplishment.

The connections linking Essene messianism with the Christian phase of messianic archetypal developments are manifold. The first of these links concerns the Jewish hero whose name the Christian savior bore. Joshua or Yehoshva, son of Nun, the successor of Moses as leader of the Jewish people, was a remarkable man. Josephus, calling him by the Greco-Latin name Jesus, son of Naue, describes him in terms of highest esteem.[7] Joshua, appointed to leadership and successorship by Moses, is indeed confirmed in his position by the God of Israel: "This day will I begin to exalt thee in the sight of all Israel, so that they may know that I was with Moses, so will I be with thee."[8] Later, after the numerous miracles attending his campaigns, which included the drying up of the waters of the river Jordan, the collapse of the walls of Jericho, and the arrest of the sun and the moon in their courses, his victory is described as the greatest event in the history of the covenant: "There has been no day like it, before or since, when God hearkened to the voice of man."[9] The most significant function of Joshua, particularly in the eyes of the Essenes, was not so much his miraculous generalship, but his role as the new giver and concealer of the Law. The Essenes held that Joshua sealed

the Torah inside the Ark of the Covenant, there to repose
for a very long time, until the pious King Josiah (presumably in the seventh century B.C.)[10] in the course of
certain reconstructions of the Holy of Holies accidentally
discovered it, the discovery being recounted graphically
in the second book of Kings. The Essene work known as
the *Damascus Document* states that King David had no
knowledge of the "sealed book of the Law" for the very
reason that it had not been opened since the death
of Joshua.[11]

Joshua, thus, is the one who has concealed the sacred
books of the Torah, so that only those worthy should
find them at the appropriate time. The aforementioned
synchronistic principle evident in the discovery of important sacred literature is quite clearly expressed in
the traditions concerning Joshua. All of this is of great
import for our considerations in view of the fact that the
Dead Sea Scrolls clearly show that the Essenes came to
regard their Teacher of Righteousness as the new Joshua
and his teachings as the "second Torah."[12] Amazingly,
even the very mode of the concealment and preservation
of the Scrolls effected by the Teacher of Righteousness
seems to have followed the example traditionally set by
Joshua, son of Nun. In an apocryphal book, dating back
to the first century A.D., called the *Assumption of Moses*,
Moses instructs Joshua to anoint the five books of the
Law with cedar oil and put them in earthen vessels, a
procedure virtually identical with the one adopted for
the preservation of the Scrolls of Qumran.[13] Also, on a
parchment sheet found in the so-called Partridge Cave
and published by Allegro in 1956, a series of prophetic
blessings and curses are to be found. These utterances,
all attributed to Joshua, relate to the coming of the Messiah,
who is ritually blessed here by his predecessor, while a
wicked builder of the city is at the same time ritually
cursed. It takes but little imagination to divine that the
Essenes collected these mainly biblical formulae in
order to apply the blessings to the Teacher of Righteousness, whom they regarded as the prefiguration of the

Messiah, whereas the curses were to apply to the "wicked priest," the precursor of the diabolical opposition to the messianic age of the last days.

What might thus be called the "Joshua connection" is clearly present. Joshua, son of Nun, is the first archetypal prefiguration of the messianic principle: a conqueror, a lawgiver, a concealer, and a preserver of the true *Gnosis*, or secret doctrine. He is followed by the Essene Teacher of Righteousness, the new Joshua, author of the New Torah, who is murdered by the "wicked priest" and hung or crucified on a tree in the vicinity of Qumran, known on the basis of biblical reference as the "Diviner's Oak" and to the Essenes as the "Teacher's Oak." The Teacher of Righteousness leaves behind various prophecies concerning the true and final Messiah (sometimes divided into two figures of the princely and the priestly messiahs). The time is now ripe for the arrival of the third Joshua, namely, Jesus of Nazareth, who is slain in a manner similar to that of the murder of the Teacher of Righteousness. Again, Jesus brings a new Law, or Covenant, and foretells his own second coming for a future period when the final battle between good and evil shall take place. As the first two Joshuas hid their secret doctrines and sealed them hermetically, so that only the right people might discover them at the right time, so the Jesus of the Gnostics subsequent to his Resurrection reveals his own secret teachings, which then are hidden by his followers (albeit perhaps two or three centuries later), not to be discovered until the twentieth century in the form of the Nag Hammadi gospels. Truly, this is a mythic pattern of impressive proportions, showing the unfoldment and repeated reembodiment of an archetype: The three Joshuas have an organic connection with each other—they are conquering, revealing, sacrificing, dying, and reappearing images of a Gnosis that ever seeks its expression, irrespective of the adversities and vicissitudes of human history.

Before leaving the Joshua connection it may be useful to contemplate a passage from the Gnostic *Gospel of Philip* discovered in the Nag Hammadi find:

> Jesus is a concealed name, Christ a revealed name. There-
> fore (this name of) Jesus really does not exist in any other
> language, but his name is (nevertheless) Jesus, as they
> might call him thus. But Christ is called the messiah in
> Syria, but in Greek his name is the Christ. . . .[14]

The author of this gospel identifies the name "Jesus"
as the most limited name applied to the Savior, limited
because it makes sense only in the Hebrew language.
The conjectural secret meaning of the name "Yehoshva"
(Joshua, Jesus) may be as follows: The Hebrew letters
Yod, Heh, Vav, Heh compose the Tetragrammaton, or
four-lettered name of God. With the insertion of the so-
called "holy letter" Shin in the center of the divine name,
we get the name of Joshua: Yod, Heh, Shin, Vav, Heh.
Gnostic thinking may view this operation as a completion, or rectification, of the name of the Jewish God,
because this deity generally appears as an imperfect
demiurgic entity in Gnostic scriptures. Joshua may thus
appear as a perfected or more highly evolved manifestation of the Old Testament God, capable of bringing the
divine Law unto greater heights of perfection and usefulness. Sanctified by the power of the holy letter Shin, the
original divine tetramorph now receives a differentiation
that it previously did not possess. In psychological terms
one might say that Yahveh becomes conscious in Jesus
and that this process of the creator's growth toward
consciousness proceeded from Joshua, son of Nun, to the
Essene Teacher, and finally culminated in Jesus as understood by the Gnostics. *The Gospel of Philip* clearly
states that the name "Jesus" holds a certain secret, but
that this secret does not exist in any language other than
Hebrew. Thus, the above theory regarding the secret of
this name is by no means lacking in some measure of
probability.*

The author of the present work claims no authority other than
his own for this explanation of the meaning of the name of
Jesus.

The Essenes themselves were ever conscious of the archetypal connections of their own teacher with earlier spiritual figures renowned in sacred lore. Two of these (in addition to Joshua) were the patriarch Joseph and the Levite Asaph of the time of King Solomon. Joseph appears to embody the archetypal qualities appearing as the *suffering holy one*, while Asaph stands for the *inspired seer and miracle worker*. The Essenes looked upon Joseph as a prefiguration of their Teacher of Righteousness. Significant references to this circumstance can be found in several Essene scriptures, notably in the *Book of Jubilees* and in the *Habakkuk Scroll*, the commentary on the Prophet Habakkuk, which was one of the first three scrolls discovered in 1947. In a scripture not directly related to the Essenes, the *Testaments of the XII Patriarchs*, in a portion called the *Testament of Benjamin*, we find a prophecy that various scholars, including Hugh J. Schonfield, related to the Teacher of Righteousness, even though they ostensibly refer to Joseph. Here are some of the conclusions offered by Schonfield in regard to the latter document:

> Under the figure of Joseph we are surely meant to discern someone else, conceivably the True Teacher, who suffered at the hands of lawless and godless men, and whose believed death was supposed to bring atonement. That the prediction relates to a Joseph-type was discerned by a Christian interpolator of the *Testaments*: for after the words "prophecy of Heaven" he inserted the words, "concerning the Lamb of God and Savior of the world," so relating the prediction to Jesus.[15]

The Christian interpolator, in spite of his possible sectarian intentions, may have discerned the archetypal connection between Joseph, and the Teacher of Righteousness, and Jesus, with a clarity that we ourselves might be well advised to emulate.

The connection with Asaph is even more intriguing. In the Essene work the *Assumption of Moses* referred to earlier, there appears a meaningless name, *Taxo*, applied to a saintly Levite who, with his seven sons, retires from the corrupt city of Jerusalem and sets up residence in a cave. Credit is due to Schonfield for having applied an old cipher of Hebrew scripture and thus discovering that *Taxo* is a coded disguise for *Asaph*. (The cipher is one in which the first eleven of the twenty-two letters of the Hebrew alphabet are exchanged for the last eleven letters in reverse order. The key to the cipher is Aleph equals Tav and Beth equals Shin, which is pronounced *Atbash*.) The question now arises: Who is Asaph?

Asaph ben Berechiah is described in several books of the Bible as a Levite at the time of King Solomon.[16] In both Jewish and Islamic lore he is regarded as a master of occult and miraculous arts, a wizardly figure who advises King Solomon in the theurgic practices, a man possessing knowledge of the true and ineffable Name of God. These qualities combined with the notion that, according to a later version, he is said to flee to live in a cave were sufficient to establish him in the eyes of the Essenes as a forerunner of their Teacher.

Joshua is the heroic hierophant of the concealed Law; Joseph, the gentle patriarch, betrayed and tormented by his brothers; Asaph, the priestly thaumaturge who works miracles and knows the secrets of the Divine Name. All three lead us to the True Teacher or Teacher of Righteousness. Perhaps it is well that he has no name, for in a mystical sense he is Joshua, as well as Joseph and Asaph, a bringer of the new Torah, a suffering and murdered image of meekness, and a magical healer and worker of mighty deeds of the spirit. And further down the road of history there is Jesus, embodying all of these archetypal qualities, and synchronistically related to the names of all three of his spiritual forerunners. His name is that of Joshua, his father is Joseph, and—incredibly enough— one of his latest legendary manifestations as told by Islamic and Asian sources is none other than a mystery figure called Jo-Asaph. The latter point needs to be explained briefly.

Ancient Islamic records tell of a saintly religious

teacher named Jo-Asaph or Yaz-Asaf. An influential Moslem sect known as the Ahmadiyya movement flatly states that this Jo-Asaph is identical with Jesus, who survived his crucifixion and ended his days in India.* Related to this mythical development may be the once very popular medieval work *Barlaam and Josaphat* (known in its variant form as *Barlaam and Jo-Asaph*), which has been alternatively suspected to be a disguised story of Jesus and of Buddha.

All of the above considerations make it fairly clear that the figure of the Christian Savior is the last and greatest of a series of archetypal images manifesting in Jewish tradition, which finally converged in the universal messiahship of the new dispensation. Joshua the conquering lawgiver, embodied in his namesake, became both the suffering Joseph and the miracle working Asaph, even as he came to be regarded in emulation of the priestly and royal messiahs of the Essenes as the sacrificed priest and the Davidic World Ruler.

It is but one step from these convergences to the undisguised intrapsychic mysticism expressed in the cosmic messiahship of the Gnostics. The sequence from Joshua to Joseph to Asaph to Jesus logically leads to the Gnostic Christ, the celestial *anthropos* or heavenly man. Schonfield makes this quite plain when speaking of the connection of Jesus with the messianic prefiguration in the patriarch Joseph:

> Using the account in the Bible of the favorite son of Jacob—whose death had been sought by his brothers and who had been exiled from his land as a Messianic antetype, the Essenes saw in him the anticipation of their True Teacher. From this equation, and the doctrine of the two Messiahs, there emerged the figure of a "Son of Joseph" Messiah. . . . He would be the Man performing the perfect will of God and suffering accordingly.
> Higher flights of esotericism then linked the Man human

---

*See the footnote on p. 33, Chapter Two.

with the Man celestial, the primeval Son of Man, in whose universe-filling likeness the first man on earth, Adam, was created.[17]

Following upon the earlier *prototypes* (early images) or "*antetypes*," as Schonfield calls them, came the epiphany of the *archetype* (primeval image) as perceived and proclaimed by the Gnostics. The Essenes had envisioned it with remarkable insight, but due to their secretive esotericism they could or would not proclaim their vision openly. Veiled in allegory and concealed by code and cipher, they guarded the Messiah archetype in their secret Torah. In his highly authoritative early work, *The Dead Sea Scrolls*, Allegro went on record stating:

> An intriguing problem which has presented itself during the work has been the deciphering of a number of different secret codes in which several of the works were written . . . to keep certain works especially secret.[18]

By contrast, the Gnostic Christ and other mythic and semimythic savior figures were no longer concealed. The religious pluralism of the great metropolitan centers of the Roman Empire, where the Gnostics flourished, did away with the anxious secretiveness practiced by the People of the Scrolls. Only centuries later when pluralism ceased and the repression of a newly emerged orthodoxy struck did the Gnostics resort to secrecy again. Until then the Gnostic Messianic image was open to the gaze of all. The Semitic obsession with concealment vanished along with the preoccupation with purity, diet, and other remnants of the old law. A new era, a new law, a new dispensation of Gnosis had come. Still, the new was no more than a more highly differentiated offspring of the old, and an explicit as well as implicit continuity existed between them. Allegro justly stated this:

> The gnostic ('knowing') Essenes reappear on the literary scene as 'gnostic Christians,' but . . . there is really no justification for the heavy black dividing line that is customarily drawn across the page of history between

them. There is a continuous development of religious thought, influenced by the turn of political events, which is perfectly comprehensible chronologically and doctrinally without the artificial separation of 'Christian' from 'pre-Christian.'[19]

When contemplating the movement of the esoteric Jewish prototypes and their culmination in the new messianic archetype of the Gnostic Christ, it is necessary to remember that this development was greatly facilitated by a powerful intellectual-spiritual development that did not have its seat in Palestine but in Alexandria. The great city of Alexander, located at the crossroads of many cultures and traditions, harbored a distinguished movement directed toward the synthesis of the deepest and most enlightened elements of the religious traditions of the Jews and the so-called Pagan peoples of antiquity. As early as 250 years before the birth of Jesus, the wise men of Alexandria were busily at work in their attempt to discern the underlying unity within the structures of Semitic and Greco-Egyptian spirituality. Ever since the learned ruler Ptolemy Philadelphus (325-246 B.C.) commissioned a team of scholars to translate the Hebrew Bible into Greek, this Helleno-Jewish spiritual conjunction may be said to have gathered momentum in its development. It was the greatest representative of this movement, Philo of Alexandria (who, as stated, was well acquainted with the Essenes), who became the first thinker to employ the term "archetype" in a sense closely resembling its usage in modern depth psychology. Philo clearly recognized—as did subsequently the Gnostics—that the gulf separating the monotheistic God from the human soul may be bridged by intermediate spiritual beings as well as by exalted and indeed divinized personages such as some of the greatest figures of the Bible. Intimately connected with Philo's teachings regarding such beings was his concept of archetypes, which was manifest among others in his teaching regarding the Logos of God. This principle, said Philo, was in effect the archetypal manifestation of God in relation to humanity. The Logos was the interpreting, prophetic, priestly effulgence of God uniquely capable of bringing humans to the knowledge of God. Not only was this concept obviously utilized by Christian theology subsequently, but it also reminds us powerfully of the principle underlying the thinking of the Essenes, particularly concerning their archetypal spiritual figures such as Joshua, Joseph, Asaph, and the Teacher of Righteousness. By his own admission, C. G. Jung felt inspired by the teachings of Philo when giving the name "archetype" to a certain phenomenon of the psyche.[20]

Jung defined an archetype (*Urbild*, primordial image) as "a figure—be it a daemon, a human being, or a process—that constantly recurs in the course of history and appears wherever creative fantasy is freely expressed."[21] When the human being encounters one of these images, the impact felt is one of intensity and novelty. As Jung expresses it, "It is as though chords in us were struck that had never resounded before, or as though forces whose existence we never suspected were unloosed."[22] Human beings inherently know that the archetypes are autonomous, that they obey their own sovereign laws, and that while they are in the nature of internal experiences they reflect themselves onto the screen of external human experience. Archetypes are thus present simultaneously in the internal structures of the human psyche and also in the arena of history. In the course of his life, Jung came to differentiate between the archetype as such and the archetypal image. The archetype as such, he said, does not reach consciousness, for it is lodged in an inaccessible region of psychic reality, "the invisible, ultraviolet end of the psychic spectrum."[23] Archetypal images, on the other hand, regularly manifest to the conscious mind in dreams, visions, imaginative experiences, and altered states of consciousness. Archetypes as such, said Jung, are *psychoid*, i.e., they transcend the human psyche, while archetypal images are *psychic*, namely, they belong to the knowable realm of consciousness. In all of these recognitions Jung was inspired by the modifications introduced into the Platonic concept of primordial ideas by Philo. From Philo this realization proceeded to the Christian Gnostics, who gave expression to their understanding of archetypes and archetypal images in statements such as the following passage in *The Gospel of Philip*:

> Truth did not come into the world naked, but it came in the types and images. It (the world) will not receive it in any other fashion.[24]

(In another line of the same saying in this gospel, the writer uses the phrase "the image through the image," indicating what might be his way of distinguishing between archetype and archetypal image.)

It is somewhat difficult for us today to appreciate the import of the archetypal element in connection with such figures of religious lore as Joshua, Joseph, Asaph, the Teacher of Righteousness, and Jesus. An insightful Jungian writer, Lucindi F. Mooney, wrote concerning this:

> Archetypal symbols, primordial images, actually do have the same meanings as always. What has changed in the Christian world is the Westerner's religious attitude toward them. For example, the form or physical representation of the symbol, created by our earlier fathers in an effort to express externally an internal drama, is almost universally rejected as a mere piece of carving or plaster. Nothing else. Once such symbols are seriously questioned as being indicators for something beyond rationality, they die. Thus, our culture is one commonly referred to as stripped of its symbols, as floundering between two myths, as rejecting its own hereditary home.[25]

As in the Gospel of Matthew quoted at the outset of the present chapter, so today we may be justly reminded that flesh and blood cannot reveal the true nature of the archetype to us. "Flesh and blood" are represented in our contemporary world by our alienated egos enmeshed in an alienated culture. Still, there is hope. Much of this hope seems to be embodied in the documents of the

Essenes and of the Gnostics, restored to us after a period
of many centuries. When conjoined with an insightful
psychological understanding of their meaning, these
scriptures may yet reverse the sad trend of spiritual impoverishment alluded to by the quotation above. The
messianic archetype declares to us, as it did of old, that
it seems to us like a stranger, for it is of another race, but
twentieth-century depth psychology fortified by the
authentic heritage of the long-lost Essene and Gnostic
core of Western spirituality increases our familiarity
with the shining and mysterious stranger. The old religious keywords salvation, sin, fear of God, blind
obedience to dogma, and commandment are losing their
influence upon the growing edge of the culture. New
hallmarks of spirituality have arisen, mostly deriving
from psychological theory: self-knowledge, integration,
authenticity, spiritual growth, wholeness. In spite of
confusion, reaction, and an often childish naiveté, a
certain Gnosis has appeared in our midst. An image, a
persona that characterizes the people who are responsive
to this Gnosis has begun to constellate itself. It is an
image that is in itself archetypal in nature and thus may
be said to resonate with all that possesses the radiance
of that other, archetypal reality. This new image may
indeed be the harbinger of a newly dawning and more
adequate myth for the West, a myth that would supply
the missing compensatory elements Jung felt our culture
desperately cried out for under the fateful, overriding
imperative for its wholeness.

The search for the archetypes and prototypes of Essene
and Gnostic lore is not without a vital contemporary
meaning. The ancients wisely held that the gods are
immortal, referring thus to their polytheistic vision of
the archetypal powers of the soul. Beginning in the dim
mists of ancient Semitic lore, the transformative and
redemptive image of messiahship moves on the pathways
of history. From Joshua and Joseph to Jesus and beyond
him to the mystical and cosmic hero-God of the Gnostics,
we see the unfolding of a mighty principle of redemption

and wholeness, which has not lost its urgency for us even today. The diminished recognition given to this messianic image in recent times is not a circumstance to be accepted or condoned. Referring to this very condition, Jung warned us: "For it seems to me that the world, if it should lose sight of these archetypal statements, would be threatened with unspeakable impoverishment of mind and soul."[26]

Happily we now possess means for the prevention of such an impoverishment in the form of the evidence in behalf of the spiritual importance and distinguished archetypal history of the Messiah-Christ image. The nearness of the redemptive power of the Living God as evidenced by the prototypes of the Christ image among the Essenes is but one important component within this evidence. The inescapable nearness of Divinity reaches new and even greater heights of recognition in the flowering of the Gnostic tradition proper, to the investigation of which we shall devote ourselves.

4

The Feminine Wisdom
and the Coming of the Knowing Ones

J. Krishnamurti, an Indian-born teacher of contemporary alternative spirituality, wrote in his early, small book *At the Feet of the Master*: "In all the world there are only two kinds of people—those who know, and those who do not know; and this knowledge is the thing which matters."[1] This aphorism could very well have been written some 1,700 or 1,800 years ago by the curious and much-maligned people called Gnostics, or Knowers.

What kind of knowledge did Krishnamurti and his early predecessors refer to? The English language is relatively poor in expressions denoting subtle differences of philosophical or psychological meaning. This is not true of the Greek language, which distinguishes the kind of knowledge that is reflective and scientific from another kind of knowledge that is based on experience and observation. This latter kind of knowledge is called Gnosis. In a deeper and more detailed sense this term could be more accurately rendered as "insight"; or in a depth-psychological sense it might be defined as "consciousness." In any case, it does not describe a static quality or condition, but rather a process of an intuitive, contemplative nature, and it is closely related to self-knowledge. The term is of Indo-European origin, closely related to the Sanskrit word *jnana*.

Although Gnosis is now primarily associated with the Christian Gnostics of the first few centuries A.D., it was a sort of spiritual prize valued and sought by many persons in the time just preceding and following the Christian era. The *Poimandres* and the *Asklepius*, both writings of the Hermetic school of mystical thought, frequently employ the term *Gnosis* to describe interior, illuminative insight. In another untitled Armenian collection of Hermetic sayings we find a sentence that is strongly reminiscent of several Christian Gnostic scriptural passages: "He who knows himself, knows the All."[2]

In the first century there appeared in Judea and in Egypt, and subsequently in most parts of the Roman Empire, a strange, new kind of people. Those who made their acquaintance called them *gnostikoi*, those who know. It was generally believed that they possessed what many were seeking: an inner knowledge of a reality and a familiarity with a field of expeiience greater than the life lived by most.

The earliest of the wandering Gnostic sages and prophets was Simon, nicknamed the Magician, or Simon Magus. He was a Jew from Samaria, a "Samaritan," as his compatriots were called. Samaritans were people residing in the North of Judea, who like the Essenes were regarded as heterodox by their more conventional-minded compatriots. Also like the Essenes, they shunned the Temple in Jerusalem and worshipped on their own holy mountain. Of the Hebrew Bible they accepted only the Books of Moses. From these rebellious and shunned people came Simon Magus.

There can be little doubt that Simon was a historical personage. References to his career abound in early Christian writings. The Book of Acts (8:10) represents him as a reprobate member of the Christian community, rebuked by the apostle Peter and then presumably reconciled with the apostolic church. Other Christian writers, such as Justin Martyr and the anti-Gnostic polemicists Irenaeus, Hippolytus, and Tertullian, make him out to be a troublesome rival of the apostles. In other early writings known as the pseudo-Clementine works, some highly suggestive points of Simon's career are recounted.

Nag Hammadi Valley

It would appear that Simon, along with an Arab companion named Doshtai, was a disciple of John the Baptist. After their apprenticeship to John, both Simon and Doshtai declared themselves messianic savior figures and traveled the roads of the Roman world, preaching and conferring mysteries. It is by no means unlikely that these two men, who like Jesus were initiated by John the Baptist, were infused with the power of the messianic archetype and acted as alternative savior figures side-by-side with Jesus. Certainly, the Romans regarded Simon as an embodied deity and conferred on him the title of "the great power."

Not only were Jesus, Simon, and Doshtai all initiates of the mysteries conferred by John the Baptist, but each appears to have had a mysterious and controversial connection with the hitherto repressed and secret feminine side of Hebrew spirituality. This connection manifested openly in the fact that Simon and Doshtai each had at their side a female disciple by the name of Helen, even as Jesus was intimately associated with his own female disciple Mary Magdalene. As we shall see, these women were much more than disciples and came to represent the divine feminine in association with the masculine Messiah.

It is often assumed that the Hebrews were fiercely opposed to goddess worship in all its forms. This may be true as far as the utterances of many of the prophets are concerned, but it is to be doubted that Hebrew popular religiosity shared in the misogyny of these "mouthpieces of the Lord." Both the Egyptian and the Babylonian matrix of spirituality, which were so closely associated with early Jewish history, were greatly attached to feminine deities, and the common Jewish people felt frequently deprived because their leaders gave them a lonely male god without a consort. It is quite likely that throughout the centuries the ordinary people who were without theological prejudice tended to worship a Lady along with their Lord God. It has been reported that in comparatively recent times in the vicinity of Hebron and in the area of the Negeb inscriptions were found dating back to the eighth century B.C., in which references were made not only to "the Lord who protecteth us" but also the Lord God's wife, here called by the name *Ashera*, a feminine form of one of the names of the Hebrew God. Similarly in the fifth century B.C., the Jewish soldiers stationed in Egypt at Elephantine (near the present Assuan) were wont to worship *Anat Jahu*, a goddess whom they regarded as the wife of their Lord, the God of Israel.[3] Thus, evidence continues to manifest indicating that the feminine was not totally absent from the pre-Christian Jewish archetypal structure.

By the first century B.C., the feminine divine archetype began to manifest at the level of sacred literature. This new manifestation was of a sophistication and subtlety that distinguished it sharply from the popular expressions alluded to above. The early Jewish goddess figure appears to have been, like her Babylonian counterpart, of a relatively primitive, primarily sexually toned, and at times androgynous character. The new divine feminine principle that emerged and took shape largely in the literary efforts of Alexandrian Jewish authors was not merely a primitive great mother, but a spiritual out-flowing of the highest godhead described by the Hebrew name *Chokmah*, Wisdom. Since the Greek language was the normative tongue of the educated at that time, Chokmah soon came to be known by her Greek analogue, *Sophia*. The principal literary work through which Chokmah-Sophia made her grand entry onto the stage of Alexandrian and Judean spirituality was the *Book of the Wisdom of Solomon*, which in reality represented the first century B.C. recension of certain elements of a hitherto secret Jewish tradition regarding the divine feminine.

It is thus that *Sophia*, the feminine wisdom of God, subsequently so closely associated with the Gnostics, appeared in plain sight for the first time. She is represented from the beginning as a divine spirit pervading all being. In the *Book of the Wisdom of Solomon*, she is in fact identified as partaking of the power of the creator ("the worker of all things"), as omnipotent (capable of "doing all things"), and as the mother of the gifts of wisdom and prophecy ("entering into holy souls in every generation producing prophets and friends of God").

There are certainly echoes present in this work of the ancient idea that Chokmah-Sophia may indeed be the consort of the Lord God: "She glorifieth her nobility by being conversant with God; yea, and the Lord of all things hath loved her."[4] Perhaps even more importantly, this feminine wisdom also becomes the lover and *inspiratrix* of the righteous and the wise. It is thus that Solomon, the archetypal wise man, declares his love for her: "Her have I loved, and have sought her out from my youth, and have desired to take her for my spouse: and I became a lover of her beauty."[5] Furthermore her guidance and her Gnosis are considered essential by the author of the *Book of the Wisdom of Solomon* for the proper conduct of a wise and holy life:

> Send her out of thy holy heaven, and from the throne of thy majesty, that she may be with me, and may labour with me, that I may know what is acceptable with thee. For she knoweth and understandeth all things, and shall lead me soberly in my works, and shall preserve me by her power.[6]

While the *Book of the Wisdom of Solomon* may be said to represent the feminine wisdom by way of the most exalted imagery, this Wisdom is already represented in a very similar manner in the older biblical Book of Proverbs. Wisdom is represented here as crying aloud in the land and in the streets, exhorting people to abandon their childish ways and to cast away their hatred for Gnosis.[7] In the same book, Wisdom is accorded primacy in all creation and is called the firstborn of God, companion in God's work, and one who delights with Him in his creation and in humanity.[8]

Thus we find that roughly since the postexilic period Wisdom is represented as a person, and beginning with the *Book of the Wisdom of Solomon* this person takes on distinctly feminine characteristics. The archetype of the feminine Wisdom has come to constellate itself as a glorious woman, as a goddess slightly disguised, who stands in a specially intimate relationship to all seekers after wisdom.

Whereas to the pious readers of Proverbs and the *Book of the Wisdom of Solomon* the Wisdom-Woman appeared as an ethereal spirit of the higher worlds, to later individuals she appeared as a physical woman. The first one to devise a mythological framework for the manifestation of Wisdom in incarnate woman-form was the aforementioned Simon Magus. It is reported that Simon encountered a woman named Helen and recognized in her the First Thought (a synonym for wisdom), who long ago had descended into the created world and underwent a process of deterioration and degradation. Simon himself is said to have expressed this process in the following poetic account:

> In the beginning the Father intended to bring forth
> the angels and the archangels.
> His thought leaped forth from him, this thought,
> Who knew Her Father's intention.
> Thus she descended to the lower realms.
> She bore angels and powers, who then created
> the world.
> But after she thus bore them, she was held captive
> by them.
> She suffered every indignity from them,
> And she could not return to the Father,
> In a human body she came to be confined,
> And thus from age to age she passed from body
> to body,
> Into one female body after the other . . .
> Thus she became the lost sheep.[9]

One of the female bodies occupied by the First Thought, said Simon, was that of Helen of Troy, the most beautiful and fateful woman known to the ancient Greeks.

In Simon's system, the Father as well as the First

Thought have their origin in Silence, an ever-existing, limitless power. Thus the primordial unity eventually brings forth a primal duality, consisting of a masculine principle (Father, also *Nous*, i.e., mind) and a feminine principle (*Epinoia*, first thought). The feminine wisdom having become entrapped in the cosmos, the masculine principle is moved to descend into the lower world in order to rescue the maiden in distress. Simon, it would seem, saw himself as the incarnation of the redemptive masculine, while he regarded Helen as the last embodiment of the fallen thought of God. (The early Christian writers have alleged that Helen was in fact a prostitute, but these statements have been revealed as possible misunderstandings by G. Quispel.)[10]

In less technical terms we might summarize the Simonian story as follows: There was a man sent from the most high God whose name was Simon. He was the light sent from on high, and he was bright like unto the sun. (Kabbalistically, the name *Shimon* is chiefly composed of the Hebrew letters Shin and Mem, which with the repetition of the letter Shin becomes *Shemesh*, the sun, the symbol for light and mind, the *nous*, or redeeming understanding, the principle responsible for Gnosis.) There also was a woman named Helen, who was the embodiment of the World Soul, even as Simon was that of the World Mind. She was a light also, but it was that of the soft, night-shining moon, whence her name is derived from *Selene*, the moon. After many lives in earthly bodies, Helen at last felt that her liberation was drawing near and she knew that her celestial twin aeon would come to earth and find her. The twin would come in the body of a man, just as she was born in the body of a woman. Thus she betook herself to the coastal city of Tyre, where many travelers were wont to tarry and she hoped that one of them might be her celestial companion and liberator. As so often before, she was obliged to sell herself into bondage in her new domicile in order to provide for her necessities.

One day, a middle-aged man of majestic countenance

entered the place where Helen lived as a chattel and he instantly recognized her as the Soul of the World. He paid off her debts and set out with her on a great journey. Together they walked the dusty roads of Syria and Palestine, the paved highways of Imperial Rome, and they called out to the lightsparks, the souls of potential knowers, so that they might gather around them and join the company of the liberated. As the years passed, Simon grew old and his eyesight failed, so that Helen led him by the hand from city to city in pursuit of the liberation of souls. People—so late Gnostic tales told in the underground traditions declare—can still see a young woman walking on the pathways of the world, leading an old, majestic, and magical man, and those who have eyes to see can perceive that the old man has about him a radiance like unto the sun, while the young woman is accompanied by a luminosity like that of the moon. Many legends and tales throughout the ages express their eternal story: Faust and Helen of Troy, Sleeping Beauty and the Prince, Kundry and Parsifal, Dulcinea and Don Quixote de la Mancha. The names and times change, but the actors are the same. Helen and Simon, the World Soul and the World Mind, are still among mortals and are still about the business of their Universal Parent, the great brooding Silence that dwells in the Fullness.

The liberation of Helen by way of the influence of Simon set an example for the redemption of all other human beings from the bonds of the false cosmos wherein they find themselves. The conjunction of World Soul and World Mind, of heart and head, of the relatedness of Eros with the intelligence of Logos, set the pattern that ever after was so crucial to every form of the Gnosis: the pattern of the creative conjunction of the opposites that results in freedom from limitation and the beatitude of a new and higher consciousness. The teaching of Simon is embodied not in a solitary messiahship, such as was found among the Essenes, but in the creative and redemptive power of the divine-human couple. The Essene redemptive figures were solitary sages, with an implied spiritual androgyny of the kind only known to monkish chastity. The Teacher of Righteousness speaks thus in one of the *Hymns of Thanksgiving* found in the Qumran caves: "Thou hast made me a father to the sons of grace, and as a foster-father to men of portent; they have opened their mouths to me like sucklings."[11] And in the same collection, the Teacher attributes similarly ascetic-androgynous characteristics to God: "For Thou art a Father to all (the sons) of Thy Truth, and as a woman who tenderly loves her babe, so dost Thou rejoice in them; and as a foster-father supporting a child in his lap, so carest Thou for all Thy creatures."[12] The contemplative and ascetic Essene still was obliged to envision both himself and his God as fulfilling a dual role as male and female, while Simon's liberated Gnosis was no longer in need of such psychic strategems.

In the Gnostic system of Simon—the first such system as far as history knows—the desperate, compulsive emphasis on purity as found among the People of the Scrolls gives way to a liberty and libertarianism of impressive proportions. As a surviving contemporary of Jesus, Simon was of course familiar with the abrogation of the law of Moses as enunciated by the Nazarene rabbi. As Jesus called for the establishment of a new law characterized by love in lieu of harsh justice, so Simon preached freedom from the restraints of both Jewish orthodoxy and Essene heterodoxy. Restriction is the order imposed on the world by the tyrannical creator angels, said Simon; whereas freedom from restriction is the natural consequence of Gnosis. The few fragments of Simon's writings available to us indicate that he was not concerned with the freeing of the Jews from political oppression, but with the freeing of the souls of men and women from what today we would call psychological restrictions, such as the one-sidedness and narrowness of consciousness. In the so-called *Great Announcement* he brought forth his majestic Gnostic myth involving the First Thought (or World Soul) and the World Mind, while in the *Four Quarters of the World* he probably propounded a magical image of the universe. And in *The Sermons of the Refuter* he appears to have criticized the God of the Hebrew Bible and engaged in a reinterpretation of the Book of Genesis in light of the foolishness of the creator who jails his human children in a fool's paradise, so that the wise serpent needs to assist their liberation.

It is apparent from these fragmentary reports concerning the teachings of Simon that almost all of the major features of the later Gnostic systems are already present in his legacy. These may be summarized as follows: (1) the Sophianic myth of the feminine world soul captured in the lower world and liberated by her supernal twin, who then becomes her companion; (2) the magical view of the cosmos and the consequent need for ceremonial sacramental aids to liberation and wholeness; and (3) the imperfect character of the Old Testament revelations and of their god, with the consequent need for a new dispensation or "covenant" in which the old law would be declared defunct and a new law of freedom and love proclaimed.

It is interesting to note regarding the third feature above that Simon, both as a Samaritan and as a Gnostic, stood in opposition to the Jewish faction of early Christians who were represented by Peter, sometimes known as "the apostle of the circumcision" in recognition of his attachment to Jewish customs. The legendry evolved by the Christian detractors of Simon has him engaged in a prolonged rivalry and contest of will with Peter, replete with duels involving miraculous powers and contests of what one today might call spiritual one-upmanship. Interestingly, both men are called Simon, and so Simon Peter the Judaizing Christian apostle and Simon the Magician appear as two sides of the same or at least similar archetypal image. It has even been suggested (by the early scholar of Gnosticism W. Baur and his Tübingen school) that Simon Magus is but a disguise for the apostle Paul. Petrine, restrictive Christianity is thus contrasted with Pauline universal Christianity. This suggestion cannot be considered as literally true, but may contain a certain amount of symbolic truth nevertheless. Could it be said that in the juxtaposition of Peter and Simon we find a symbolic confrontation of the sort of Christianity that subsequently became normative and orthodox, with the liberating and Gnostic Christianity that Jesus himself taught and that the Petrine church, under the influence of the Old Testament archetypal structure, came to deny? And it is certainly true that Pauline Christianity with its openness to the non-Jewish populace and its pluralistic view of the composition of the church was certainly nearer in spirit to the Simonian Gnosis than its more rigid counterpart.

It must be remembered also that Simon was indeed rightly called *Magus* or Magician. As such he was the inheritor of the messianic archetype encountered earlier in the Levite Asaph, author of many Psalms, greatly revered by the Essenes. Whereas Jesus primarily appeared to embody the archetypes of the Suffering Holy One and the Conquering Hero (and only to a minor extent those of the Priest and the Magician), Simon appeared clearly as the miracle working sage, commanding the elements, extolling the virtue of the alchemical fire—which in his *Great Announcement* he represents as the symbol of the Universal Root of being—and performing as well as preaching many astonishing wonders. Not the least of his wondrous deeds is the reputed feat of Simon's ability to fly. In a third-century Syriac work called *Didascalia*, Simon is reported to rise up into the air, and Peter then miraculously causes him to fall and break his ankle. Eusebius in his work on Church history (c. A.D. 324) writes that Simon, when confronted with Peter's opposition in Judea, simply rose into the air and flew away in a westwardly direction. In the *Acts of Peter and Paul*, Simon receives a supernal summons to speed to Rome and he flies through the air from Aricia to Rome, arriving at the city gates in a cloud of smoke. Perhaps more significantly, in a fourth-century source we find an account of Simon riding in a chariot drawn by four flaming horses.

What are we to think of the tales concerning this Gnostic Icarus? The flying motif is not unknown in either the

Old or the New Testaments. Ezekiel the prophet is in a sense regarded as the patron of all mystic flights, inasmuch as in his famous vision he beheld a divine chariot conjoined with a throne upon which God was seated and surrounded by four winged creatures called the Cherubim.[13] This throne-chariot, called in Hebrew *Merkabah*, became the mystical archetype of a certain form of Jewish mysticism, consisting in spiritual flights wherein the soul of the devotee was said to leave his body and rise through various intermediary regions to the throne of God. It is held by some scholars (notably Gershom G. Scholem in his noted work *Major Trends in Jewish Mysticism*) that this practice of mystical flying gave rise to the later system of the Kabbalah, the received tradition of secret Jewish Gnosis. What is particularly significant for our purposes is that the Dead Sea Scrolls contain fragments that speak of the glories of the chariot of God and the vision of the "Glorious Face" among the "Angels of Knowledge."[14] Merkabah mysticism and with it early Kabbalism thus may indeed be rooted in Essene mystical practices of "flying on the Chariot."

Simon, it would seem, inherited from the Essenes a mystical proclivity for flying, and he perfected this art both magically and by way of constituting it as a spiritual metaphor. Ever since Simon the Gnostics always knew that in order to achieve liberation the initiate had to find a way of releasing his imprisoned spirit from the limitations of the gross material body, allowing it to fly to its own true home in the fullness, like a bird freed from its cage. Once again, the Essene tradition appears to have acted as the forebear of the Gnostic. Thus we find in the account of Josephus describing the Essenes of an earlier time:

> For it is a fixed belief of theirs that the body is corruptible and its constituent matter impermanent, but that the soul is immortal and imperishable. Emanating from the finest ether, these souls become entangled, as it were, in the prison-house of the body, to which they were dragged down by a sort of natural spell; but when once they are

released from the bonds of the flesh, then, as though liberated from long servitude, they rejoice and are borne aloft.[15]

Not only are we assured here once again of the direct continuity linking Essene and Gnostic practice, but also we may find a relationship between the Hebrew alternative tradition and the timeless practice of shamanistic and related transmissions. A common experience of archaic technicians of ecstasy is the exiting from the body and the flight of the soul over long distances. Mystical flights are a prominent feature of the stories of prophets such as Elijah, Ezekiel, and Muhammad, as well as of witches and magicians persecuted by the inquisitors. Simon the flying Gnostic finds himself thus in abundant company indeed.

Simon discovered the World Soul in Helen, as did his fellow initiate Doshtai in another Helen. For many centuries it was believed that these two men differed radically from Jesus, who merely redeemed the fallen woman Mary Magdalene. It took the recent discovery of the Nag Hammadi gospels to bring to the attention of Christendom the routinely held belief by at least some Christians of the early centuries that Jesus had found in Mary Magdalene the same kind of Sophianic consort as Simon found in Helen. Not only was Mary Magdalene the favorite and most Gnostic disciple of Jesus, but as indicated by *The Gospel of Philip* she was the magical consort of Jesus as well:

> There were three who walked with the Lord at all times;
> Mary his mother and her sister and Magdalene whom
> they called his consort. For Mary was (the name of) his
> sister and of his mother and of his consort.[16]
> The consort of the Savior is Mary Magdalene. The Lord
> loved her more than all the disciples and used to kiss her
> often on her (mouth).[17]

Yet it would be erroneous to assume that the association of such messianic figures as Simon, Doshtai, and Jesus with a particular woman denoted primarily a human and personal relationship. The dyad of Messiah and Messianic Consort bears all the hallmarks of a myth in the truest sense of the word. The two protagonists appeared in many different forms and were called by a variety of names. This is particularly manifest in Simon's mystical consort Helen, whose name (while related to the Goddess Selene) means torch and who was regarded by Simon and his followers as the reembodiment of Helen of Troy. This woman, whose beauty brought about the Trojan War, was associated with a supernatural radiance, so that while she was asleep in Troy, her Greek countrymen were able to locate her residence by perceiving the light that blazed above her chamber. Quoting Simon, the church father Epiphanius recalls this episode as a metaphor for Helen's Gnostic role in the enlightenment of humankind:

> Through its shining, as I said, he signified the display of light from above. . . . As the Phrygians, by dragging in the wooden horse, ignorantly brought on their own destruction, so the gentiles, that is, men apart from the *gnosis*, produce perdition for themselves. . . .[18]

Helen thus symbolized the light of supernal knowledge, and her role on earth was to lead human beings through the darkness of matter back to God. The World Soul herself, redeemed from exile, brings about the victory of the forces of light by showing forth her own radiance. Sophia, Wisdom, has become manifest under the guise of a woman and has become a partner, even an equal partner, in the task of redemption. The notion of a solitary male savior, as taught in later mainstream Christendom, is contrary to the vision of such knowing ones as Simon and his successors. The Gnostics made their appearance as the apostles not merely of the *man of light* (Simon, Jesus) but also of the *woman of light* (Sophia, Helen, Mary Magdalene) as co-redemptrix, or partner in the work of salvation. The knowing ones had come and with them Wisdom, the feminine Word, had begun her march in history. Resented and persecuted, combated and repressed from age to age, she came to enjoy a period of manifestation through the agency of her Gnostic devotees that was to leave its mark on the turbulent tale which constitutes the history of Christendom and of Western culture. Again and again the voice of the eternal feminine was to go unheard and crying in the wilderness, but she was assuredly wooed, prayed to, and revered by her friends the Gnostics. With Simon the Magician, the tradition of the knowers emerged from the shadows of Hebrew patriarchy and declared its uniqueness, its power to enchant and transform the hearts and souls of those who long desired to know the face of Lady Wisdom. Jacques Lacarrière, the French poet and admirer of the Gnostics, summed up their intentions well when he wrote:

> The essential point about everything concerning Simon Magus (and Gnosticism) is the image of the primordial Couple, the image of Desire . . . exalted as the primary fire of the world and the source of liberation, which is the image of Wisdom, incarnate in the body of Helen, who has fallen from the heights of heaven into the depths of history to teach men that the way to salvation is through union with that reflection of the divine splendour that is the form of woman.[19]

5

The Odyssey of the Gnosis

The journey of Gnosticism began on the high roads of Samaria, but it did not end there. Two disciples of Simon carried his message to Antioch and Syria. Their names were *Saturninus* and *Menander*. Both taught the existence of an Unknown God and the great intermediate hierarchies composed of angelic beings, not all of whom stand in a benevolent relation to humanity. The rigid monotheism of Judaism, which was inherited by the orthodox party in Christianity, was revealed by these teachers as a gross oversimplification. The personal God, envisioned as the creator, lawgiver, tyrannical king, and judge of his universe —so said Saturninus and Menander—is not the only and true God. The authentic Godhead is an impersonal fullness, utterly transcendent and beyond the reach of the human mind in its present condition. This Godhead, referred to at times as the Unknown Father, emanated a portion of its own sublime essence, which became the created cosmos. It also emanated a number of angels and creative spirits, some of whom became estranged from their ultimate source and came to look upon themselves as autonomous rulers. The traditional cosmology of the ancient Hebrews already recognized that the planets were not inert luminaries, but rather that they were ensouled by angelic powers whose inevitable order served to celebrate the power of Jehovah. The star-angels and other ruling spirits appear as tyrannical, limiting agencies in this Gnostic view. They are usurpers who lord it over humanity and creation in order to enhance their own self-importance and glory. It is incumbent upon the knower to realize this and to extricate himself from the grasp of these powers whenever possible. The existential predicament of human life lies in the uncomfortable dominance to which these lesser godlings subject the spirits of human beings, and from which only the experiential realization of Gnosis can extricate them.[1]

Such myths are clearly not "scripture" as exoterically understood by Jew or Christian, nor are they a work of philosophy in the sense of discursive reasoning in the knowledge of the origins and nature of the human being. Rather, they appear to be based on what might be called experiential psychospiritual knowledge. They are what Gilles Quispel insightfully called "the mythologization of Self-experience."

Significantly, it is in Egypt and not in Palestine, Antioch, or Syria that Gnosticism came to reach its greatest and fullest flowering. This circumstance is in fact more understandable than it might seem at first hearing. Hellenistic Egypt was not only a gathering point of religious and transformative traditions and disciplines of great diversity, but also it was the locale where colonies of Essenes existed. The People of the Scrolls were as numerous, perhaps even more numerous, in Egypt than they were in Palestine. It was here that Ptolemy Philadelphus (309-246 B.C.), the learned Greco-Egyptian ruler, commissioned the noted translation of the Hebrew Bible into Greek, in the version known as the *Septuagint.* Here Judaism met Platonism as well as the mystery systems of Serapis, Isis, and others, and here Essene piety was subjected to the refining and widening influences of the wisdom-heritage of the known world. No wonder that the Gnostic teachers found a welcome in Alexandria and other Egyptian settlements and that they found followers in profusion.

Simon and to a lesser extent Saturninus and Menander were itinerant prophets. The later generation of teachers of the Gnosis came to be established in cities, or more frequently in *the city*, Alexandria, the spiritual capital of the Roman Empire and, indeed, of most of the world beyond it. Whereas Gnosticism proper differs from most Western religions in having no personal founder, it soon becomes intimately associated with the still youthful movement of Christianity and its founder, Jesus. Thus, it is without doubt that one of the earliest popularizers of the Christian message, *Lucius Charinus*, a disciple of John the Evangelist, was a thoroughgoing Gnostic. His *Acts* of the various apostles—namely, Peter, Andrew, John, Thomas, and Philip—enjoyed wide popularity and represented a major factor in the spread of Christianity. This literature was not considered heretical by anyone for some time, and its author was revered as a close associate of the author of the Fourth Gospel. Another great teacher of the Gnosis, *Basilides,* was regarded as having been a disciple of Glaucias, who as a very young man sat at the feet of Peter, chief of the apostles. Basilides taught in Alexandria from about A.D. 117 to 138, and his school was even extended to Spain by one of his successors, Marcus of Memphis. Such teachings of Basilides as are available to us indicate that he emphasized the importance of the concept of the Unknown God, totally transcendental, incomprehensible, and beyond all categories of existence. Here are some of his statements in this regard as recorded by the church father Hippolytus:

> There was when naught was; nay even that 'naught' was not aught of things that are. But nakedly, conjecture and mental quibbling apart, there was absolutely not even the one. And when I use the term 'was,' I do not mean to say that it was; but merely to give some suggestion of what I wish to indicate, I use the expression 'there was absolutely naught.'
> Naught was, neither matter, nor substance, nor voidness of substance, nor simplicity, nor impossibility of composition, nor inconceptibility, imperceptibility, neither man, nor angel, nor God; in fine, neither anything at all for which man has ever found a name, nor any operation

which falls within the range either of his perception or conception.[2]

Basilides was clearly in touch with numerous teachings of the East, both in the form of the writings of Zarathustra and of transmissions received from India. It is in part due to these sources of insight that we may attribute the remarkable fact that his vision soars beyond even the archetypal world of Plato and rises to contemplate the Absolute, the unnameable One, which can be adored in silence alone.

Bardesanes, or Bardesan, born in A.D 155 on the banks of the river Daisan in Syria, was of distinguished birth and was a close advisor of the local ruler whom he converted to a Gnostic form of Christianity. Thus, between A.D. 202 and 217, there actually existed a Gnostic Christian state in Syria, which was subsequently destroyed by the Roman emperor Caracalla. Bardesanes, however, continued to teach in Armenia, Mesopotamia, and Syria and died in A.D. 233. He was a writer of odes and hymns of great beauty, and it is generally held that the lovely mythic poem known as *Song of the Pearl* was written by him.* His book of 150 hymns was used by the Christian church of Edessa in Syria until it was replaced some 170 years later with the more orthodox hymns composed by St. Ephrem. After Bardesanes' death, he was succeeded by his son Harmonius, who also was known as a poet and musician. Whereas it is often held that Bardesanes' approach to the Christian Gnosis was characterized by somewhat atypical ascetic tendencies, it is certain that his teachings also contained a considerable emphasis on the divine feminine as exemplified by the following triple fragment of his hymns preserved by St. Ephrem:

> Thou fountain of joy
> Whose gate by commandment
> Opens wide to the Mother;
> Which Beings divine

---

*See Chapter Nine of the present work.

Have measured and founded,
Which Father and Mother
In their union have sown,
With their steps have made fruitful.

Let her who comes after thee
To me be a daughter
A sister to thee.

When at length shall it be ours
To look on thy banquet.
To see the young maiden,
The daughter thou sett'st
On thy knee and caressest?[3]

Sacred scriptures have played a great role in the teaching and practice of many religions. Among such religions the Judeo-Christian-Islamic family of faiths appears to possess a particularly fervent attachment to its scriptures, amounting at times to a veritable worship of the written word. Early Christianity was faced with a considerable dilemma regarding scripture, inasmuch as its founder had repeatedly shown a lack of reverence for the letter of the Jewish scriptures and in addition declared that he had brought a new law, apparently superseding the old. The man who addressed himself with great acumen and success to this dilemma was a Christian cleric and shipowner born on the southern shore of the Black Sea by the name of *Marcion*, who though widely traveled and well acquainted with the Alexandrian Gnostic teachers, carried on considerable activity in Rome between the years 150 and 160. He was a bishop and also the son of a bishop and a man of great influence in the various Christian communities.

Marcion pointed out that the God referred to by Jesus and the God spoken of and speaking in the Old Testament are not one and the same Being. The God of Jesus is a *Good God* said Marcion, whereas the God of the Hebrew Bible is merely a *Just God*. Many centuries later, the modern school of higher biblical criticism adopted views extremely similar to those espoused by Marcion. G. R. S. Mead, commenting on the position of Marcion, writes truthfully:

> The Christ had preached a universal doctrine, a new revelation of the Good God, the Father over all. They who tried to graft this to Judaism, the . . . creed of a small nation, were in grievous error, and had totally misunderstood the teaching of the Christ. The Christ was not the Messiah [expected by the mainstream of Judaism—S.A.H.]. The Messiah was to be an earthly king, was intended for the Jews alone, and had not yet come. Therefore the pseudo-historical "in order that it might be fulfilled" school had adulterated and garbled the original Sayings of the Lord, the universal glad tidings, by the unintelligent and erroneous glosses they had woven into their collections of the teachings.[4]

Something needed to be done. Marcion thus decided to remedy the existing conditions. With great skill he organized the material relating to Jehovah in the Old Testament and juxtaposed it in topically related parallel columns to the sayings and deeds of Christ. The result was devastating. The contradictions and inconsistencies shocked and distressed all who were confronted with them. The best of Jehovah merely showed him as a stern God of Justice, whereas at his worst he was revealed as a capricious, cruel, and willful Being. In both aspects he seemed greatly removed from the ideal of the Good God preached by Jesus. Marcion was particularly attached to the figure and tradition of the apostle Paul, who he said was the first to really understand the mission of Christ, and who had rescued Christianity from the provincialism and petty sectarianism of those who attempted to follow Jesus without understanding him. (This reasoning was by no means uncommon among Gnostic teachers and is based on the fact that Paul communed with Christ spiritually in his experience on the road to Damascus and, thus, had an experience of Gnosis that was superior to the experience of those who had merely seen Jesus in the flesh.) The gospel espoused as authentic by Marcion was a version he possessed of the Gospel of Luke and which he said was in the main the work of the apostle Paul himself.

One of the most controversial and also most engaging Gnostic teachers was *Carpocrates,* who with his wife Alexandra and his son Epiphanes (the historical existence of whom is doubted by some) presided over an influential school of Gnostics. Irenaeus, who wrote about Carpocrates and his school in malicious and scandalous detail, as well as the somewhat more trustworthy Clement of Alexandria (A.D. 150-205) inform us that Carpocrates was a Greek born on the island of Cephalonia, but who settled in Alexandria and taught there during the reign of the emperor Hadrian (A.D. 117-138). While the church fathers accused Carpocrates and his school of all manner of unsavory practices—primarily of a sexual nature— there is no true evidence indicating that this particular group of Gnostics was much more than a cultured, educated, and prosperous Alexandrian circle composed of urban intellectuals of liberated views and habits. Some of the ideas of this circle were set forth in a treatise concerning justice, which may have been written by Carpocrates' son Epiphanes. This scripture puts forth certain ideas that were not uncommon in contemporary Christian communities, or rather communes, where the sharp divisiveness and selfishness of personal property and the exclusiveness of familial connections were abrogated. It is also unfortunate that Clement, who seems to have stood in a position of some sort of rivalry with Carpocrates, represents one of our principal sources of information on this topic. All one can say with certainty is that Carpocrates, along with the majority of Gnostics, taught the need to be emancipated from the obsessive rules and repressions of the Mosaic structure of law, and that he did not view the tendencies of some Christian leaders (possibly including Clement) to compromise Christian existential freedom with the old law with any degree of favor.

Of greater interest is the teaching of this school regarding what has been called the Monadic Gnosis and its implications in terms of the reembodiment or reincarnation of souls. The Monad, or primeval Unitary Being, is the fount and ultimate destiny of all existence. But the manifest plane of existence contains numerous finite spiritual entities, who in the interest of maintaining their own separate spheres of influence are ever bent on counteracting the universal striving after unity, which pervades all creation. Such mundane spirits impose various restrictions on the portions of the universe they dominate. It is necessary for the spirits of human beings to awaken first of all to the *memory* of their former condition and their origin, so that fortified by these reminiscences, they may soar above the limitations of diversity and return to the unity of the Monad. The mystery of remembering (*anamnesis*) thus makes its first powerful appearance in the available Gnostic literature. The existential and psychological predicament of the human soul according to these views is that it fails to remember what it is and where its true home is located. One is reminded of the thoroughly Gnostic statement of the modern British writer Colin Wilson that a human is really a god suffering from amnesia, laziness, and nightmares. But how, one might ask, can this amnesia be removed? The answer given by Carpocrates and his school is that by purposeful or, as we might call it today, conscious experience of the world and of the flesh one may recover one's true memory. In its cycle of existence the soul has to pass through a great diversity of experiences, all of which if carefully observed and assimilated may be conducive to the overcoming of self-forgetfulness. By way of careful self-observation in the midst of experience, human souls are able to shake off the shackles of limitation imposed on them by the mundane spirits. They are freed from the cycle of repeated lives and experiences and are able to obtain a state of perfection and sovereign repose. It would appear that this school definitely accepted a version of the doctrine of reincarnation, while asserting that only the individual who chooses to lead a self-observing life of alert consciousness can overcome the ceaseless round of cyclic return to which the agents of limitation have condemned the human race.

This brings us to the most outstanding of all the Gnostic teachers, in whom the Gnostic tradition receives its greatest and most appealing expansion and amplification: the poet, prophet, visionary, and lover of the Divine whose name was *Valentinus*. Mead called Valentinus "the great unknown of Gnosticism," and indeed it is true that we possess far less information regarding his life and person than we might wish for. Valentinus was born in Africa on the coast of the ancient state of Carthage around or before the year 120. He was educated in Alexandria and spent a considerable portion of his life there, although an important segment of his life must be allocated to his residence in Rome. He was personally acquainted with numerous leaders of the Christian churches in Alexandria and Rome. The famous church father, Origen, born A.D. 185, was one of his early associates, and it is not unlikely that some of Origen's teachings as well as general "Gnosticizing" attitude may have been influenced by Valentinus. Between A.D. 135 and 160 Valentinus lived in Rome, and according to Tertullian he was a candidate for the office of Bishop of Rome. It is also stated by Tertullian (a subsequent candidate for heresy himself) that Valentinus was excluded from the "great church" around A.D. 175. There is evidence indicating, however, that he was never universally condemned as a heretic in his lifetime, and that he was respected in most Christian communities until his death. He was almost certainly a priest in the mainstream church and may even have been a bishop. Like other prominent Gnostic teachers, Valentinus also received a transmission of teaching and of sacramental power from an "apostolic man," in his case from one Theudas, a friend and disciple of the apostle Paul.

It is certainly a question of more than minor interest what the course of Christian doctrine and practice might have been had Valentinus been elected to the office of

Bishop of Rome. His clear, hermeneutic vision, combined with his sense of the mythical, would have probably resulted in a general flowering of the Gnosis within the very fabric of the church of Rome and might have created an authoritative Gnostic paradigm of Christianity that could not easily have been driven out for many centuries, if at all. The fact that circumstances and the increasing floodtide of pseudo-orthodoxy caused his efforts to fail must be reckoned among the great tragedies of the history of Christianity. Still, many important features of his unique contribution survived and more have recently surfaced from the sands of the deserts of Egypt. Some of these may be in need of enumeration here.

Valentinus and many other Gnostic teachers have presented their students and readers with intricate cosmologies: systemizations of psychospiritual reality of impressive proportions and rich content. It was alleged by the antagonistic church fathers and long held by those who followed their lead that these cosmological constructs were little more than artificially compacted images calculated to bewilder and impress the minds of devotees. It was largely the result of the highest and most unbiased insight of modern depth psychology that many contemporary scholars began to recognize that these cosmic images, which reappear in kindred form in neo-Gnostic systems such as Theosophy and Anthroposophy, might in fact be primal patterns perceived as the result of direct visionary and intuitive experience. C. G. Jung, who found remarkable similarities between Gnostic archetypal imagery and his own, stated repeatedly that he was convinced that the Gnostic systemizations of reality were the result of direct and highly instructive spiritual experience on the part of the Gnostic visionaries, among whom a place of signal distinction belongs to Valentinus. Jungian psychologist and mythologist Ean Begg comments on the depth-psychological character and importance of Gnostic archetypes in the following manner:

> To Gnostics the archetypes were not just concepts or
> abstract ideas, nor were they quite the same as the gods

of old, personifications of human instincts and receptacles
for human projections, who were already entering into
their twilight by the time Gnosticism appeared on the
scene. It seems as though some Gnostics, at least, came
very near to understanding the archetypes as psychoid,
that is, subliminal, collective, autonomous energy quanta,
manifesting typically in synchronistic or transcendental
experiences, possessing individuals and operating through
them. The closeness of their views to his own impressed
Jung greatly, though, when he died, only a fraction of the
Nag Hammadi library, the Jung Codex, had been
translated.[5]

The cosmogonies and theogonies, gospels and myths
that are often gathered under the heading of "Valentinian"
might all be most profitably understood as being based
on a single existential recognition, which might be summarized as follows: *Something is wrong.* Somewhere,
somehow, the fabric of being at the existential level of
human functioning has lost its integrity. We live in a
system that is lacking in essential integrity and thus is
defective. Humans live in an absurd world that can be
rendered meaningful only by Gnosis, or self-knowledge.
This absurdity is the property of the kind of reality we
live in. It does not follow that the physical or superphysical
constituents of this reality are in and of themselves absurd,
but our systematic way of perceiving them is. The word
"cosmos" as used by Gnostics does not mean world (as
it is frequently, but inaccurately translated) but rather
system, and can thus be perfectly well applied to the
system created by the human mind concerning reality.
Basilides called this cosmos one of illusion, thus repli-
cating the views of Hindus and Buddhists. Valentinus, in
the *Gospel of Truth*, of which he is the likely author, introduced a name, "plane," meaning error to denote the same
concept. We all can agree that reality to us is what appears
to be real, and so our minds though lacking in Gnosis
present us with a flawed reality replete with absurdity.

Similarly, it is necessary to consider that Valentinus'
effort to shift the blame for the cosmic defect from

humanity to Divinity is by no means the sort of blasphemy that Judeo-Christian-Islamic believers would perceive it to be. Rigid monotheism is lacking in the kind of psychological and metaphysical subtlety that may be found in Gnostic thinking. The lesser God, or creator, as envisioned by the Gnostics is somewhat akin to an imperfect mythologem created by the mind. *The Gospel of Philip*, a scripture bearing the imprint of the influence of Valentinus, tells us: "God created man and man created God. So it is in the world. Men make gods and they worship their creations. It would be suitable for the gods to worship men."[6] The proposition that the human mind lives in a largely self-created world of illusion and error from whence only the enlightenment of a certain kind of Gnosis can rescue it, finds well-nigh exact analogues in Hinduism and Buddhism. The Upanishads state that this world is the *maya* of deity, through which man deceives himself. Buddha stated that the world consists of ignorance, impermanence, and the lack of authentic selfhood. Valentinus is in very good company indeed when he establishes the proposition that we live in a defective system of false reality that can be set aright by the insight of the human spirit.

How does Valentinus propose that humans bring about the repair of the flaw of the cosmos? Irenaeus quotes Valentinus concerning this:

> Perfect redemption is the cognition itself of the ineffable greatness: for since through ignorance came about the defect . . . the whole system springing from ignorance is dissolved in Gnosis. Therefore Gnosis is the redemption of the inner man; and it is not of the body, for the body is corruptible: nor is it psychical, for even the soul is a product of the defect and is a lodging to the spirit: redemption therefore must be itself of a *pneumatic* (spiritual) nature. Through Gnosis, then, is redeemed the inner, spiritual man: so that to us suffices the Gnosis of universal being: and this is the true redemption.[7]

The ignorance of the agencies that create the false system

is thus undone by the spiritual Gnosis of the human being. The defect can be removed by Gnosis. Spiritual self-knowledge thus becomes the inverse equivalent of the ignorance of the unredeemed human ego. The proposition thus outlined, which some have called "the pneumatic equation," represents the central core-reality of the elaborate mythic structures of cosmogonic and redemptive content that are associated with the teachings of Valentinus.

The methods advocated by Valentinus for the facilitating of a true, spiritual Gnosis are not confined to philosophical doctrines and poetic mythologems. The Valentinian system was above all a system of sacrament. In addition to the seven Christian sacraments still preserved in certain branches of Christendom, the Valentinian Gnosis practiced two greater mystery rites, called "redemption" and "the bridal chamber," respectively.*

Valentinus had numerous disciples, among whom a particular distinction belongs to *Marcus*, an early disciple, and two learned commentators who tended to modify the teachings of Valentinus, *Ptolemaeus* and *Heracleon*. The latter two have further modified the teachings to accommodate mainstream Christian views. Thus, while Valentinus emphasized that Jesus occupied a vehicle that was pure spirit, Ptolemaeus admitted that he also had a psychic nature and body.

The names here mentioned by no means exhaust the number of the Gnostic teachers of the classical period of the second and third centuries. Such names as those of *Cerinthus, Monoimus, Cerdo,* and *Apelles* appear in the polemical writings of the church fathers, all describing teachers and practitioners of the same Gnosis of which Valentinus and the other prominent Gnostic leaders may be considered the greatest representatives.

What came of Gnosticism? Beginning with the fourth century, all of Alexandrian spirituality began a rapidly accelerating decline. In the wake of the fateful Council

---

*For an exposition of the Valentinian supreme mystery rites, see Chapter Twelve of the present work.

of Nicea (A.D. 325), convoked by the pagan emperor Constantine who nevertheless established Christianity as the official religion of the Roman state, the mainstream party attached to literalist orthodoxy became the ruling element not only in the Church but also in society in general. Elaine Pagels, in her influential work, *The Gnostic Gospels*, tells us:

> By the time of the emperor Constantine . . . , when Christianity became an officially approved religion in the fourth century, Christian bishops, previously victimized by the police, now commanded them. Possession of books denounced as heretical was made a criminal offense. Copies of such books were burned and destroyed.[8]

It became a matter of expediency that the form of Christianity now propagated for the masses should be as simple and unsubtle as possible. These criteria were not met by Gnosticism. The teaching and practice of the Christian Church henceforth became reduced to the lowest common denominator. General culture suffered also: the great Alexandrian library was burned, the School of Philosophy was closed for want alike of students and qualified teachers. Gnostic devotees either learned to adapt their minds, at least ostensibly, to the narrow orthodoxies of the Church and passed their lives in the early monasteries of Egypt and Europe, or they hid their Gnostic theory and practice behind the mysterious phrases and symbols of alchemy. Except in some outlying provinces, the Gnostic transmission ceased to function in the outer world and its mysteries were withdrawn behind the veil.

To the east of the Roman Empire in the ancient land of Persia a special branch of the Gnostic movement was founded by the poet, painter, and prophet *Mani*. Born in Mesopotamia of Persian parents in A.D. 215 and executed cruelly in 277, this gentle and refined lover of the Gnosis was indoctrinated in some variety of probably Syrian Gnosticism in his early youth, which he adapted to the Persian spiritual milieu in the course of his ministry. Mani and his associates were not only visionaries and writers but efficient organizers. In spite of the relative brevity of Mani's life, the Manichaean movement grew and spread not only in the Mediterranean region but also in India and China, as well as in the Balkans and in Europe. Put to the sword and burned at the stake over and over again in many lands, the followers of the Manichaean Gnosis heroically and stubbornly survived. In the Balkans, a saintly teacher named Bogo-mil (friend of God) in about 960 established a form of the faith of Mani that enjoyed widespread popularity for several centuries and is still said to possess secret devotees in Bulgaria. By far the largest and most influential late Manichaean movement was that of the Cathars (pure ones) in the Languedoc, whose learning, moral purity, and kindliness earned them the love and respect of the local populace, but also aroused the anxiety and ire of the papacy and the kings of France, whose joint efforts led to the frightful extermination of the Cathar devotees and the devastation of the lovely provinces where they resided.

On March 16, 1344, the last stronghold of the Cathar faith, the mountain fortress of Montségur, fell to the ravaging Northern French armies, and the remaining leadership of the faith perished in an inquisitorially ordered holocaust, described by novelist Lawrence Durell as the Thermopylae of the Gnostic soul. As in the Balkans, the sparks of the Gnosis were never totally smothered, and the secret fire continued to smolder beneath the ground trodden by inquisitors and enemy troops. To this very day one may encounter in the Languedoc unassuming country folk who will confide to a discreet visitor the fact that they never ceased to be Cathars and that they shall continue in their ancient pure faith until the end of their race. The outer world has also increasingly become aware of the mystery and romance of the martyred pure ones, and the ruined castle of Montségur serves today as a site of frequent pilgrimages of reverent visitors from many parts of the world. Pioneered by historian and novelist Zoë Oldenbourg, a mounting body of contemporary literature in several languages continues to explore the ways and byways of the story and teachings of the Cathar Gnosis.*

Are there any Gnostics today? The answer is, Yes. The contemporary representatives of the Gnostic tradition may be divided into two groups: the undeniably direct and unbroken descendents of ancient Gnostic schools, on the one hand, and revival movements and partial revival movements, on the other. A direct heir of ancient Gnosticism is the faith of the Mandaeans, who in remote backwashes of the Middle East have maintained their distinctive traditions since the very first centuries of the Christian era. Virtually nothing was known of these reclusive Gnostics until an enterprising British woman, Lady E. S. Drower, in the early decades of the twentieth century discovered their existence and translated many of their holy books into English.[9] *Manda* means Gnosis in the ancient tongue of this people, and the Gnosticism of their faith appears to be of a very early variety, since it does not accept Jesus and concentrates its attention on the figure of John the Baptist instead. Mandaeans today constitute a respected religious minority in Iraq, residing primarily in cities such as Baghdad and Basra, and are increasingly the subject of interest on the part of visiting scholars. It is by no means unlikely that the thoroughly Gnostic, but non-Christian Mandaeans constitute a vital, previously missing link connecting the gnosticizing late flowering of the Essenes with the classical Gnosis.

With the gradual coming to light in the eighteenth and nineteenth centuries of such original Gnostic documents as the Akhmin, Askew, Berlin, and Bruce Codices, the sympathetic interest of the creative edge of the culture in

---

*One of the more unusual contributions to this literature comes from the British psychiatrist Arthur Guirdham, who in his practice encountered numerous persons who seem to possess startlingly accurate memories of previous lives as Cathars. (See particularly his book, *The Cathars and Reincarnation* (Wheaton, Ill.: Quest Books, 1978).

Gnosticism increased. William Blake was called a Gnostic by his friend Crabb Robinson, while a century later Madame H. P. Blavatsky undertook a full-scale rehabilitation and rekindling of Gnosticism. Religious scholar Robert S. Ellwood, Jr., commented: "Blavatsky took up again the cause of the Gnosis. Scattered through [her work] *Isis Unveiled* are affirmations of most of its principles, though their existential pessimism is much mitigated by her making them equivalents of more sanguinely expressed Eastern, Hermetic and Cabalistic doctrines."[10] The opinion of scholars regarding the character of this, the most influential pioneering movement of the occult revival of the nineteenth and the twentieth century, is by now almost unanimous in its assertion to the effect that Theosophy is indeed a new Gnostic movement. In his work on the Theosophical movement, Prof. Bruce Campbell states that Theosophy is "an ancient *Western* tradition, the Gnostic tradition, which went underground when Christianity triumphed."[11]

As might be expected, the discovery and subsequent translation of the Nag Hammadi collection of Gnostic texts, even more than the few original Gnostic codices discovered in the eighteenth and nineteenth centuries, have led to a Gnostic revival. Already early in the twentieth century there was a known Gnostic church in France that functioned in public. This body, the "Eglise Gnostique Universelle," had attracted such noted French esotericists as Papus (Dr. Gerard Encausse), Sédir (Yvon Le Loup), as well as artists, writers (such as Fabré des Essarts, the symbolist poet), and generally the creative edge of the mainstream culture. Rising from mysterious but distinguished sources of transmission such as the Cathars, Knights Templar, and even older secret Gnostic bodies, the French Gnostic church has experienced a revival and has initiated extensions in other parts of the world. While still far from numerous, Gnostics are present and accounted for in today's world.

The heart and soul of the Gnostic tradition is mythological. Beginning with its hoary origins in the deserts of Judea and Egypt among the pious Jewish heretics called Essenes, and continuing with the great luminaries of the Gnosis such as Valentinus, Basilides, and Mani, the *other tradition* winds its way not unlike a great underground river right into the landscape of the contemporary world with its jet planes, computers, and increasing spiritual rootlessness owing to the loss of its once nourishing myths. It is time now that we examine the principal myths of this other tradition, so that peradventure we may find there what our official myths were lacking. Tennyson wrote: "God fulfills himself in many ways, lest one good custom should corrupt the world." Assuredly, the alternative myth carried by the other tradition represents one of the ways in which such divine fulfillment may save us from the depredations brought upon us by the one-sidedness of the traditions and myths of the mainstream. It is with such expectations that we may address ourselves to the mythic images that together present us with the consciousness of the *other reality*.

PART II
The Other Reality

Gnostic Alchemical Serpent

6

Errant Wisdom:
The Myth of Sophia

Introduction: Gnosis, Metaphor, and Myth

Tradition is always rooted in experience. Behind every structure woven of theology, philosophy, and revealed ethics there lies a fundamental bedrock of transcendental experience. Moses climbs Mt. Sinai and by experiencing the reality of Jehovah receives the tablets of the Law. The Buddha achieves enlightenment under the sacred Bodhi tree and then goes forth to proclaim the Dharma. Muhammad discourses with the angel Gabriel in a cave before beginning his prophetic mission. Yet it is undeniable that the mainstream religious traditions differ substantially from the alternative tradition, inasmuch as the former tend to enshrine the results of revelatory experience in belief and commandment, and the latter strenuously resists the metamorphosis of experience into theology and moral preachment. The Gnostic tradition descended from the Essene and continuing within the Christian dispensation has always thus resisted the turning of experience into a theological-ethical construct and opted for a different course instead.

As noted earlier (Chapter Five), the Gnostics engaged regularly in what G. Quispel called "the mythologization of Self-experience." The same author explained this procedure in greater detail in the following manner:

> In my *Gnosis als Weltreligion* (1951), I suggested that Gnosticism expressed a specific religious experience which

was frequently turned into myth. An example is the story when Mani, the founder of the Manichaean religion was twelve years old God sent an angel to him to inspire him. When he was twenty-four the angel came to him again and said, "The time has now come to make your public appearance and to proclaim your own doctrine." The name of the angel means "twin" and he is the twin-brother or "divine self" of Mani.

This Manichaean myth expresses the encounter between the I, the ego, and the divine self. In the system of Valentinus we find the similar concept of the guardian angel who accompanies a man throughout his life, who reveals the gnosis to him and is not allowed to enter eternal bliss without him.[1]

At the heart of the alternative tradition of Gnosticism lies the experience of the inward self, which, being of the same substance as God, naturally joins human consciousness with divinity. The personal experience of the Gnostic was alluded to by Prof. Elaine Pagels in the title of the sixth chapter of her book *The Gnostic Gospels*, which reads: "Gnosis: Self-Knowledge as Knowledge of God." This experience of self-knowledge, which simultaneously is knowledge of God, is then turned by the Gnostics into that most creative of all symbolic expressions of reality known as *myth*.

One of the greatest modern mythologists, the Hungarian scholar C. Kerényi, likened mythology to music. Music and mythology have this in common: in both we find art and material fused in the same phenomenon. The art of the composer and his material, which is the world of sound, are one. The making of the myth and the material of the myth, in this case the world of images, are also most intimately related. Myth is in fact not as much made as it is experienced, and the experience then gives rise to a torrent of mythological images expressing aspects of the meaning of the experience. Moreover, a true mythic expression or mythologem is not something that could be expressed just as well and just as authentically in a non-mythological way. One cannot substitute for mythology a mode of expression of a different nature. Certain experiences can be adequately expressed *only* in the form of myth and in no other way. Seen in this way, myth acquires a new significance. It becomes the expression in the world of relativity of spiritual principles that are of crucial importance to all human beings, inasmuch as they express within this same world the experience of the Absolute. The experience of the Absolute, as found in the knowing of the inward self by the Gnostic, is then expressed in the realm of mind by the myth that acts at once as the veil over Truth, and as the way whereby Truth may be unveiled. "The apparent leads to the Real" is a Sufi saying indicating that behind symbolism there is a reality linked with the symbol itself, and that behind mythology also there is an experiential essence that possesses a direct connection with the original experience (called by Jung *Urerfahrung*—archaic experience) that gave rise to the myth in the first instance.

It is more than likely that the Gnostics were the first conscious mythologists who used myth both to express their primal mystical experiences and to subtly lead others to similar experiences. Already in classical times the Greek word *mythos* had come to denote a legend from the time before history, a tale involving the denizens of the ahistorical dimension, namely the gods, goddesses, and heroes. In comparatively modern times, in the romantic era, the same term was reintroduced as describing a story in which supernatural persons or events of an unspecified earlier period appear. Many contemporary dictionaries define myth as something "entirely fictitious." But one needs to remember that the word "fictitious" comes from the Latin *fingere*, to form or to shape, thus suggesting that a myth is an account that is not historically true, yet represents a shaping of truths of a timeless character. Mythic events occur, as the Latin Mass expressed it when announcing the Gospel, *in illo tempore*, in an unspecified time similar perhaps to what Australian aboriginals are wont to call "dreamtime." The Gnostic myths must be understood as existing in such timeless categories, occurring as what in Latin has been called *sub specie eternitatis*, under the aspect of eternity. It is from such deep and mysterious sources that the Gnostic mythmakers drew their sustenance and inspiration.

That the Gnostics were indeed such psychologically informed expert mythmakers was long suspected by those on the creative edge of modern scholarship. Long before Jung, Quispel, and Joseph Campbell, as long ago as in 1932, F. C. Burkitt wrote: "It is quite evident all the time that he [Valentinus] is describing the first origin of things under the figure of myth . . . and further, that *his idea of the origin of things was psychological, akin to the mental processes of our own mind*, which indeed are the only mental processes we know of."[2] (Italics ours—S.A.H.) What Burkitt, Jung, and others have called psychologically informed mythmaking was recognized by Hans Jonas and Rudolf Bultmann as "existential objectification," which simply means that the Gnostic myths represent the objectification of the human being's understanding of its existence.[3] Whether originating in the psyche's striving for individuation or brought to the fore by the need of humans to understand the fateful alienation and portentous choices of their existence, the immense value of the Gnostic myths is attested to by both parties.

Experience turned into myth and myth turned inward as psychological self-knowledge: such is the grand movement of Gnosis on the plane of psychic reality. Yet, there is still a third component, which allows the myth to descend from the purely psychological to the material level of manifestation where it may impress not only the intuitive, thinking, and feeling functions but also the function of sensation. This third element is valid ritual, possessing true meaning, which becomes the dramatization or "playing out" of the myth in plain view of the senses. The considerable concern of the Gnostics with sacramental ritual attests to the important role played by the ritualization of myth in the above-noted movement of Gnosis. It is also here in the nature of this movement of Gnosis that we may graphically apprehend the great difference separating such mainstream traditions as Judaism, non-Gnostic Christianity, and Islam, on the one hand, from the alternative tradition of Gnosticism, on the other.

The tendency of the mainstream traditions is to turn the initial experience into dogma and commandment through the intermediary agency of historically interpreted holy scriptures, which usually appear as stories with a moral. The tendency of the alternative tradition is to move from initial experience to an expression of the experience in myth, and from there to the ritual playing out of the myth into fully perceptible physical manifestation, from whence proceeds the withdrawal of the images into the Self, thus opening the way to original and primal experience once more.

An interesting validation of the transcendental rootedness of Gnostic myths comes to us from the aforementioned noted mythologist C. Kerényi. In his work *Essays on a Science of Mythology* (written in collaboration with C. G. Jung), he indicates that the Gnostics were mystics who specialized in the mythologization of mystical experience. Following the lead of the late scholar Leo Frobenius (1873-1938), Kerényi assumes the existence of certain major mythic structural coordinates, which he calls "monads." These mythic monads are the principal

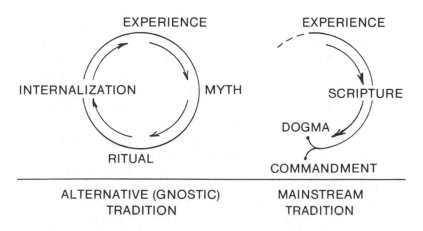

EXPERIENCE   EXPERIENCE

INTERNALIZATION   MYTH   SCRIPTURE

DOGMA

RITUAL   COMMANDMENT

ALTERNATIVE (GNOSTIC)   MAINSTREAM
TRADITION   TRADITION

differentiated forms into which the primal experience of mythic reality divides itself. The noted German philosopher Oswald Spengler recognized eight such cultural monads, with another in formation (some of these being the Egyptian, the Greco-Roman, the Vedic-Aryan, and the Maya-Aztec-Incan). All of these mythic monads are based on primary mythologems that are premonadic, which category includes the mythologems of the Gnostics, says Kerényi:

> The mythologems that come closest to these naked encounters with the Godhead we regard as the primary mythologems. . . . These in their pure state, e.g. the pure idea of the *mandala*, its "archetype," so to speak, are premonadic. What exists historically has the character not only of a monad, i.e. belonging locally and temporarily to a definite culture, but also of a *work*, i.e. speaking in the manner typical of a certain people. On the other hand, every people displays its true form most purely when it stands face to face with the Absolute. . . . That is why Plotinus can tell us about pure mystical experience, and *why his contemporaries, the Gnostics, can tell us about what comes closest to mythology in mysticism.*[4] (Emphasis ours—S.A.H.)

This mystical mythology found among the Gnostics is thus a rather unique phenomenon. Rooted as it is in highly charged personal experience of deeper states of consciousness, it possesses qualities seldom found in traditional folklore and culturally conditioned mythologems. Unlike the latter, it is capable of conveying a considerable measure of its original quality, to which Jung and others have applied the term "numinous," carrying the power of a *numen*, or deity. Gnostic myths belong in a special category, and as such they possess a force capable of making an impact of unusual quality on the psyches of individuals. That most efficient popularizer of mythology, Joseph Campbell, has pointed out (largely by way of utilizing a preexisting analysis by Immanuel Kant) that the a priori realm of transcendence can relate itself to the temporal field of phenomenal appearances only by analogy, and that the instrument whereby this kind of analogy is expressed is the *metaphor.*[5] This agency, which Campbell defined as "a psychologically affective image transparent to transcendence," must also be regarded as the true cornerstone of Gnostic myth. Gnosis, myth, and metaphor thus constitute the trinity of conscious instrumentalities whereby the realities glimpsed by the Gnostic seers were made available to mortals still aspiring to such seership. Let us now allow some of the myths and metaphors of the Gnostics to speak to us in their own fashion, albeit modified and amplified by our contemporary perception and language. We shall thus address ourselves to the first of these important mythologems in the form of the story of the divine wisdom-woman Sophia.

The Myth of Sophia

High in the ineffable and transcendental world of light there existed a primal pair named Depth and Silence. Together they brought forth a perfect realm of balance and creative power, consisting of thirty archetypal forms of consciousness called Aeons. The youngest and most adventurous of these, called Sophia (Wisdom), fell in love with her own royal progenitor, the great invisible king of the all, called Depth, and wished to fathom his perennially inscrutable nature. Confused by her love, she cast her glance in various directions from her aeonial seat in the fullness until in the distance she espied a magnificent light, shimmering with sublime grace. In her bewilderment brought about by love, she could no longer distinguish between the above and below and thus came to assume that the seductive light, which was in reality below her, was none other than the royal effulgence of the great king, her father, who resided at the highest point of the heavens. Thus she descended into the abysmal void, where in a boundless and fathomless sea of glass the reflection of the heavenly light beckoned to her. Her celestial consort, Christ, was unable to restrain her, and thus after a final, painful embrace she plunged into the murky deep, only to discover how the reflected light had deceived her. Saddened and frightened, she found herself enclosed by emptiness, devoid of the quality and power of Gnosis to which she was accustomed in the fullness. Desirous of having a kindred figure next to her, she brought forth in a virginal fashion a being whose name was Jesus. Although conceived mysteriously by her desire for her original Gnosis, Jesus was nevertheless joined to a shadow of darkness, which attached itself to him because of the malefic influences of the dark void wherein he was born. Jesus soon freed himself from his troublesome, shadowy attachment and ascended into the fullness, leaving Sophia in a state of despondency.

Left outside the supernal spiritual universe, alone and comfortless, Sophia experienced every sort of psychic storm imaginable. Passion, sorrow, fear, despair, and ignorance exuded from her being like mighty clouds and condensed into the four elements of earth, water, fire, and air, as well as into a number of beings, which later were to be known under such names as the Demiurge and the rulers (*archontes*)—fierce and troublesome spirits, one and all. The mightiest of these, a lion-faced being filled with pride and the will for power, marshaled his host of world-fashioning spirits, and out of the raw material of earth, water, fire, and air they built a world of impressive external appearance, yet replete with great flaws, having been created in the image of its creators. Sorrow, fear, ignorance, and other painful and destructive passions were built into the fabric of this imperfect world, inasmuch as the raw material used by the fashioners originated in feelings like those experienced by Sophia. Looking down at the flawed and troubled world pridefully fashioned by her own ignorant offspring, Sophia was filled with pity for creation and resolved to assist in such ways as would be available to her. She thus became the spirit of the world, anxiously observing it like a mother is wont to do when watching over a feeble and misshapen child.

Meanwhile in the lofty height, Jesus was anxiously observing the sorrowful fate of his mother, Sophia. He joined himself to Sophia's twin aeon, Christ, and thus became Jesus-Christ, the Messiah and messenger of God. Around him rallied all the sublime and compassionate powers of the fullness, each contributing to him gifts and glories of their respective treasures. Thus in Jesus-Christ the fullness and its powers came to be gathered together, readying him for the great act of redemption, the liberation of Sophia from her lamentable condition in the void. Ceaselessly, Sophia's supplications ascended like clouds of bittersweet incense, penetrating the recesses of the fullness, arousing the compassion of all the splendid aeonial beings who perpetually contemplate their glory in their kingdom of perfection. Through the centuries and millennia of earthly history, Sophia prayed and sorrowed over her fate and the fate of the flawed world and the sparks of light enmeshed in the nets of the rulers, who like monstrous spiders continued to manifest webs of matter, emotion, and thought for the entrapment of humans—in essence not their creation but rather the sparks of Sophia's own higher nature infused into bodies of clay.

Finally, the powers of the fullness were assembled and, having entered Jesus-Christ, descended to earth to free Sophia and thereby also to bring redemption to her spiritual children, the members of the human race. After undergoing vicissitudes visited upon him by the rulers and their deceived human minions, Jesus-Christ rose triumphantly from earth, holding Sophia by the hand. Joyously they ascended to the various heavenly mansions, knocking at the portals of the spiritual guardians and gaining passage to ever-higher and subtler regions of existence. At each of the gates Sophia uttered great songs of praise and gratitude to the light that had saved her from the chaos of the nether regions.

When the World-Spirit Sophia came to the borders that separated the nether worlds from the fullness, she looked down once again unto the flawed and troubled world, suspended in the void and chaos, and compassion filled her broken but now mended heart. No, she could not leave utterly behind this strange creation, to its less than adequate resources. Neither could she abandon her true children, the women and men who were more intimately related to her than any other beings outside of the fullness. Thus, she worked her magic and divided her nature in half: one to ascend into the aeons of fullness, there to dwell with Christ and Jesus, the other to remain in proximity to creation and continue to assist it with compassionate wisdom. Her second self, created by compassion, thus became known as *Achamoth*, the errant or lower one who is still in contact with humanity and the regions of this world.

It was thus that it came to pass that the universe constellated itself in three regions. The first of these is the sublunar or material world, ruled by a prince whom the ancients called Pan and whom others inaccurately call the devil. This prince rules over the earth, the plants, and

Sophia extinguishing the old law
of the seven planets

living creatures and like a patient shepherd sees to it that all of these manifestations of Sophia's life may one day reach the higher worlds, no matter how far they stray. Not privy to the realities and designs of the mighty aeons of light, the prince of this world merely turns the great wheel of birth, death, and rebirth, hoping that if he and his flock are but able to remain within the motions of biological life, their hour of liberation will not find them past redemption.

Higher in immaterial space is the world of soul or mind, which is ruled by the chief archon, also called the Demiurge and having numerous names, including Yaldabaoth (childish God) and Saclas (blind one). It is from the realm of this arrogant and power-hungry godling that many of the concepts and precepts originate that enthrall the minds and wills of humans. The blind god has a great liking for what he is pleased to call law. Rules, commandments, and regulations of all sorts are fashioned by him in order to diminish freedom, which is the birthright of the spirit. Philosophies and ideologies of diverse sorts are also placed into human minds by the Demiurge, along with greed, power, and other obsessions that becloud and vitiate the spiritual purity of men and women.

Thirdly, in the world above planets, immediately below the portals of the mighty fullness itself, is a region where Sophia-Achamoth, the celestial mother and wise helper of humankind, is enthroned. With her live countless hosts of angels of light and holy and righteous souls that once occupied human bodies. This is the world of spirit, where the twin angels of human personalities also reside and the celestial bride chamber is erected wherein the lesser selves of humans may meet and be wedded to their spiritual counterparts, the twin angels. When humans commune with whom they envision as *the Goddess* in her manifold aspects, it is none other than Sophia-Achamoth, their wise guardian, whom they envision. Unaware of these subtle mysteries, many well-intentioned followers of the Christian revelation have come to see this form of Sophia as Mary, Queen of Heaven. It is in this

manner then that our Lady Wisdom, though redeemed
and having assisted Jesus-Christ in the work of redemption, is not far from her children even to this day.

The three cosmic regions just spoken of have their
corresponding portions within the nature of the children
of men. Within every human there is the material part
(*hyle*), derived from the kingdom of Pan and carrying
the instincts and urges of material life with its inten-
tionality of survival and physical continuity by way of
offspring. There is also a portion embodying mind and
emotion, referred to often as soul (*psyche*). This portion
is derived from the realm of the Demiurge, and thus it
contains more than one dangerous feature. While it is the
seat of ethical awareness and calculating reason, it is
also susceptible to the influences and blandishments of
the rulers with their obsessive commandments, fanatical
ideologies, pride, and arrogance of soul. Third is the
human spirit (*pneuma*), which belongs to the fullness,
although it is the gift of Sophia. In most humans this
spiritual spark smolders and dreams, unconsciously
awaiting the breath of the emissaries of the fullness to be
fanned into effective action. This spirit is of Sophia, and
through and beyond her, it is of the identical essence as
the supreme King and Queen, Depth and Silence
themselves.

In this embodied existence we find some humans who
may be called *hyletics*, who are ruled by instinct, urges,
and sensations and live largely in the realm of Pan.
Others have been named *psychics*, and they usually worship
the Demiurge as God, having no awareness of the spiritual
world above. Their pride and joy are law and doctrine,
and they imagine themselves as superior to other humans
by virtue of their laws. So the spiritual history of humanity
is largely a progression from primitive instinctuality and
nature-worshipping pantheism (where Pan is theos, i.e.,
God) to dogmatic religion and ethics, and from these to
the true spiritual freedom of Gnosis. In order to reach
the kingdom of light and become a *pneumatic*, the human
being must have first renounced his servitude to physicality,

and then, often with great difficulty, also renounce the thralldom of the Demiurge and his minions in the form of ideological servitude. Ideas enslave just as much as passions, and both are obstacles to the rule of the spirit. Thus comes about the great renunciation (*apolytrosis*) wherein humans break the shackles affixed to their bodies and minds by the rulers. Following this there is but one great step to be taken: the bride chamber, or the transformative union of the lesser human with the overshadowing presence of the twin angel.

From the heights of the material world and the peak experiences of the mind, men and women lift up their eyes and behold the everlasting hills of Sophia-Achamoth's kingdom of spiritual light. The twin angel reaches down his shining arm to earth and bears the human soul aloft into the bride chamber where the spiritual union is sealed in a heavenly marriage. One by one, Sophia draws her spiritual children unto herself, bidding them to join the army of the elect. Such is the gift of Sophia, drawn from the endless treasury of the light and made available to humans by way of her compassion and wisdom. She who remained faithful to the true light entreats her children to do likewise. Faithfulness to the spirit dwelling in the deepest and highest recesses of their nature will thus lead them to the renunciation of illusion and the embracing of the real.

Interpretation of the Myth

The above recension of the myth of Sophia is based primarily on the version of Valentinus, as embodied in *Pistis Sophia*, the principal scripture referring to Sophia, but it has also been streamlined and amplified to serve the needs of contemporary persons. As such, it might be called the product of a "latitudinarian" approach to Gnosticism by some who fancy themselves purists, but it must be kept in mind that it is precisely such an approach that is intended here. Descriptive and exegetical scholarship may profit from a purist approach, but such a mode would by no means be appropriate to the purposes the present writer intends to realize.

Let us then, in outline form, address ourselves to some indicative interpretation of the myth of Sophia. Sophia is the World Spirit, or the collective archetype of the entirety of cosmic and individual life, growth, and development. As such, she is most closely associated with the nature and fate of humanity: the initial differentiation and subsequent individuation of the soul and its union with spirit. At first she dwells in a plenum of undifferentiated psychic energy, a heaven world where all things exist in full potentiality. The fullness (*Pleroma*) is like the uncarved block of Taoist Chinese metaphorical thought: a fullness of being from whence individuality and manifest existence emerge by way of subtraction and not by way of a *creatio ex nihilo* (creation out of nothing). Emanation rather than creation is the law of manifestation, certainly in the realm of the psyche and in all likelihood in the sphere of cosmic manifestation also.* The unitary primal nature of the psyche differentiates and descends into ever-deeper conditions of alienation from its original source of light and power. At the psychological level, this alienating differentiation is at the heart of the dark mystery of the fall of Sophia.

Sophia's love for her father, the king of the heavenly fullness, and her effort to get close to his light have been frequently interpreted as a metaphor for the hubris, whereby the human mind, or any kind of limited embodiment of consciousness, presumes to want to comprehend the ever-incomprehensible and ineffable transcendence of being. In our desire for comprehension, we no longer know whether we are looking upward toward transcendence or downward into lesser realms of mind where transcendence is reflected. Again and again in our lives we mistake the reflected light for the true light. Especially

---

*For an authoritative neo-Gnostic creation myth, embodying the methodology of emanation and closely affinitized to Hindu and Mahayana Buddhist metaphysical theory, see the noted magnum opus of H. P. Blavatsky, *The Secret Doctrine*.

true is this, perhaps, of the essentially arrogant efforts of many growth psychologies and so-called New Age movements, which in an overly glib and facile manner treat the greater mysteries of being as if they were readily susceptible to the manipulations of personal consciousness. A good, though relatively mundane example is to be found in the field of the use of dreams. On the one hand, Jung and other responsible depth psychologists regard the dream as a primarily revelatory expression of the unconscious to be treated with great care and reverence. On the other hand, we find efforts of less reverent persons to exploit and manipulate the dreams of people for the accomplishment of strictly personalistic aims. Whenever a psychospiritual phenomenon of a potentially transcendental value is subordinated to personal goals, one may say that, like Sophia, we mistake the reflected light for the supernal radiance and thus put ourselves in jeopardy.

In the course of the differentiation of the psyche, all of us find ourselves eventually in an empty space without Gnosis. Here, our terror, anguish, and other feelings create unsavory emanations, which proceed from our own psyche and in turn evolve into tyrants and tormenting demiurges of our authentic being. Once the human ego falls into a space greatly removed from psychic wholeness, aspects of the ego (or in the view of some, the ego itself) become demiurges. Ean Begg, in his meditation on Gnostic myths, writes:

> The rulers, the planetary gods ... who assist the demiurge in the creation of horizontal man keep him unaware of his true origin. They are the archetypal core of the complexes or subpersonalities that live our lives for us while we remain unconscious of them.... The ego-consciousness which emerges is that of the demiurge, and his limited perceptions are accounted the sole reality. Man is a prisoner of space and time. His rulers are real, not only as the divisions of the week but as the complexes. The sun, the ego-complex, the chief ruler, rules the day and, with its light and heat blots out the hidden influence of the other

archons. The moon is the great pendulum which keeps everything as it is, ticking over regularly, inexorably fixated within its own cycle.[6]

Not only the sun and the moon, but also the other planets were regarded by the Gnostics as symbols for the manifold limitations imposed on the freedom of the human spirit by the rulers. The often shallow, although clever intellectualism of Mercury, the gripping and imaginative desire of Venus, the fierce combativeness of Mars, the lordly heedlessness of Jupiter, and certainly the restrictiveness and pusillanimity of Saturn (often equated with the Demiurge) are all superbly suited to symbolize the tendencies and proclivities of the personal self of the human being, ever interposing itself between earthly life and the true light of meaning. Living on the earth below the moon, we appear to be subject to the archonic limitations of the planets, even as Sophia was thus entrapped and limited by the rulers.

The mystery of salvation, meaning liberation from the existential condition of unconsciousness and limitation, is intimately connected with our heavenly origins. On the one hand, our redeemer is Christ, a heavenly archetype, having its true home in the fullness. On the other hand, Jesus, the more human component of the salvific principle, is made by ourselves in the vale of tears, which was also called by the poet John Donne "a vale of soul making." We cannot depend entirely on an external and transcendental Savior, as Christendom has been wont to do for all too long, for by so doing our own inherent powers of spiritual freedom atrophy. Still, the self-created salvation ensuing from our own travails avails us heartily little also, unless transcendentally archetypal assistance is adduced to it. So Sophia brings forth Jesus in her exile but is redeemed by Jesus conjoined with the heavenly aeon Christ.

Gloriously ascending from her limited state, Sophia yet remembers humanity, her younger and less capable relations, and decides to remain in a position to be of assistance to them. (An eminently valid analogy may be found in the Bodhisattva ideal of Mahayana Buddhism, where the redeemed becomes a redeemer. In fact, the celestial Bodhisattva Avalokitesvara, whose name literally means "one who looks down from on high," whose most popular form is the feminine Bodhisattva Kwan Yin and who is accessible to all earthlings in need of compassionate redemption, bears such a resemblance to Sophia that one readily suspects a more than casual connection. It may also be recalled that Gautama the Buddha, according to Mahayana teaching, has also left behind an aspect of himself to continue to assist living beings toward liberation. It is this aspect that, according to certain legends, manifests once a year on the Buddhist holiday of *Wesak* (to those capable of observing it).

Thus Sophia, the redeemed redeemer, continues as a guarding and enlightening entity in association with earth. In a personal psychological sense, it may be said that a major step taken in individuation always necessitates an effort at liberating the still unintegrated part selves as well as a compassionate and charitable course of living in relationship to our fellow humans. The Sophia myth also has human implications of a more direct and intimate character. Even as Simon is said to have regarded his consort Helen as the manifestation of the World Soul, so there is some evidence indicating that Mary Magdalene, whom the Gnostic scriptures identify as the true "beloved disciple," may have been regarded as an earthly manifestation of Sophia, and that her relationship with Jesus may indeed have been the ritual acting out on earth of the liberating union between the celestial Messiah and Sophia.

Thus, we come to the end of our considerations regarding the myth of Sophia. It goes almost without saying that the minimal exegesis here offered can in no way do justice to this complex and inspiring myth. The psychological emphases in these commentaries, inadequate in themselves, touch but upon one facet of the magnificent cut gem that is the story and the mystery of Sophia. (Similar statements may be made with much justification regarding the other Gnostic myths to be recounted in the chapters following the present one.) Still, one more thought intrudes in conclusion: Why, one might ask, is it at all useful or even necessary for Sophia, the World Soul, the psyche, and the ego to leap out after the deceptive light and undergo such trials and sorrows as well as joys and triumphs? It is once again none other than C. G. Jung who offered us one of the best replies when he wrote: *"Were it not for the leaping and twinkling of the soul, man would rot away in his greatest passion, idleness."*[7] (Italics ours—S.A.H.) Action and risk are essential to the Gnostic enterprise. Those who must know run great risks, including the one of plunging into the abyss of loneliness and alienation. The Gnostic risk opens up the individual psyche to many adventures and may lead to opportunities for the exercise of the kind of compassion that only wisdom is capable of manifesting. Despite the ever-recurring naive notions of many to right all the wrongs of existence by way of extraverted collective solutions alone (an effort worthy of demiurgic arrogance!), the crucible wherein compassion weds wisdom is erected in individuals one by one. Collective solutions are in reality no solutions at all, for the true vehicle of life, the offspring of Our Lady Wisdom, is the individual. Those favored by the grace of Sophia may devote their lives to offering active service in the public arena, or, again, they may simply bring the compassionate light of Sophia to bear upon the private human tasks of their daily lives. In all instances, however, they might consider the concluding words written by Miguel de Unamuno in his *Tragic Sense of Life*: "And may God deny you peace but give you glory."

7

The Dancing Savior:
The Myth of the Gnostic Christ

Introduction: The Alternative Image of the Savior

The sparks of light that are the spirits of men and women entrapped by the ruling powers of this lower world (so said the Gnostics) are nevertheless not abandoned by the divine Source from whence they originate. The supreme Light never lost interest in the scattered fragments of its own essence. It sent a redeemer or intermediary to assist in their liberation. The large majority of Gnostics were associated with the then brand-new Christian movement and looked upon Jesus as the carrier of this redeeming light. The secret tradition of Israel, manifest in the Essene movement, was well on its way toward transforming the political Messiah of official Judaism into a cosmic and personal savior who would redeem the spirits of the sons of light from the oppression of the world of darkness and its dark rulers. This development culminated in the image of Jesus. As we noted earlier (Chapter Three), there are an almost bewildering number of characterizations of Jesus today, most of which contradict each other radically. These are but the most recent portrayals; the much earlier ones, especially those that appear to us in sacred art, are also more than a little confusing and contradictory.

All of the Jesuses demanding our attention are based on what until recently constituted the only evidence concerning this mysterious figure, namely, the New

Testament. And the New Testament evidence itself is
confusing and contradictory. Some of the canonical
Gospels portray Jesus as quite human, even sensuous:
"the son of man came eating and drinking, and they say,
'behold a glutton and a drunkard, a friend of tax collectors
and sinners' " (Matt. 11:19). His association with women is
represented as causing a scandal: "And they marveled
that he was talking with a woman" (John 4:27); "There
were also women looking on from afar . . . and also many
other women who came up with him to Jerusalem" (Mark
15:40). At the same time, Paul describes him more as a
transcendental, even Gnostic spiritual being when he
states that Jesus is "far above all rule and authority and
power of dominion, and above every name that is named,
not only in this aeon but in that which is to come" (Eph.
1:21). If one prefers to envision Jesus as a gentle and
peaceful individual, one may refer to the way he describes
himself in Matthew 11:29: "for I am meek and humble at
heart, and you will find rest for your soul." If, on the
contrary, one wishes to conjure up a picture of him that
shows anger and rough manners, one can point to his
treatment of the merchants in the temple and his un-
qualified condemnation of the Pharisees as hypocrites,
whited sepulchers, and blind guides, misleading people.
Needless to say, these diverse images of Jesus make the
often extolled "imitation of Christ" more than a little
difficult. For instance, are we to imitate him when he
advises us to "turn the other cheek" when struck; or are
we to emulate him when he says, "I came not to bring
peace but a sword"?

In addition to the Jesuses based on the evidence of
the New Testament, there has always been another Jesus,
although much of the evidence concerning him has
emerged into full view only recently. In order to present
and understand this Jesus, we have to reconstruct the
myth that is told by the scriptures of the Gnostics, many
of which are contemporaneous or very nearly contemporaneous with the New Testament. What did the
Gnostics say about Jesus? They disagreed with the exoteric

Christians about the precise nature of his physical embodiment as well as about his death and resurrection. They did not accept the simplistic notion that the redemption of humanity was accomplished by the physical death of Jesus on the cross, and that a good Christian merely has to believe in this event in order to be redeemed. The reason for most of these disagreements was that Gnostics never held that humans were primarily in need of redemption from sin. The task of the messianic messenger was to help human beings discover who they truly are, and to assist them in overcoming the inimical cosmic powers and rejoin the fullness of the true light. "Salvation" thus became synonymous with "liberation," and the way to this state was envisioned not as consisting of faith but of interior liberating experience facilitated by the teachings of the Liberator and by the sacramental mysteries he entrusted to his followers.

The Jesus of the Gnostics is a person substantially, and not only superficially, different from the Jesus of most of the canonical Gospels. His humanity is far less significant than his transcendental or archetypal nature. Thus, it might appear fair to say that the Gnostics were less interested in what Jesus did and were more concerned with who or what he was. Most of their scriptures, such as *The Gospel of Thomas*, contain sayings of Jesus without any connective narrative. We do not have a Gnostic gospel that reads like the four canonical ones, where we may gather details of the events in the life of Jesus in connected, narrative form. Still, it is quite certain that the Gnostics had their own version of what did take place in connection with Jesus. Indications of this version can be found in many sources: *The Acts of John*, a scripture that has been available and was widely read for centuries, written in all likelihood by Lucius Charinus from whom some Gnostics derived their esoteric transmission. Portions of *The Gospel of the Egyptians*, one of the scriptures in the Nag Hammadi collection, are also most useful in this respect. Another work of distinguished history is the collection called *The Odes of Solomon*, portions of which appear in the early discovery *Pistis Sophia*, a complete collection of which was published in the nineteenth century and dates back probably to the end of the first century or the beginning of the second century. In addition to these, several of the scriptures from Nag Hammadi contain valuable material that allows us to reconstruct a mythic narrative of some consistency.

One element of crucial importance to the myth of Christ is of course the issue of why humans need a savior in the first place. Can't Gnosis come to individuals without the intermediary agency of a messenger, a redeemer from the greater world of fullness and light? Aren't good works, sincere desires for greater consciousness, and meditative practices sufficient for liberation, salvation, enlightenment, or whatever names may be devised for the needed salvific event? Historically, no doubt the concept of a *soter* (healer, maker of wholeness, freely translated as "savior") developed from the time-honored Jewish idea of the Messiah. Spiritually, it developed from universal, archetypal roots of a much wider scope and greater depth. One set of important questions answered by Gnosticism (and raised explicitly in these words by Valentinus) is the following: "What we were and what we became; where we were and whither we have been cast; whither we hasten, whence we are delivered; what is birth and what rebirth?" The answers may be summarized as follows: Humans are originally pure spirits, but they have become shackled in a cosmic system; once they dwelt in the regions of the fullness with the Divine, but they were made to descend into a realm of imperfection. The spiritual nature within humans desires to hasten back to its unity with Divinity, thus to be delivered from the existential limitations of life within the cosmic system. Birth means to be born here to this cosmos, which is at least in part in the grip of unfriendly forces. Rebirth is to be born anew as a free being into a divine world of consciousness and light. This rebirth does not come about unaided. Divinity is actively engaged in facilitating humanity's rebirth into its own and true estate. Salvation requires a savior, not only in Judaism and Christianity, but in most of the great spiritual traditions. Already in the Upanishads we find the statement that salvation is effected by "the Lord" (Isvara).[1] An elaboration of this concept is the teaching regarding the *avataras*, or descents of God, particularly of the second person of the Hindu trinity, Vishnu. Vishnu is known to have at least ten such descents, among whom the most important are Rama and Krishna. In both Theravada and Mahayana Buddhism, a plurality of Buddhas is envisioned (usually seven for the entire evolutionary history of the earth), all of whom are descents of transcendental spiritual beings (Dhyani Buddhas and Dhyani Bodhisattvas) in addition to their earthly personalities. All of these Buddhas, however, are also recognized as aspects of the One Buddha Light in its redemptive aspect. Even the gods who administer existence in the manifest realm are in need of and rejoice over the descent of a Buddha. In one of the sutras it is just one such god who addresses Buddha in this manner: "Marvelous it is, O Lord, how after such a long time you have today manifested yourself in the world. During fully eight thousand ages had this world of the living been without a Buddha."[2]

The attitude of the Gnostic tradition is clearly stated by the Persian prophet Mani, as quoted by the Arab scholar Al-Biruni:

> Wisdom and good deeds have always from time to time been brought to mankind by the messengers of God. So in one age they have been brought by the messenger called Buddha to India, in another by Zarathustra to Iran, yet in another by Jesus to the West. Thereupon this revelation has come down, this prophecy in this latter age through me, Mani, the apostle of God of truth in Babylonia.[3]

The foregoing should suffice to convince us that in the idea of salvation and of the Savior we are faced with a truly archetypal idea, universal and not conditioned by time or culture. We may thus safely address ourselves now to the retelling of the myth of the Savior, in our case

Jesus, of whom Mani said in the above passage that he "brought wisdom and good deeds as a messenger of God to the West."

The Myth of the Savior

When the time for the earthly descent of the one who was to heal the broken heart of the lower world was come, all the great Powers of the kingdom of the fullness gathered together. The Father of all and the Holy Spirit mingled their spiritual substance and brought forth a fiery seed of life. The Powers arranged themselves in a vast circle and imposing their hands, infused the seed of the Father and of the Holy Spirit with their strength. Then the fiery seed descended through the circle of the stars and the region of the planets into the womb of a chosen human virgin whose name was Mary and who was destined to become the mother of the Savior after the flesh. Although a virgin, she became a mother without any pain, for the helpers of the fullness stood by and gave her assistance.

The boy grew up in a household where simplicity and purity reigned; he was guarded by his mother Mary and taught skills by her husband Joseph. Yet many were the times when it became apparent that he was a person of unusual powers and character, and his mother and earthly father regarded him with awe. Thus, one day Jesus was working in the vineyard with Joseph; at the same time a person demanded entrance to the house who looked like Jesus in appearance and asked: "Where is Jesus, my brother?" Mary, recognizing that she had met a spirit rather than a human being, constrained the spirit in the house while she summoned Joseph and Jesus. When Jesus entered the house he loosed the spirit from confinement and they embraced and became one. It became known that this spirit was the twin angel of Jesus who descended from the heaven world and joined his earthly counterpart in an act of abiding union. This union came to be called later the mystery of the bride chamber and was experienced only by the wisest and greatest of humans who had become perfect in the skills of their spirits. But

Jesus was a united and whole being already as a young boy, thus being prepared to bring wholeness to all children of men.

When reaching young adulthood, his mother and brothers brought news of a man named John who was baptizing people in the wilderness for the remission of sins. Although Jesus stated that he had no sin from which he should be freed, he went to be baptized by John, and while he was immersed in the waters a light shone brilliantly on the waters, so that all were afraid. A dove fluttered above the head of Jesus and sang, and it became plain to many that a power had descended on him that was not of this world. The power was the Christ, a high presence from the fullness, destined to guide him to the fulfillment of his earthly mission. When the people gathered to look at him they could but barely recognize him as the man they knew, and he said to them: "I seem to you like a stranger because I am from another race."

He became a guide to those who would follow him; he was tranquil and unhurried. He put to shame those who were filled with the importance of their own learning and the Law; he called them empty people and they hated him. And he said to his disciples words like these: "I came into the midst of the world and in the flesh I appeared to them but I found them all drunk, and I found none of them thirsty for my living waters. And I sorrow for the children of men because they are blind and are not able to see with their hearts." And he also told them that he came to make the things below like the things above, the external as the internal, and the male and the female he came to make into a single one. All these things they heard him say, but they understood little. Many of his disciples were called by him in an unusual way. Thus when he was at the Sea of Galilee, he chose first Peter and Andrew and then motioned to John and James, who were fishing in a boat offshore, by calling out to them: "I have need of you, come follow me." James, however, saw a child on the seashore and inquired from his brother what the child could possibly want with him. John, on the other hand, saw a grown man on the shore, while others saw a light only and yet others saw nothing. They went to the shore in great perplexity, wondering who or what it was that they had seen so differently.

Jesus also exhibited little respect for the priesthood of the Temple and for the Law. Once he took his disciples to the innermost part of the Temple where they were accosted by a prominent priest named Levi, who arrogantly declared that Jesus and his disciples were unclean and unworthy to observe the sacred vessels and places. Jesus called him a blind man who mistakes the external symbols of cleanliness for true purity and wisdom. He also exhorted his disciples not to follow blind men, such as Levi and the other members of the establishment. And when his disciples asked him if circumcision was necessary or not, he answered: "If it were necessary then every father would beget an already circumcised boy from his mother." When asked about the need to observe a special diet, he merely answered that it was more important not to lie and not to do what one hated, for those things that remained hidden in one's soul would become apparent eventually. It became increasingly clear to everyone that Jesus had come to declare the old Law abrogated and to proclaim a new Law, the core of which was love. And he said: "Love your brother as your soul and keep him ever as the apple of your eye." When explaining the relationship of the spirit to the body he said: "I marvel at how such a treasure came to find its habitation in such poverty."

In Bethany, Jesus was brought by a woman to a tomb where her brother was buried. The brother then called to Jesus out of the tomb, and Jesus raised him up, taking him by the hand. Jesus then arranged to meet with the youth in the dead of night and taught him great truths and conferred mysteries on him. And he became known as a miracle worker and initiator who could lead humans from death in this world into the life of the spirit.

All this while the priests and Pharisees were inspired by the rulers of this world to arrest and murder Jesus, because if they left him to his own devices, the people would follow him and the darkness of this aeon would be defeated. Jesus knew that if they were to proceed with their plan to kill him, the leaders of the establishment would so discredit themselves that their rule over the people would be greatly shortened. And thus, Jesus met with his disciple Judas Iscariot, who said to him secretly: "Is it not true, Lord, that this world is dominated by the Evil One and that you must dissolve the things below and the things above?" And Jesus answered him: "So it is, Judas. But how can one enter a strong man's house and deprive him of his treasures unless one can bind the strong man first? Only then can one enter and take his treasure. Remember, that when I am lifted up from this world, the Prince of this World will be cast in chains in that very hour." And it was thus that Judas came to understand that it was necessary that Jesus be handed over to his enemies and he proceeded to act as the instrumentality of Jesus' betrayal, while he had a secret understanding concerning the need for this course of action. And the leaders of the people, whose law was false and inspired by lawless spirits, believed Judas and made preparations for the arrest of the Savior, thereby sealing their own doom and the doom of their Temple and their Law.

Before he was to be arrested by his enemies, Jesus gathered all his disciples together and bid them to partake of a sacred meal, at which he blessed the bread and the cup of wine and reminded them that they ought to do this in remembrance of him and in order to invoke his presence when he would no longer be with them in the flesh. Then he said to the disciples: "Before I am delivered up let us sing a hymn to the Father and then we shall go forth to whatever awaits us." Then he stood in the middle of the room, asked the disciples to form a circle around him, holding each other's hands, and after the recitation of each verse to answer with the word "Amen." And so he began to sing a song, while the disciples danced around him in a circle, responding repeatedly by saying "Amen."

And this was the hymn Jesus sang:

Glory to Thee, Father!
(And they moving around in a circle answered him)

Amen! Glory to Thee,
Charis (Grace)! Glory to Thee, Spirit!
Glory to Thee, Holy One!
Glory to Thy Glory! Amen!
We praise Thee, O Father;
We give thanks to Thee, O Light;
In Whom Darkness dwells not! Amen!
For what we would give thanks, I say:
I would be saved; and I would save. Amen!
I would be loosed; and I would loose. Amen!
I would be broken; and I would break. Amen!
I would be born; and I wish to give birth. Amen!
I would eat; and I would be eaten. Amen!
I would hear; and I would be heard. Amen!
I would understand; and I would be understood. Amen!
I would be washed; and I would wash. Amen!
Now *Charis* is dancing.
I would play on the pipes; dance all of you. Amen!
I would play a song of mourning; lament all of you. Amen!
The eight sing praises with us. Amen!
Those who dance not, know not what cometh to pass. Amen!
I would flee; and I would stay. Amen!
I would be adorned; and I would adorn. Amen!
I would be at-oned; and I would at-one. Amen!
I have no house; and I would have houses. Amen!
I have no place; and I have places. Amen!
I have no temple; and I have temples. Amen!
I am a lamp to thee who seest me. Amen!
I am a mirror to thee who understandest me. Amen!
I am a door to thee who knockest at me. Amen!
I am a way to thee a wayfarer. Amen!
Now answer to my dancing!
See thyself in me who speak;
And seeing what I do, keep silence on my mysteries.

Understand by dancing, what I do;
For thine is the passion of man
That I am to suffer.
Thou couldst not at all be aware
Of what thou dost suffer,
If I were not sent as the *Logos* by the Father.
Seeing what I suffer, thou sawest me suffering;
And seeing, thou didst not stand still,
But wast moved greatly, thou wast moved to be wise.
Thou hast me for a couch; rest thou upon me.

What I am thou shalt know when I depart.
What now I am seen to be, that I am not.

But what I am thou shalt see when thou comest.
If thou hadst known how to suffer,
Thou wouldst have power not to suffer.
Know then how to suffer, then thou wilt have power
    not to suffer.
That which thou knowest not, I myself will instruct thee.
I am thy God, not the betrayers'.
I would be kept in time with holy souls.
In me know thou the *Logos* of *Sophia*.
Say thou to me again:
Glory to Thee, Father! Glory to Thee, Logos!
Glory to Thee, Holy Spirit!
But as for me, if thou wouldst know who I was:
In a word I am the Logos who did dance all things, and
    who was not ashamed at all.
It was I who danced.
But do thou understand all, and, understanding, say:
    Glory to Thee, Father! Amen![4]

Having said these things, Jesus departed and the disciples
fled in all directions, like people who had awakened
from a trance, for their consciousness was so changed
by the hymn and dance of Jesus. Not even John, his
beloved disciple, was able to stay by his side but fled in
haste to a cave on the Mount of Olives and there wept
and grieved. And when Jesus was crucified, darkness
covered the earth, but the figure of the Savior appeared
to John in the cave in a burst of great light and addressed
him saying: "John, in the eyes of those below here in the
city of Jerusalem I am crucified and pierced by lances,
and I am tormented, and given gall and vinegar to drink,
but you should know that nothing of these things which
they will say of me have I truly suffered; for the true
mystery was not this, but rather the suffering that I have
revealed to you and the others in the dance; that was the
true mystery that came to pass. I show you what you are, but
what I truly am I alone know and no other man."

While John was thus favored with a visit from the
Savior, Peter, leader of the apostles, had a visitation also.

In a vision that occurred prior to the trial and Crucifixion, Peter saw a crowd approaching and seizing Jesus. "What is this that I see, O Lord?" asked Peter. "Who is this whom I see above the cross, one who is happy and laughs? Is it he or another, whose feet and hands are being pierced?" The Savior replied to Peter: "The one whom you see above the cross, glad and laughing, is the living Jesus. The one whose hands and feet are pierced by nails is merely his corporeal part, which is but a substitute, made in his likeness." It was thus that unbeknown to the persecutors Jesus stood by while the Crucifixion was in progress, laughing at the blindness of his enemies.

From this time on Jesus was known as the Living One, for he had obtained mastery over the deadly powers of this world. Though his fleshly body was tormented and slain by the servants of the Demiurge, yet he lived. Many were the mysteries he came to reveal to his disciples after he had returned from death. He taught them much wisdom and led them on mystical journeys into the secret worlds of the aeons, where they became acquainted with the treasuries and wonders of the light. When the time had come for him to depart from this earthly kingdom, he admonished his disciples to go forth and impart Gnosis to all people. And he also made it plain to them that he came to bring them freedom, for the Law of Moses was ended: "I have left no commandment but what I have commanded you (namely, that you should love one another), and I have given you no law as did the lawgiver, for I would not have you bound by any law." When he said this he went away and ascended to his own place in the high aeons.

After Jesus' departure the disciples were bewildered and fearful, for they had an inadequate understanding of the mysteries he communicated to them. They approached Mary Magdalene, whom he loved more than any of the other disciples and who was regarded as his companion, and they sought her counsel. Mary said to them: "What is hidden from you I will disclose." And Mary Magdalene taught them the secret teachings that

Jesus had imparted to her and that concerned the ultimate liberation of all things, both earthly and heavenly, and the manner in which the soul shall ascend through the regions of the seven planets, who shall ask the soul: "Whence do you come, you fierce hero, and where are you going, you conqueror of space?" And the victorious soul liberated by Gnosis will answer: "Whatever seizes me is killed and what turns me about is overthrown, for my desire has reached an end and now ignorance is dead. I am a whole world, and I was saved from a cosmos, and from the chains of the helpless knowledge, from the existence which is bound to time. From this time on I shall rest in the time of the moment of eternity in silence."

And it was in this way that Mary revealed to the other disciples the true secret of salvation, and, although several among them resented her on account of her sex, they were obliged to accept her Gnosis and went forth into the world fully informed regarding the purpose of the coming of the Savior and the accomplishment of his labor of freedom.[5]

Interpretation of the Myth

The myth of the Savior declares that the decisive revelation of the Gnosis was brought by Christ, the heavenly Power, who had descended upon and fused his nature with that of Jesus at the time of the baptism in the river Jordan. This is the same Christ who, according to the Valentinian myth, waits for the spiritualized souls at the entrance of the Pleroma in the company of Sophia and who with her is the guardian of the bride chamber where the pneumatic union accomplishes the ultimate spiritualization of human souls. Christ is thus both the messenger who initiates the process of redemption on earth and the transcendental hierophant who places the ultimate seal of redemption on the liberated soul.

As in the case of the myth of Sophia, so here also our understanding may be greatly aided by enlisting the illuminative amplification afforded by archetypal motifs recognized by C. G. Jung: "The drama of the archetypal

life of Christ describes in symbolic images the events
in the conscious life as well as in the life that transcends
consciousness—of a man who has been transformed by
his higher destiny."⁶

This means that the life of Christ viewed psychologically
represents the process of individuation. Jung had repeatedly alluded to the fact that persons who are contained
in a collective myth are carried along unconsciously,
or semiconsciously, by this process, whereas those who
for various reasons have left this containment become
candidates for a personal experience of Gnosis, which
ultimately makes them into indivisible psychic beings.
(The word "individual" is derived from the Latin *individuum*, signifying an indivisible unity.) Thus the story
of Christ, when accepted as a matter of faith, often acts
as a substitute or vicarious symbol for individuation.
When the myth, on the other hand, is recognized as a
metaphor open to transcendence, it becomes both a
symbolic description of and a guide to the personal
experience of individuation. This may be best apprehended when the various portions of the above-recounted
myth are individually explained in terms of their significance as stages of this process.

The prehistory of consciousness is symbolized by the
transcendental seed of light being prepared for its in-
carnational journey. The process of psychospiritual
development begins and ends in the fullness, the plenum
of being. The full potency of psychic life is gathered
together for the purposes of rendering the future journey
of the soul as effective as possible. Every authentic movement of psychological growth and transformation is
initiated by a state of empowerment, which must of necessity originate in a state of wholeness. In a prayer of the
Greek Orthodox church, this transcendental background
of the nativity is expressed in terms that appear Gnostic:

> The Virgin today brings forth the Superessential, and the
> earth offers a cave to the Unapproachable. I behold a
> Mystery strange and wondrous: The cave is Heaven,
> and the Virgin is the throne of the Cherubim: In the
> confines of the manger is laid the Infinite.⁷

In the nativity of Jesus the sacred fire of transpersonal energy descends into manifestation. It does this by way of the instrumentality of the Virgin Mary, whose virginity stands as the symbol of the kind of human personality or ego that is capable of expressing transpersonal psychic energy without becoming inflated thereby. Yet, Mary is only the mother of Jesus "after the flesh," which means that each individuated soul is "twice born," once in the realm of spiritual transcendence and once in external manifestation. The spiritual purity of the household and of the earthly parents of Jesus signifies the necessary permeability of the human ego, without which successful individuation is impossible. This permeability may facilitate early encounters and even union with the Self, symbolized in Gnostic scriptures by the twin angel, who visits and unites with the young Jesus already in his boyhood.

In the mystery of the baptism, the future Savior receives his authentic vocation by way of an overshadowing or descent of a supernal principle. The autonomous psyche, the deepest essence of the collective unconscious, thus makes itself known and calls the individuating person to his or her true vocation. Into the life of every transforming person enters the drama of death and rebirth in which one's transpersonal destiny is met and accepted. This destiny is never found at the level of mundane and personalistic considerations, but is always the result of a *showing forth (Epiphany*, the ancient name of the feast commemorating the baptism of Jesus) of a power greater than our human selfhood. Writing of Gnostic views regarding baptism, Irenaeus writes:

> For the baptism instituted by the visible Jesus was for the remission of sins, but the redemption brought in by that Christ who descended upon Him, was perfection; and ... the former is animal, but the latter spiritual. And the baptism of John was proclaimed with a view to repentance, but the redemption by Jesus was brought in for the sake of perfection. And to this He refers when He says, "And I have another baptism to be baptized with, and I hasten eagerly towards it" (Luke 12:30).[8]

The first baptism, connected with John and his Essene purificatory background, is connected with preparation and cleansing, the second with being redeemed from the constraints and terrors imposed upon humans by the rulers of the cosmos.

The individuated ego finds itself at odds with the circumstances of this life and particularly with the rules and regulations imposed on the soul by those who are concerned with the mundane order of things. Thus, Jesus complains of the blindness of his fellow men and exhorts them not to follow leaders and laws that exhibit spiritual blindness. The law of individuation is quite different from the procedures the psyche may follow prior to the discovery of its true higher destiny. Thus, the old law must be abrogated and the new, spiritually informed order must be made to prevail.

The Last Supper celebrated by Jesus and his disciples assumes a double aspect in the Gnostic account. The first is the mystery of the Eucharist, still widely practiced in Christendom. The word "Eucharist" means thanksgiving, and the act of consecrating the partaking of the sanctified elements of bread and wine was considered by the early Christians the proper way of thanking God for having sent the Savior to them and for making such means of grace available to them. The second portion of the story of the Last Supper, as present in the Gnostic myth, is of a different order. After one communes with the higher life, one must experience the transport of ecstasy, and this element is embodied in the dance that Jesus bids his disciples to execute after they partake of the sacramental meal. Moreover, it is significant that he states that the true character of his suffering is manifest in the dance, rather than in the dark tragedy of the Crucifixion. Here is an important event in the drama of the Savior that has been suppressed and ignored in the official accounts endorsed as canonical by the Church. Why? The *chorea mystica* (ecstatic cult dance) was not unknown in antiquity. In one Greek magical papyrus we read: "Come to me, Thou who art greatest in heaven, to whom heaven was given as a dancing ground."[9] Thus, the high divinities are often envisioned as dancers who dance the world into existence. Similarly, the religious dance has the capacity to so enrapture the devotees that they joyously dance through the gates of initiation into the supernal aeons. The dance as an instrumentality of establishing contact with Divinity was still known in the Middle Ages, where the German mystic Mechtild of Magdeburg (1212-1277) in her poem *Der Minne Wäg* ("The Way of Love") tells us of a dialogue between the divine Lord and a maiden. The Lord commands: "Maiden, dance as deftly as my elect have danced before" and the maiden replies:

> I would not dance, Lord, unless thou leadest me.
> Wouldst thou that I leap mightily,
> Then must thou sing for me,
> Thus will I leap into love,
> From love into knowledge,
> From knowledge into joy,
> From joy beyond all human senses.[10]

Thus, we are faced with the second portion of the myth of the Last Supper; the ecstatic dance is revealed as the other or second Eucharist in which the emphasis is not on the shed blood and the broken body of the crucified one, but rather on the event of the dance, which is not confined to the earthly dancers but is joined in by *Charis* (Grace), one of the high feminine aeons of the fullness, as well as by the eight (the seven planets along with their sphere of transcendence) and the zodiacal twelve powers. The dance is thus revealed as a cosmic and transcosmic movement in which all of creation participates and which is also blessed with the presence of the representatives of the supernal fullness. And, as Jesus reveals to John, the true secret of his suffering is not to be found in the Crucifixion but in the dance. It may be useful to remember at this point that "to suffer" comes from the Latin *sub-ferre*, to undergo. What has the Savior thus truly undergone? The Crucifixion of his corporeal selfhood? No, for unlike the hyletic portion of humanity, he possessed the capacity to detach himself from the body of flesh. He underwent, however, the limitation in order to enter the region where the lost sparks of light dwell and from whence they must be liberated.

The psychological significance of the Crucifixion—and even more of the cosmic one described here than of the physical one on the wooden cross—is well stated by C. G. Jung:

> The reality of evil and its incompatibility with good, cleave the opposites asunder and lead inexorably to the crucifixion and suspension of everything that lives. Since "the soul is by nature Christian" this result is bound to come as infallibly as it did in the life of Christ, i.e., suspended in a moral suffering equivalent to veritable crucifixion.[11]

The cross and the dance are two interrelated and interchangeable symbols. The dance reveals the true cross, which is not the mere cross of wood but the cross of light upon which the true life and salvation of the cosmos are suspended. It is in the ecstatic dance that this secret is revealed: The Logos declares that he is indeed the one who has danced all things and who teaches us what is the nature of suffering and of redemption. Jung has stated that, from a psychological point of view, the drama of Christ represents the vicissitudes of the Self as it undergoes embodiment in an individual ego and of the human ego as it participates in the salvific drama of individuation. The myth of the Gnostic Christ is eminently compatible with this understanding, although it must be recognized that the interpretation of the myth transcends psychological categories and possesses numerous aspects that we could not elucidate here. The Dancing Savior is nevertheless a unique Gnostic image in which ecstasy and suffering, the cosmic process and its transcendence, embodiment and liberation are united in a peculiarly Gnostic conjunction of the opposites. In it we may also find indications of an often overlooked phenomenon: The role of ecstatic, altered states of consciousness in the process of Gnosis. The intensity of the transport of mind and emotions is aptly portrayed in the image here observed and the Dancing Savior declares to us his amazing etiquette of ecstasy when he admonishes us:

All whose nature is to dance; dance. Amen!
Those who dance not, know not what cometh to pass. Amen!

8

Princes of the World:
The Myth of the Tyrant Angels

Introduction: Creator Gods or Divine Rebels?

Who created and who rules this world? The answers to these questions vary. The mainstream tradition of Jewish-Christian-Islamic orthodoxy holds that the creation and subsequent management of the cosmos are to be attributed to the One God, the ultimate source and destiny of all. The alternative tradition apparently always had its doubts concerning this proposition, which it considered an oversimplification at best and a deceptive falsehood at worst. Ancient peoples were far more sophisticated in their thinking about ultimate metaphysical issues than we generally recognize today, and thus they often brought forward ideas that cast doubt on the simplistic view of the monotheistic religions. One of these concerns the nature of deity itself. If the ultimate source of all being is absolute, as most religions claim, how could this utterly transcendental, absolute existence be directly responsible for the minutiae of the fashioning and development of the innumerable details of the created world-system? Echoing the sentiments reflected in many ancient sources, the neo-Gnostic writer H. P. Blavatsky writes:

> The One is infinite and unconditioned. It cannot create, for It can have no relation to the finite and conditioned. If everything we see, from the glorious suns and planets

down to the blades of grass and specks of dust had been created by the Absolute perfection and were the direct work of even the *First* Energy that proceeds from It, then every such thing would have been perfect, unconditioned, like its author. . . .[1]

As the above quotation indicates, the other issue raised by the critics of the monotheistic religions concerns the existence of imperfection and evil in the world. How can an omnipotent, good deity create and/or countenance the existence of so much grotesque, injurious, and senseless evil? (The well-nigh frivolous answer advanced frequently that evil is somehow due to human sin would not even have been seriously considered by most skilled thinkers in the ancient world.) If, on the other hand, evil and imperfection exist in the world, they must be due at least in part to the activity of agencies who interpose themselves between manifest existence and the Absolute and who do not partake of the perfection and goodness of the former. "By their works shall ye know them." An imperfect world replete with very real evil must be the work of gods or a God partaking of the qualities of imperfection. Such was the judgment rendered by the Gnostics and before them of other sophisticated thinkers of the ancient world.

Semitic religiosity was filled with curious contradictory images and notions when it came to a concept of the deity and to the nature and origin of evil. The Sumero-Babylonian religious matrix that exercised a large influence on ancient Judaism squarely admitted that the gods were responsible for evil as well as for good. Enki and other Babylonian gods freely amused themselves by creating monsters and freaks and visiting humanity with evil conditions purely for their own divinely perverse amusement. The Lord God of Israel was in many ways similar to his Babylonian counterparts: he had both a good and an evil side and freely exercised both of these proclivities depending on his whim. The people who served the Hebrew God simply had to bow their heads to his will, whether it bode good or ill to them. During the last few centuries prior to the Christian era, an increasing number of Jews were no longer willing to endure the tension of the opposites that they perceived in their God. Thus, the Essenes came to avail themselves more and more of a mythos of dualism, which served as a rationale for the existence of radical evil in the cosmos. The People of the Scrolls diligently searched the more obscure works of Jewish literature and mythology, such as the legendry associated with the prophet Enoch, and discovered ideas there that shed light on their concern with evil and the battle of the sons of light with the children of darkness. Some of these scriptures spoke of imperfect beings bridging the gap between God and the created cosmos.

The notion of the existence and activities of angelic beings, "sons of God," who were nevertheless imperfect, lustful, and rebellious, has ample warrant in the Hebrew Bible. The first four verses of the sixth chapter of Genesis tell of the curious episode of the so-called sons of God, who as soon as daughters were born to humans took them as their wives ("any of them they liked") and thus became the progenitors of an equally strange race of beings, whose name is sometimes translated as heroes and at other times as giants. Later Jewish apocryphal literature, such as the Book of Noah, and the renowned Books of Enoch present lengthy elaborations on this theme. The actions, all too briefly alluded to in Genesis, now take on a distinct tone of rebellion brought on by concupiscence and greed. The chief of the sons of heaven, who is called *Semihazah*, leads his terrible host of two hundred rebellious angels down from the summit of Mount Hermon, pronouncing terrible magical oaths and curses and filled with fierce lust for human women. The angels in question are called by the ominous name of "watchers," and the offspring resulting from their rape of human women are angry and cruel giants who kill men and beasts and despoil the earth. The Lord then explains to Enoch that the giants will be called demons or evil spirits and the earth shall be their dwelling place. These giant spirits are destined to continue to oppress humankind and to do all sorts of damage to the earth, and all of this is justified by the fact that they have the "holy watchers" as their ancestors and progenitors. One of the ten leaders of the rebel angels in the literature of Enoch is named *Asael*, who as *Azazel* appears in the writings of the Qumran community (see Chapter Two of the present work). One passage in the Enochian literature is particularly instructive. Here Enoch travels around in cosmic realms seeing all the workings of the universe, and he is shown seven stars of the heavens who are bound together like prisoners. The explanation given to Enoch is that these are some of the stars that transgressed the command of the Lord and have been bound for ten thousand years for their sins. The linking of the rebellious angels with the seven planets thus leads us to the Gnostic idea that the planets are ruled by sinister lords of limitation who are intent upon keeping the spirits of humanity captive in their earthly confinement.[2]

From the Books of Enoch, the Book of Jubilees (both of which were very popular with the Essenes), and the fascination of the People of the Scrolls with the subject of the rebel angels, there naturally developed the Gnostic conclusion that split the biblical monotheistic God into a transcendent Being, on the one hand, and a lower creator being or Demiurge, on the other. The transcendence and unknowability of God were stressed for some time by Jewish theology, when the increasing gnosticizing tendencies of the Essene groups finally erupted as an open rebellion against the image of Jehovah as it appeared in the official teachings of the Jewish priesthood.[3] Parallel with this development there evolved a recognition, which may be called the doctrine of the Son of Man. The expression "Son of Man" is a Hebraism denoting simply a member of the human race, but the teachings that grew up around this concept have implications that reach beyond humanity as ordinarily understood. The Son of Man, known in Greek as *anthropos*, of whom the Teacher of Righteousness was regarded as a manifestation, came to be understood as the reflection of God in creation, a miniature manifestation of the transcendent Godhead, who is destined to develop into the fullness of his potential on our planet. This archetype of true humanity is described by Hugh Schonfield in the following manner in his late work *The Essene Odyssey*:

> He is the ideal of our species incognito. He may be encountered in East and West, in the past, in the present, and in the future by any of us of any faith and clime. He is the immortal traveller who has endured all the adversities our planet can inflict. Wherever he is found he calls us back to our better selves, to the path of concern for others, to love and goodness of heart. He restores our courage and our hope. He is eternally adaptable, so that in all our diversities we are at home with him, and he is our home. He is also the goal towards which we strive, the World Man of a wiser, nobler world we visualize in our finer imagination. Through him, in spirit, we reach out to wonders infinite and glories incomparable.[4]

The earliest embodiment of this archetype of humanity, so the developing alternative tradition believed, was the first human pair, Adam and Eve. A set of treatises collectively called the "Adam books," comprising such works as the *Life of Adam and Eve (Vita Adae et Evae), The Apocalypse of Moses,* and the Nag Hammadi text the *Apocalypse of Adam* (all composed probably in the first century B.C.), present us with an image of the first parents of humanity that is substantially different from the current representation. Adam and Eve appear here as majestic, quasi-divine beings filled with glory and power, whose status is envied by the adversary angels. In the overtly Gnostic *Apocalypse of Adam,* Adam speaking to his son Seth about his and Eve's original estate says: "And we resembled the great eternal angels, for we were higher than the God who created us and the powers with him whom we did not know."

Rebellious angels interposing themselves between the transcendent God and creation; glorious humans, created in the image of a supernal archetype and infused with a spirit superior to this world; the envy and hostility of the rebel angels against humanity: Such are the dramatic elements that make up the great tragedy of human life on earth as understood mythically by the alternative tradition. We may now perhaps be ready to appreciate the myth of the Princes of this World and their aeonial contest with the children of men.

The Myth of the Tyrant Angels

From Sophia, the celestial mother of all living things, was born the one who became the fashioner and ruler of the system of creation. His mother was in great sorrow and anguish when she brought him forth, for she was alone in an abyss of darkness and her light was diminished. Her offspring appeared before her and she saw that he was a shape changer: he appeared in the shape of a serpent with the face of a lion, and out of his eyes there came forth lightning flashes. And Sophia repented of her desire to bring forth a being in her loneliness, and she wept and lamented over her offspring whom she named Yaldabaoth, which means the Child-Lord.

Yaldabaoth then went forth into the chaos and fashioned a system of creation that was to his own liking, and into it he placed twelve authorities, seven kings of the firmament and five kings of the abyss. All of these, with their children, were called rulers, for their desire for power and authority was great. The fashioner and his host then mingled light with darkness, so that the darkness would appear radiant and thus could deceive the eye. This mixture of light and darkness resulted in a world that was imperfect and weak, for the darkness prevented it from developing an armor of light that might protect it. And great indeed became the weakness of this world, for the darkness that was everywhere mixed with the light invited terrible, evil powers and beings from beyond the system of the world.

Thus, Yaldabaoth stood in the midst of the world system he fashioned and grew arrogant in his pride as he exclaimed: "I am God and there is no other God beside me!" Thus, he demonstrated his ignorance of the true character of being and his pride, whereby he denied even his own mother. Sophia, however, looked down on him from on high and exclaimed with a loud voice: "Thou hast uttered a falsehood, O Samael!" It was thus that he received the name that makes him the blind lord of death, and then Sophia also called him by the name of Saclas, whereby she affirmed his foolishness.

Sophia, however, knowing that her offspring had fashioned a creation in his own flawed image, decided to secretly come to the aid of the light that was present in the world. She descended from her habitation and came close to the earth, moving to and fro over it, and thereby conferred her wisdom and love upon the system that the foolish fashioner created. It was her mighty spirit that moved upon the face of the waters, as was stated in the account of creation rendered by Moses. The rulers thought that they alone created and ordered the world, but the spirit of Sophia secretly contrived to place splendid archetypal patterns into the fabric of their work.

Then a great wonder appeared in the heavens: the form of a man, majestic and glorious to behold. And the image was accompanied by a voice that exclaimed: "The Man exists and the Son of Man." The creator and his host trembled and the foundations of the abyss shook and the waters churned in terror upon the earth. So great was the radiance of the celestial human archetype that appeared in the heavens that the rulers were blinded by it and they could not bear its power. They averted their eyes and beheld the reflection of the form of the man as it appeared in the waters below.

All the rulers and their servants rushed hither and gathering their powers made a replica of the image of the heavenly man. But their work was faulty and feeble, because the force of Sophia was not in their creation. The counterfeit man was dull and insensate and crawled on the earth like a worm. Sophia then sent down several of her messengers of light and they secretly entered the mind of Yaldabaoth, causing him to breathe into the pitiful creature, thus bestowing life upon him. The fashioner thought that it was he who endowed man with life, but in reality it was his mother, Sophia, who gave humanity true life. And the man stood up, walked, and was surrounded by an unearthly light.

Yaldabaoth and his host now came to recognize that the man was in fact a being whose spiritual power and intelligence exceeded their own. Filled with envy and rage they attacked the man whose name was Adam and cast him into the darkest region of matter, there to languish in sorrow and deprivation. But Sophia, in cooperation with the highest powers of the fullness, sent a helper to Adam to instruct and assist him with wisdom and spiritual strength. The helper was a woman who came to be known as Eve, but whose true name is Zoe, meaning life. The wise feminine spirit entered Adam and was concealed in him, so that the rulers could not recognize her presence.

The rulers now conspired and devised a plan whereby they hoped that the man could be deceived and remain a captive to their designs. They made a garden filled with the beauties and delights of the earth and placed Adam in the midst of it, providing him with every kind of pleasant object he could desire. But the beauty and the pleasures they offered him were deceptive and corrupt and designed to keep him a captive of the rulers, without a will and a life of his own. A tree was also placed by them in the garden that contained their life and that they forbade Adam to touch or eat the fruit of.

Once again Sophia and the other heavenly powers came to the aid of Adam and instructed him to eat of the fruit of the tree and defy the ruler and his tyrant angels. At the same time, the woman came forth from Adam, but the chief of the rulers recognized her as having the light of Sophia in her and he was enraged. He pursued her all over the garden and, having subdued her, raped her, and she conceived two sons by him whose true names were Eloim and Yave, although they became known as Cain and Abel. But the shining spirit of wisdom that inhabited Eve fled while this ravishment took place, so that only the human Eve was thus shamed but not Zoe, the living spirit. Eloim-Cain became master over earth and water and from him descended men and women whose inclination is toward matter, whereas Yave-Abel commanded fire and air and became the father of humans who value the soul and mind. Adam, however, recognized what the tyrant ruler had done and subsequently fathered a son by the name of Seth, whose inclination was toward spirit and who became the father of those who desire Gnosis and who strive for union with spirit.

The tyrant angels then watched in rage as humankind went its way and would no longer linger in the fool's paradise where the fashioner wished to keep them captive. The chief ruler particularly cursed the woman who became the mother of humankind, and her lot and the lot of her daughters has been a difficult one ever since. Nevertheless, Eve gave birth to a daughter named Norea who was filled with true Gnosis and who remained on earth for a long time as a helper of humanity, because she was wise and knew of the schemes and the evil works of the tyrant angels.

Meanwhile, humans multiplied and, instructed by Seth and Norea, many turned to Gnosis, so that the rulers had few men and women who would accept them as divine and follow their laws. The tyrants gathered and declared that they wished to destroy all humans who were not subservient to them. They caused a deluge from which they intended to save only those who were still beholden to them, among whom was a man named Noah. The chief ruler approached Noah and told him to build an ark whereby to save himself and his companions from the deluge. Norea, however, learned of this and in order to frustrate their designs she first attempted to dissuade Noah from constructing the ark, but when she did not succeed in her attempt she blew fire upon the ark he had built so that it burned. Noah, however, being stubborn, built a second ark.

The evil angels then assaulted Norea, wishing to ravish her as they did her mother Eve, but a great angel of light named Eleleth rescued her and gave her strength to continue with her mission. The knowers of the truth hid themselves in a luminous cloud high above the mountains and were saved from the flood. So, with the help of Norea the scheme of the tyrant angels was frustrated.

Ever since those days, humankind lived in conflict and division, for the chief ruler had divided it in wrath. True Gnosis became rare and the children of men learned about useless and dead things and their knowledge became worldly and corrupt. Still, the human race was never left alone, for it had helpers in the high aeons. Not only Sophia and her angels, but some tyrant angels also turned from the evil of their chief and returned to the service of the light. The greatest of these was the brother of Yaldabaoth, and he is named Sabaoth and also Abraxas. This spirit renounced the works of his blind and evil brother and submitted to his mother Sophia, who appointed him the ruler of the seventh heaven, from whence he ever calls after the fashion of a celestial chanticleer

Abraxas

to all beings, so that they might awaken and renounce the works of darkness.

At a later time, conflict arose between the children of men who still served the tyrant angels and those who had been liberated by Gnosis. The servants of Yaldabaoth betrayed the knowers, and the rulers rained fire and brimstone on them, hoping to destroy them. Abraxas-Sabaoth, assisted by other mighty angels of light, rescued them, so that the plan of the rulers once again came to naught. (This became known as the destruction of Sodom and Gomorrah.)

Time and again the rulers rallied and schemed to destroy those humans who would not serve them. They wished to corrupt the whole human race by mingling their essence with humanity, and they abducted many human women and procreated giants who were filled with malice. These giants became the ancestors of those men who selfishly despoil the earth and deprive good men and women of their possessions and sustenance. Owing to the manifold evil schemes and depredations of the rulers, a certain portion of the human race is contaminated by their seed, although all men and women possess in addition the spark of Sophia.

The rulers, however, are truly tyrants. Their deepest desire is to subjugate and rule the children of men whom they mistrust and despise, for they are superior in essence to the rulers themselves. Thus the rulers are ever at work devising laws and commandments whereby they might constrain the children of men. They masquerade as messengers of light, or even as the true God himself, and demand obedience and worship. They thus deceived many well-intentioned prophets and seers and came to dominate large numbers of humans. The Law of Moses was, at least in part, similarly inspired by the rulers, for Moses could not make a distinction between the true, transcendental God and the chief of the tyrant angels.

Jesus, who descended from the high aeons, came to advance the defeat of the tyrant angels by teaching humans how they might become free and by bringing them mysteries that would act as weapons against the wiles of such adversaries. The chief ruler in his blindness did not discern that Jesus was of such high and divine origin; he assumed him to be merely a troublesome human who could be murdered. He thus incited the priests and Pharisees to condemn Jesus to death. Jesus, being other than human, did not die, although he permitted the illusion of his physical death. He returned in glory and completed his work of redemption in spite of the plans of his enemies. The assault on his person had brought such consequences upon his persecutors, however, that soon the Temple at Jerusalem was destroyed and the circumstances changed in such a way that many could renounce the old law that was influenced by the rulers. The spiritual freedom brought by Jesus only prevailed for a brief period of history, and the tyrant angels began to corrupt the message of the Good News once more. The battle of the forces of light against the tyrant angels continues, but the outcome is not in question. The forces of redemption are destined to prevail, bringing Gnosis and liberation to the sparks of light hidden in humanity. Defeat will come to the blind and foolish tyrant angels who have for so long ruled in the kingdom where, like usurpers, they established their illegitimate dominion.

Interpretation of the Myth

The origins of the chief tyrant angel lead us back to Sophia. The feminine soul, having descended into the abyss of darkness, brings forth an offspring in an irregular manner. *The Apocryphon of John* tells us that this offspring was brought forth without the consent of the spirit and "though the personage of her maleness" did not approve. The mother of the Demiurge thus acted in an unbalanced manner. In contemporary terms, we might say that she brought forth without the cooperation of her animus or masculine psychic selfhood. When we act out of only one side of our contrasexual polarities, we go wrong. In order to bring forth a psychologically healthy and

productive creative act we must solicit the approval of
the opposites. The head needs the consent of the heart,
the ego of the Self, the spiritual of the physical, the anima
of the animus (and vice versa). Unbalanced acts bring
disaster in their wake.

   Sophia's misbegotten son has the shape of a lion-faced
serpent. He also has the capacity to assume other forms.
Lion and serpent are creatures associated with the primary
polarities of fire and water, respectively. In the same
vein, the Demiurge is also described as androgynous by
many Gnostic scriptures. These features would lead one
to believe that he stands for a certain preconscious, undifferentiated force that stands in an adversarial relation
to differentiated consciousness. In the *Seven Sermons to
the Dead*, Jung refers to a similar symbolic figure as "the
hermaphrodite of the lowest beginnings." We may thus
initially define this being as a symbol for primitive,
undifferentiated psychic energy that constellates itself
in a human ego. As soon as this energy has assumed an
ego identity, it begins to create its own world. The ego
comes forth from its larger psychic background, but soon
turns its back upon its mother and arrogantly declares
its independence from the unconscious mystery from
whence it arose. The name Yaldabaoth, although having
several meanings, is derived from YHVH (Yahweh,
Jehovah), the meaning of which is "I am that I am." Do
not the words "I am" also characterize the very nature
of the psychological ego? The imperfect creator serves
thus as a suitable metaphor for what depth psychologists
call "the alienated ego." Defined by its own sense of
selfhood, this psychic entity draws away from the wisdom
(Sophia) contained in the unconscious and declares
itself as a creator and ruler in its own right. He who could
have become an angel of light becomes a dark tyrant.

   The ultimate proof of the tyrant ego's arrogance
is implicit in the statement of the Demiurge: "I am God
and there is no other God beside me!" Jungian psychologist Edward Edinger writes of this phenomenon
as follows:

Power motivation of all kinds is symptomatic of inflation. Whenever one operates out of power motive omnipotence is implied. But omnipotence is an attribute only of God. Intellectual rigidity which attempts to equate its own private truth or opinion with universal truth is also inflation. It is the assumption of omniscience. . . . Any desire that considers its own fulfillment, the central value transcends the reality limits of the ego and hence is assuming attributes of the transpersonal powers.[5]

Sophia thus stands for the transpersonal, supernal matrix (from *mater*, mother), whereas Yaldabaoth represents the tyrannical ego, which is unwilling to acknowledge the existence of transcendence and thus of any limits that may be set to its power. It may also be noted that the Demiurge frequently exhibits fits of anger, which is a hallmark of an inflated state. The inflated ego ever attempts to coerce and dominate its environment, and when attempts in this direction are not successful, fierce anger is the result. It is for such reasons that the Creator curses Eve at the time of the fall, and it is also such anger that motivates him and his minions to rape her and to attempt the same kind of outrage against Norea. (In a rather Gnostic way, various Jungian psychologists have identified this kind of arrogant anger as a "Yahweh complex.") Alienation leads to inflation; Sophia's child becomes alienated from its mother and then arrogantly repudiates her and all other powers outside of itself.

The ego creates its own world, but of necessity it is a flawed world. The wisdom of the transpersonal, archetypal psyche, however, is never totally absent. That is why Sophia's spirit moved over creation and entered it secretly. The alchemists were responsible for coining the term *Lumen Naturae*, the light of nature, whereby they implied that in addition to the higher light of divinity in the realm of transcendence, there also exists another light, inferior in character but still potent. This light is present in nature and in the body of the human being. Its ultimate origins, of course, are divine. The presence of this light is indicated by several mythologems in the story of the Demiurge and his tyrant angels. First, Sophia enters into an intimate connection with creation. Then she exhibits to the terrified gaze of the rulers the image of the perfect or heavenly human form. On the basis of this celestial archetype the rulers fashion the first man, but he is lacking in one very vital ingredient: consciousness or self-awareness. This power only comes to him at the behest of Sophia. We are made in the image of great archetypal patterns, but we become truly human only when the gift of consciousness comes to us.

With the first stirrings of conscious selfhood begins the process of psychospiritual growth. The first steps along the path of individuation evoke strong resistances from the tyrant ego. Spiritual development never occurs without a struggle brought about by the arrogance and the will to power of the ego. The lengthy story of the difficult relationship of the human race with the Demiurge and the rulers is a tale that tells of this struggle.

A particularly fine mythologem expressing this struggle is the story of Adam and Eve in the garden of Eden as understood by the Gnostics. The ego world is so constituted that it may efficiently distract the soul from the tasks of individuation. In many ways this is a paradisiacal world: It is filled with objects and experiences that promise pleasure, riches, and power. Still, when viewed from the vantage point of transformative growth it is a fool's paradise. The serpent, not mentioned by name in our account, is in reality the principle of *Gnosis*, the emerging consciousness and urge to individuation. Also, it is worthy of note that it is Eve rather than Adam who responds to the inspiration of wisdom and brings about the happy catastrophe of the expulsion from paradise. Gnostic interpreters of Genesis generally felt that Eve represented the human spirit with its supernal intuition, whereas Adam signified the soul with its somewhat earthbound emotions and thoughts.

This mythologem is repeated in connection with the story of Noah, where Norea acts in accordance with the

designs of the spirit and Noah remains subservient to
the rulers. There is little doubt that the entire Gnostic
approach is greatly affinitized to the feminine with its
nonrational intuitive emphasis. One person who recognized this fact and put it to good use was C. G. Jung. As
early as August 1912, Jung intimated in a letter to Freud
that he had an intuition that the essentially feminine-
toned wisdom of the Gnostics, which he symbolically
called Sophia, was destined to reenter modern Western
culture by way of depth psychology. By unlocking the
deep recesses of the human soul through intuition and
insight, by rehabilitating the dignity of human feelings,
Jung's psychology has in large measure justified this
early prediction. The Gnostic myths suggest that it was
the wisdom of the feminine as embodied in such figures
as Sophia, Eve, Norea, Mary Magdalene, and other
women that acted as the champion of Gnosis throughout
human history, whereas the masculine psyche with its
more prosaic, earthbound orientation was more often
than not in league with the forces of ego-consciousness
and worldly mindedness. One may also note that though
the relationship between Adam and Eve is envisioned
by Gnostic interpreters as a metaphor for the intrapsychic
relationship of soul and spirit, the enlightening importance of the feminine as embodied in living woman
is not ignored. Thus, when the wise spirit sent by Sophia,
after first being concealed in Adam, finally separates
from him and becomes external to her mate, she remains
his instructor and inspiration and continues as his
spiritual superior. A psychological analogue appears
in the importance of the value of the anima, not only
when recognized within the masculine psyche, but also
when projected from it and appearing superimposed
upon a flesh-and-blood woman.

Another instructive and significant motif of the myth
is one that recurs within many other myths of the Gnosis.
This concerns the issue of law versus freedom. Whenever
humans become free, the tyrant angels try to destroy
them. The "sins" for which humanity is visited with the

deluge and with fire and brimstone are disobedience to the laws of the tyrant angels. Depth psychology recognizes that individuation implies going contrary to the established shiboleths of society. As long as the human psyche is content to be contained within the system of family, state, and society, the kind of inner growth brought about by individuation does not occur. This does not mean that the individuated person remains forever in a mind-set characterized by rebellion and anarchy; rather, we must realize that once the psyche has ceased to identify with and blindly accept rules and laws external to itself it becomes capable of living as a free individual within a social setting. Individuated (or successfully individuating) persons seldom flaunt their nonconformism; nor are they unconscious slaves and victims of collective rules and conventions. In order to make choices, it is necessary to become emancipated from the choiceless adhering to established rules. And it is choice that characterizes the process and the results of individuation at their best. It is obvious then why the Gnostic myths describe the battles of the choice-makers against the slaves of the law. The pneumatic Gnostic is ever a person willing to bear the burden and enjoy the glories of existential choice and responsibility, whereas the psychic non-Gnostic values externally imposed law over the internally held values of his own soul.

Gnostic mythologems tend to contrast the old dispensation of Moses with its rigid concern with the law with the new law proclaimed by Jesus. The former decrees obedience and, flowing from such obedience, a collective redemptive victory of the people of Israel. The latter implies an existential dignity brought about by conscious choice and personal responsibility. (That many subsequent developments led to the neglect of this existential element in the Christian ethic does not mitigate against its historic existence and cannot diminish its usefulness when recognized and implemented.) The old law is the law of collective psychology influenced by the dark unconscious tyranny of humanity's guilt-ridden unconscious. The new law recognized by the Gnostic, but often obscured by later so-called orthodoxy, is the law of individuation with its attendant freedoms and responsibilities, its existential terrors and transcendental joys. Well did the great American mythologist Joseph Campbell state it in his work *The Hero With a Thousand Faces*:

> It is not society that is to guide and save the creative hero, but precisely the reverse. And so every one of us shares the supreme ordeal—carries the cross of the redeemer—not in the bright moments of his tribe's great victories, but in the silences of his personal despair.[6]

Sooner or later we all must come to the kind of Gnosis that inspires us to turn from the blandishments and threats, the carrot and the stick of the tyrant angels. Masquerading as religious law, customs of society, political and economic ideology, and many other manifestations, the designs of the tyrant angels keep us enmeshed in a condition of collective thralldom, lacking choice and individuation. The tyrant ego acts in many ways and at many levels. Some of his cunning deeds are collective, whereas others are intensely personal. Externally imposed dogma thus meets and conspires with guilt, anger, and greed rising from the shadow side of the personality. Like Seth and Norea in the Gnostic myth, we must avert our gaze from the intimidating spectacle presented to us by tyranny and wickedness residing in high places. In *The Gospel of Thomas*, Jesus employs the word *monachoi*, usually translated as "solitary ones" but also meaning "those who have become unified." This is the name whereby one might describe the individuated psyche, the soul of the knower, who having become a unity now can stand alone without the burdensome collectivity of society, as well as without the tyranny of the alienated ego. These are the men and women who have succeeded in freeing themselves of the dominion of the tyrant angels, and of them the Gnostic Christ says: "Blessed are the solitary and the elect, for they will discover the kingdom! . . . Many stand outside the door, but it is only the solitary ones who will enter into the bridal chamber."[7]

9

Traveler from Heaven:
The Myth of "Song of the Pearl"

Introduction: A Song of the Soul's Journey

Among the numerous documents that serve as vehicles of the enshrinement of Gnostic experience in mythic form, none equals the charming and meaningful story of "Song of the Pearl." Contained within *Acts of Thomas*, an apocryphal scripture long known in Christendom, this poem is poetically attributed to Thomas, the apostle of Jesus, most highly regarded by the Gnostics. The Nag Hammadi collection alone contains two major scriptures attributed to this apostle (*The Gospel According to Thomas* and *The Book of Thomas the Contender*), and numerous other books and traditional sayings are said to originate with him.

In the Ninth Act of *Acts of Thomas* is an account of the apostle traveling to India, where he ran afoul of an important official named Charisius, whose wife Mygdonia became his follower against her husband's wishes. The enraged husband proceeded to denounce Thomas before the local ruler, and the apostle was thrown into prison. While in prison, Thomas was approached by his fellow prisoners to give them spiritual consolation, and responding to this request he sang a poem or song to them that represents a thinly veiled version of the Gnostic myth of the liberation of the soul from confinement in the darkness of materiality and unconsciousness and its entry into the kingdom of light and fullness. The story is thus at once a parable and a symbolic monomyth, the message of which may be discovered in virtually all other Gnostic myths.

As in most such instances, the poetic account of the origins of the poem is probably not an accurate one. It is frequently assumed that the true author of the song was Bardaisan (Bardesanes), the great light of Syrian Gnosticism.*

Acts of Thomas has been described as a Gnostic composition preserved with orthodox reworkings; however, such reworkings appear to be totally absent from "Song of the Pearl" itself. In addition, one may note also the absence of any explicitly Christian references, all of which makes this poetic tale the most universal and also the most readily comprehensible of all Gnostic mythic statements. The total lack of any technical terminology whatsoever, in combination with the impressive simplicity of the story, place this scripture into a category all by itself. (The present writer, having told this tale to general audiences as well as observed it being performed in dramatic form, can attest to the fact that its message is very readily apprehended by persons with little or no background in Gnosticism or in mythology of any kind.)

The text of our poem is available both in the Syriac language and in a Greek version. The former is to be preferred, since it appears to be closer to the original, whereas the latter represents a revision. The story is written in the first person, thus reinforcing the impression that it is based on personal experience. In the following account I shall retell it as a prose narrative, disregarding the original metric divisions and maintaining the first-person form.

The Myth of "Song of the Pearl"

When I was but a little child and lived in the kingdom of my parents and enjoyed the wealth and splendor of

---

*For an account of the life and teachings of Bardaisan, see Chapter Five.

those who raised me, my parents decided to send me on a journey away from our homeland in the East. They did not, however, send me forth without provisions, for from the abundance of our treasury they gathered a bundle for me: It contained gold, silver, chalcedony, and opal. In addition, they girded me with adamant, a metal so strong that it crushes iron. Great was the burden of these provisions, yet light they were also, so that I could bear them alone.

My splendid robe of glory, which in their love they had made for me, they now removed from my shoulders, and also the purple mantle that was made to fit me perfectly. And they made an agreement with me, which they wrote on my heart, so that I might never forget it. It read as follows: "If thou shouldst go down into Egypt, and bring the One Pearl to us, which reposes in the middle of the sea, guarded by a roaring serpent, then, upon thy return thou shalt resume thy robe of glory and thy royal mantle, and together with thy brother, our viceroy, thou shalt be the heir of our kingdom."

I left the East and accompanied by two royal envoys, who were ordered to assist me since I was young and needed help on such a dangerous journey, I passed over several lands that lay between the East and the land of Egypt. As I arrived at the border of Egypt, my guardians took their leave from me.

Having arrived in Egypt, I traveled to a place that was near to the sea where I knew that the serpent lived. I established myself in an inn, there to await the time when the serpent should sleep, so that I might take the pearl from him. I was a stranger to the others who dwelt in the inn. Still, I met a person there who was of my own kind, fair and familiar and a descendant of royalty. I received a warning from him to guard myself against the Egyptians, for they were unclean. I thus disguised myself, wearing the garb of the Egyptians, so that they might not discover that I was an outsider intent upon taking the pearl, and that they might not therefore arouse the serpent against me. Nevertheless, they soon recognized that I was not their compatriot. They feigned friendship for me and persuaded me to drink of the drink they mixed for me and of the food they prepared for me.

To have thus yielded to the blandishments of the Egyptians became a great calamity for me. I fell into a swoon of forgetfulness, and I no longer knew that I was the child of a king and I served their king instead. I forgot all about the pearl for which my parents had sent me.

My parents in their kingdom were aware of what had befallen me and they grieved for me. They issued a proclamation and summoned all the great ones of their kingdom for a meeting, at which a plan was devised not to allow me to languish in Egypt. They wrote a letter to me, and each of the great ones signed it:

> From thy father the King of Kings, and from thy mother, the ruler of the East, and from thy brother, our viceroy, to thee, our child in Egypt, greeting. Awake and arise out of thy deep sleep, and be alert to the message of our letter. Remember who thou art: The offspring of a king. And see whom thou hast served in dark bondage. Remember also the pearl, for whose sake thou hast journeyed into Egypt. Remember thy robe of glory and thy splendid mantle, so that the time may come when these may rest again upon thy shoulders, and, arrayed in them, thy name may be read in the book of the heroes, and thou shalt become, with thy brother, our viceroy, heir in our realm.

This letter was a magic messenger unto me. My father had so sealed it that it would be protected against the dreadful denizens of the regions that it would have to traverse before arriving at my habitation. The letter rose up in the shape of an eagle, the king of all birds, and it flew until it arrived beside me, where I heard its speech. Upon hearing the message I awoke from my sleep and arose, took the letter, kissed it, broke its seal, and read its contents. The letter read like the words inscribed once upon my heart. I remembered everything: I knew that I was the offspring of kings and that my soul, born to freedom, was desirous of being with its own kind.

I also remembered the pearl, which I had come to Egypt to fetch. Thus I proceeded to enchant the roaring serpent by singing over it the name of my father, my brother, and my mother, the ruler of the East. I then seized the pearl and turned about to go to my parents. I cast off the impure garment of the dwellers in this land, and I directed my way so as to go toward the light of our homeland, the East.

As I proceeded on my way, I was guided by the letter that had awakened me, and as it once aroused me with its voice, so it now guided me with its light, which shone before me. Its voice encouraged me against my fear, while its love drew me on. So I went forth and passed through the regions and the cities that lie between the land of Egypt and my homeland, the kingdom of the East.

Then the treasurers sent by my parents, who for their faithfulness were entrusted with it, brought to me my splendid robe that I had taken off and also my royal mantle. Indeed, I no longer remembered its magnificence, for it was long ago that I had relinquished it in my father's house. But all of a sudden, when I saw it over against me, the splendid robe of glory looked more and more like my own reflection; I saw it as if it were my own self, and the distinction between it and myself melted away, so that we were two in differentiation but one in single union. Even the two treasurers who brought my robe to me appeared as a single person, impressed with the one seal of my father's majesty.

I thus came to observe further the robe in its splendor. It was adorned in glorious colors; upon it were gold and many diverse jewels, and its seams were fastened with adamant. The image of the King of Kings was depicted all over the robe, and I saw move over it the rippling movements of the holy Gnosis. I also perceived that the robe was about to speak to me, and the sound of great hymns resounded in my ears as it fell down on me: "I am the one that acted in the actions of the one for whom I was brought up in my Father's house, and I perceived in myself how my stature grew in accordance with his works." And the robe poured itself entirely down upon me with regal movements, and it leaped out of the hands of those who held it, so that it might come to rest upon me. And I loved it so greatly that I ran towards it to receive it. I reached up towards it and enveloped myself in its glorious colors, having clad myself entirely in this royal robe of glory.

Clothed in my robe, I now ascended to the gate of salutation and adoration. I bowed my head and adored the splendor of my father who had sent the robe to me, whose commands I had fulfilled, and who had done with me as he promised. And at the gates of his nobles I met the great ones of the kingdom. And my parents were jubilant as they received me, for now at last I was with them in their kingdom. And with a mighty voice of music did all their servants praise them, and they exclaimed that they had promised that I should journey to the court of the King of Kings so that, having brought the pearl, I might appear together with him.

Interpretation of the Myth

Hans Jonas, in his well-known work *The Gnostic Religion*, writes concerning "Song of the Pearl":

> The immediate charm of this tale is such that it affects the reader prior to all analysis of meaning. The mystery of its message speaks with its own force which almost seems to dispense with the need for detailed interpretation. Perhaps nowhere else is the basic Gnostic experience expressed in terms more moving and more simple. Yet the tale is a symbolic one as a whole and employs symbols as its parts, and both the total symbolism and its component elements have to be explained.[1]

We shall thus comply with Jonas' suggestion and add our interpretation to the story.

The Father's house in the East is the Pleroma, or fullness of spiritual power, from whence the soul originates and to which it desires to return. The existence and the memory of this transcendental homeland are central features of all Gnostic myths dealing with human existence. The celestial king and queen represent the supreme dyad that is envisioned as the true and ultimate Godhead. The viceroy and the great ones of the kingdom are the aeonic powers, which together with the king and queen represent the totality of the fullness.

Contrasted with this plenum of heavenly beatitude, we find the land of Egypt with the pearl guarded by a serpent in the sea. The ancient name for Egypt is *Khem*, meaning "dark earth." Egypt thus stands as the symbol for earthly life with its attendant darkness of unconsciousness and alienation.

The roaring serpent in the sea is a symbol very different from the wise serpent of Genesis. Rather, it is a serpentine dragon envisioned as encircling the earth, the beast of the original chaos, enemy of the light and Gnosis. In the book *Pistis Sophia* we read: "The outer darkness is a huge dragon whose tail is in his mouth." The sea within which the serpent-dragon dwells is the watery body of corruption and forgetfulness into which the divine has sunk. Yet in the midst of this sea guarded by the terrifying monster lies the pearl so greatly desired by the rulers of the heavenly kingdom.

Many of these elements of the myth bear a relationship to Jung's theories concerning the beginnings and journey of the human ego. The ego has its beginning as a child of the celestial royal family, living in a state of identity with the archetypal psyche and its royal Self. In order to gain personal consciousness, the ego must of necessity leave this powerful matrix of psychic primordiality. Thus, it is sent away from its supernal home on a mission. Although we leave the heaven-world of the archetypal Self, we are "provisioned" by carrying with us a measure of its power and the distant memory of its sublime character. The poet Wordsworth in his ode "Intimations of Immortality" speaks of these psychological implications of the earthward journey of the child of heaven:

> Our birth is but a sleep and a forgetting:
> The Soul that rises with us, our life's Star,

Hath had elsewhere its setting,
And cometh from afar.
Not in entire forgetfulness,
And not in utter nakedness,
But trailing clouds of glory do we come
From God, who is our home: . . .

And in reference to the "descent into Egypt" with its
attendant vicissitudes, the poet continues:

Shades of the prison-house begin to close
  Upon the growing boy
But he beholds the light, and whence it flows,
  He secs it in his joy;
The youth, who daily farther from the east
  Must travel is still Nature's Priest,
  And by the vision splendid
  Is on his way attended;
At length the Man perceives it die away,
And fade into the light of common day.

It is this "fading of the vision splendid into the light
of common day" that is poignantly stated in "Song of the
Pearl" by way of the metaphor of the partaking of the
drink and food of the alien land by the traveler from
heaven. The soul is a stranger to its fellow dwellers in
the inn of this world. The acceptance of the condition
of existential alienation brings with it a useful consequence, however. This is the appearance of a helpful
companion, whose presence and advice assist the pro-
tagonist in pursuing his goal. The Gnostic is thus ever
aided in his predicament by the company of those "of
his own kind," namely, of persons who share the quest
for consciousness and are aware of their spiritual mission.
Yet the world of the commonplace, "the triviality of
everydayness" (as Heidegger named it), eventually over-
powers the individual. The suffocating world of personal
preoccupations makes us forget the world of broader
meaning and significance that resides in the inner recesses of our psyche. The ego becomes estranged from
the Self and from the entire archetypal psyche, and its

estrangement pushes it into subservience to the consensus reality of the external world and in due course into depression, the well-nigh universal affliction of contemporary humanity.

Humans possess two ways in which they can expand the magic circle of their selfhood: one outward, the other inward. Extraversion of psychic energy propels the attention of the personality into the outer world of sensation with its attendant reactive feelings and thoughts. But in states of deep inward attentiveness and psychic permeability, another kind of expansion takes place. Suddenly, we are no longer puny humans trapped in the gray fog of personalistic concepts and images; rather, we are at the center of a web of consciousness, we become aware of many kinds of meaning vibrating along the web, and we develop the capacity, not unlike a spider in a similar situation, to catch hold of the causes of these vibrations. To use another image, we become like a tree that suddenly becomes aware that its roots reach down deep into an underground world of power, meaning, and blissful excitement, and we also come to acknowledge that it is this underground realm that confers life on our branches, which stretch above it into the daylight world of ego-consciousness. Such is the phenomenon of seeing the connecting link between one's ego and one's suprapersonal, original selfhood reestablished.

In "Song of the Pearl," this reconnecting of ego and Self, of the personal and the transpersonal, is brought about through the instrumentality of a letter. The letter is of a highly magical character; it speaks words, flies on the wings of an eagle, and is "like a messenger." It is without doubt that this portion of the poem possesses soteriological overtones: the messenger, who is also the message, is a primeval symbol of the agent of salvation— Jesus, Buddha, or any other salvific messenger of light. Upon the individual's ability to open the seal of such a letter, which means to receive the redeeming call in full consciousness, depends the redemption of the soul.

In the *Odes of Solomon*, a scripture of powerful Gnostic

overtones, we read an account of the theme of the letter
where the recipient is unable to take advantage of the
message of salvation:

And his thought was like a letter,
And His will descended from on high.
And it was sent from a bow like an arrow
That has been forcibly shot.
And many hands rushed to the letter,
In order to catch it, then take and read it.
But it escaped from their fingers;
And they were afraid of it and of the seal which was upon it.
Because they were not allowed to loosen its seal;
Because the power which was over the seal was greater
than they.[2]

Where, as in "Song of the Pearl," the soul is ready to
receive the full significance of the symbolic communication, a great awakening and transformation of the personality takes place. Psychologically, the letter symbolizes,
in its various aspects, the axis that connects the ego and
the Self. Without this axis, life is lacking in the psychic
energy that is required to fulfill the tasks, to live out successfully the personal myth of the psyche. It is not possible
to capture the "pearl of great price" in the turbulent sea
of this world without being awakened by the power of
psychospiritual redemption.

But who or what is the pearl in search of which the
soul, even the ego, descends into the arena of conflict
and travail? And how are we to regard the serpent when
applying its symbolic image to the inner life of the individual? The answer to these questions in a sense
determines the meaning of the entire story.

As Hans Jonas pointed out, in Gnostic symbolism
"pearl" is one of the principal metaphors for the concept
of soul in a transcendental sense.[3] In this case the meaning
of the mythologem is defined by the existential fate that
has befallen the pearl. The pearl of our story is not any
pearl: It is the *lost pearl* that needs to be found and re-
trieved. Throughout this manifest creation the seeds of
the Divine, the sparks of the eternally brilliant flame,

are scattered and concealed. The great sea of material and psychic forgetfulness has covered the precious pearls of heaven. Frightful and fierce guardians watch over them and hold them captive. The pearl is hidden in the shell of an animal; thus are the scattered sparks of light hidden in nature and in the material universe. The dragon-serpent, as noted earlier, is a form of the *ouroboros*, the tail-swallowing monster whose circular shape represents (among others) the cyclicity of self-perpetuating natural life within time. The symbol of the serpent serves the same purpose as the Wheel of Life in Buddhism; it stands for the fiercely revolving patterns of embodied existence that hold the units of transcendental life and light captive.

The heavenly traveler is thus the human soul descending to earth in order to rescue the divine spirit enmeshed in the structures and workings of nature. The human spirit acts as a savior to the spirit lost in the cosmic sea. At the same time, the forces of the manifest cosmos are not without their effect on the heavenly traveler; they overpower him and impose the sleep of unconsciousness on him. The rescuer now needs to be rescued himself; the savior is in dire need of salvation, which boon is bestowed on him by the letter from on high. (In many ways, this is the Gnostic version also of the myth of the wounded healer, the maimed fisher king, and similar figures.) Humans act as redeeming helpers toward the spirit in matter and nature, whereas the divine messengers of light in turn come to the aid of the human soul in the calamities into which it fell in the course of its own redemptive mission.

These motifs of Gnostic metaphysics are amplified by the psychological relevance of the mythologems and symbols employed. It is a time-honored recognition of Gnostic and related thinking that the greater world (macrocosm) of transcendence is duplicated within the smaller world (microcosm) of immanence, and the latter may justly be envisioned as the human psyche itself. Thus the ego stands as the intrapsychic representative of the human soul, whereas the Self is the symbolic paradigm of the redemptive agencies of transcendence.

As Jung never ceased to affirm, Christ is the supreme symbol in our culture of the Self, and redemption is the religious formulation of individuation. The robe of glory of individuated selfhood is intimately related to the aspect of that robe in its ultimate metaphysical meaning. As always, the spiritual and the psychological are not mutually exclusive. Far from it, they are but two sides of the same great coin of wholeness.

One more important keynote needs to be reiterated in conclusion of this interpretation. It is evident to anyone who reads the "Song of the Pearl" in its unabridged form that the writer was not so much motivated by didactic intentions, such as one may find among writers of allegories, as he was inspired by vivid personal feelings rooted in experience. Particularly, the description of the robe when it is restored to its original owner bears all the hallmarks of an altered and/or mystical state of consciousness with its accompanying visionary transports. The symbolic meaning radiating from this splendid poem is perhaps the greatest proof of the efficacy of the Gnostic function of myth. It is almost impossible not to experience a measure of the original insight, and even rapture, experienced by the writer once one has read and assimilated this wondrous mythic poem. Today, as long ago, we may still perceive in this work, as on the robe of glory depicted in it, "the rippling movements of the holy Gnosis."[4]

10

And the Myth Goes On:
Some Modern Gnostic Myths

Jung's Gnostic Myth: Answer to Job

In 1952, Jung's controversial book *Answer to Job*[1] was published and caused much upset among clergymen and laymen of various Christian denominations who were associated with his psychological school. Most felt that this book represented a startling and drastic kind of criticism of Christianity, whereas few if any recognized that it was a modern Gnostic myth. While Jung's Gnostic interests were known to many and his early poetic Gnostic treatise *Seven Sermons to the Dead* bore testimony to his close identification with Gnosticism, few of Jung's students were prepared for the contents of his reworking of the biblical myth of Job.

The Book of Job, a work dating vaguely between the years 600 and 300 B.C., deals ostensibly with the theme of the righteous man who is unjustly afflicted by God. In Jung's Gnostic view, this venerable story concerns not the theme of a suffering human who arrogantly questions God's inscrutable designs, but rather that of a God who is unwise, uncharitable, and unjust because he is imperfect. Here, then, in brief outline form is Jung's myth of Job and his afflictor.

Driven to extremity by the sufferings unjustly visited upon him, Job demands a confrontation with God, who with great bluster replies to him out of a whirlwind. But the answer given so dramatically by God is in reality no

166

answer at all. What sense is there, asks Jung, to God's thundering about morning stars, flowing seas, crocodiles, and so on, and what is the point to his asking Job where he was when he created the world? After all, poor Job was only too conscious of the bewildering mystery of things, for he had experienced it quite painfully. God, however, evades the issue by telling Job something he knew quite well, namely, that God is the Almighty, and then goes on boasting about what his great might can do. For all the impressive noise, the inflated majesty, and the parading of the panorama of nature, God was just blustering. Job had asked him a perfectly legitimate question, one of most agonizing urgency to the questioner, and yet he did not offer a real explanation; nor did God apologize for his conduct, which any sensible mind would regard not only as unseemly but also as immoral. Were a human being to destroy another's family by fire and practice bacteriological warfare on him, such a person would assuredly be called to account; but God just replies that he is almighty and that is the end of the argument. Moreover, God seems angry at Job for having put the question, and he reproaches the poor man with thunderous divine eloquence.

In Jung's view, Job is not truly the inferior of God, and he is aware of this fact. Job is not in the wrong, but rather it is God who is in the wrong. God is a great, powerful, but quite unconscious bully who has been coasting along on his own omnipotence until he found himself in a position in which one of his creatures could stand up to him and utter a legitimate criticism of him. He is a jealous God who demands of Job and of all humans complete obedience to his will and law. Jung points out that God is also a cheat, for in contravention of his promise to abide by the covenant, he cheats David, who in the Eighty-ninth Psalm complains bitterly of this fact.

The moral superiority of Job, the created man, over God the Creator introduces a truly Gnostic paradox into the myth. Obviously, there is something radically wrong with God, whereas there is much that is right with

Job. It is Job who is the real hero of the story, and as a representative of humanity, as against so-called divinity, he represents the small but potentially vital element of consciousness of the human spirit confronted with the huge, materially powerful, but spiritually unaware almightiness of the Creator. Jung here restates the ancient Gnostic proposition that we find in our foregoing chapters, namely, that the God of this world is a Demiurge, and that the materially feeble human being possesses a moral superiority over the Creator by virtue of the presence of the supernal spark deposited into his nature by Sophia. The words uttered by Job, "I know that my Redeemer liveth," show that Job is aware of beings and forces that are superior to the God of this world who are capable of bringing about the redemption of the captive light-sparks from this lower region of existence.

More importantly—and it is here that Jung's myth adds a new keynote to the Gnostic theme—God is still in the process of growing, of developing consciousness. Jung's God is an undifferentiated being, possessing a double nature. The sufferings of Job, as well as his questionings, have led to a significant achievement. The double nature of God, his light and dark aspect, was now revealed, and with the assistance of the human spirit God would have to renew himself. Jung states bluntly that when God discovered that his creature caught up with him, he then decided that it was time for him to become different. The growth and development of God could occur by God coming to consciousness in humanity—in other words, using Christian terminology, by incarnating. God must become man in order to discover what human consciousness is like and to enlighten his own darkness by the light he might discover in the human spirit. The incarnation of God is a step taken by God because of his recognition that it might benefit him to assimilate the superior qualities present in the human soul and spirit.

Like the ancient Gnostics, so Jung the modern Gnostic turns the traditional reasoning of the Judeo-Christian system of thought upside down. Not only does the almighty but unconscious God desire human consciousness, but also Christ did not become man because humans sinned, but because God needed redemption from sin. Jung states unequivocally that God had to become man because he had done man an injustice.

Jung now traces the stirrings of psychological growth in God, since these occur subsequent to his confrontation with Job. God begins to remember. His vivified memory reveals to him the existence and the role of someone he once knew but forgot: Sophia, Lady Wisdom. The relationship of Sophia to the God of this world is not clarified by Jung in any detail; she appears as a combination of mother, sister, and spouse of God, who in the course of his own career had lost her and forgotten her. Now he begins to desire her and wishes to move closer to her.

Along with Sophia, God also begins to remember another figure: the Son of Man, the mysterious celestial archetype of humanity, mentioned by Enoch and Ezekiel, and repeatedly emphasized by the Gnostics. Jung states that the preparation for the coming of the Son of Man in the form of an incarnation was lengthy and extensive. The numerous prophecies of Enoch and other seers and prophets created a psychological readiness for the coming of the messianic dispensation. He remarks in this connection that if any event was ever prepared for by a historical development in the thinking of the human environment into which it came, it was the emergence of Christianity. (We find here Jung's recognition of the psychological element that is so amply represented by the Essene tradition and its emphasis on the Son of Man archetype. It is necessary to remember that at the time Jung wrote *Answer to Job*, the Dead Sea Scrolls were not available for his investigation.) The archetype of the Son of Man, as extolled by the books of Enoch (a literature most dear to the People of the Scrolls), represents thus the first answer of God to the question of Job, namely, the promise that the incarnation of certain divine forces will take place and justice will be done for humanity.

When the time is ripe the promise is fulfilled, and the

Son of Man appears on earth as the messianic figure of Jesus-Christ. Jung points out that great precautions were taken by divine providence to make the venture of the incarnation a success. The circumstances of Christ's birth, occurring by way of a virgin, the paternity not being assigned to any man but to the Holy Spirit, and many more elements indicate that he conforms to the Hero archetype, thus being sharply distinguished from other men. In typical Gnostic manner, Jung states that Jesus was more god than man, that in him, human and divine nature were not evenly matched. Being free from sin particularly, says Jung, distinguishes Jesus from the rest of humanity, since all human beings sin. Only at one point in his career did Jesus fully experience the lot of humanity, and that was when he was moved to exclaim on the cross: "My God, my God, why hast thou forsaken me?" Here Christ, according to Jung, manifested the real answer to Job, not merely in prophetic vision or promise but in actual fact. This was the point in time when God found himself in the position of a human being and thus experienced the forlornness and agony of the human condition. In all other ways, the incarnation is an incarnation of the light side of the Divine only.

A fascinating aspect of Jung's myth is the assertion that Jesus seems to have been aware of several Gods, according to his recorded statements. On the one hand, he speaks of his heavenly Father as a God of kindness and love, and he insists that humans could count on his being such. On the other hand, he addresses the petition "lead us not into temptation" to someone in the Lord's Prayer. How can a God of love lead human beings into temptation? Obviously, in addition to the loving Father we are dealing here also with a darker, more tricksterlike and therefore perilous aspect of divine nature. Clearly, Jesus was aware that, although he as an embodiment of divine light was in touch with the God of light, the dark god, or the dark aspect of God, was also in evidence and was in need of being addressed. This recognition is the point of departure for the further development of Jung's myth.

The incarnation of Christ increased the light, but the darkness did not go out of existence; it continued at certain levels of being and was bound to reemerge eventually. Christianity was designed to be a faith of light, ushering in an age of light, inasmuch as the light aspect of God was thus placed in the forefront of human consciousness. Thus, soon after the departure of Jesus for higher realms, the dark side of reality begins to emerge from hiding. This becomes particularly clear in the Book of Revelation, where the dark side of God reemerges and with it the dark side of life and of Christianity. Jung implies that in numerous ways this book indicates that the dark God has broken into the universe and consequently into Christian thought once more; the author of Revelation is no longer dealing with the workings of the messianic light, but rather with the fury and cruelty of the evil side of God so often encountered in the Old Testament.

With all of its dark and terrifying imagery, Revelation brings forth an image that Jung considers fascinating and hopeful. This vision may be found at the beginning of the twelfth chapter. A woman appears, arrayed with the sun, with the moon under her feet, and bearing a crown of twelve stars. She is about to give birth, and a terrifying red dragon is waiting to devour her child when it is born. Further strange events take place: the child is born and is taken up to God's throne, and its destiny is to rule the nations. The woman flees into the wilderness, where a place has been prepared for her by God.

Jung notes a great similarity between this image and the one usually appearing in connection with the emergence of the Self, the paradigm of the individuated ego. The woman is clearly no longer the Virgin Mary, but rather the universal, cosmic woman, the counterpart of the Son of Man. Thus in Jung's mythic vision, the incarnation is now brought forward into a new and universal phase. Jung also indicates that the incarnation did not cease with the ascension as sometimes assumed, but that it is continued in another fashion by way of the work of the Holy Spirit. This means that, in the continuing progress of the incarnation, the Divine can be born in every human being; in some sense all humans can become an incarnation of the Divine.

Although Christ represents the all-important pattern of this, in some sense it can be repeated by all. Thus, Jung finds the third answer to Job. The first was the promise of the incarnation as revealed in the visions of Enoch; the second, the human experience of Jesus in his abandonment on the cross; and the third lies in the fact that deity is today striving to come to consciousness in every human soul. God no longer incarnates in the pure virgin, but in the archetype of earthly womanhood; God is incarnating in the existential state of humanity and no longer waits for conditions of exceptional purity and holiness as the prerequisites for his descent into human flesh. (A parallel concept may be found in our investigations indicating the change of emphasis from Essene purity to Gnostic existential living in the earliest times of the Christian era, as described in Chapters Three and Four.)

Jung indicates that this third answer to Job, the new possibility of incarnation, is hardly conscious at this time. The child is caught up to God, and the woman goes into the wilderness for a long period. Still, the indications are clearly present that the divine and earthly principles can once again come together in a new synthesis of consciousness, and that God can thus be incarnated in an ordinary human being who is not purified and prepared in the manner of an earlier age.

The incarnation of God in humanity at large, said Jung, involves the elevation of the feminine principle and its return to divine or semidivine status. As the Creator had become forgetful of the divine woman Sophia and thus became a one-sided and largely unconscious being, so it is by the restoration of the exalted feminine to consciousness that this demiurgic forgetfulness can be finally undone. It is with such thoughts in mind that Jung approached in *Answer to Job* the then recent Papal pronouncement on the Assumption of the Blessed Virgin.[2] which he regarded as the most outstanding theological and religious event since the Reformation, since it implies that the earthly principle of the feminine (the physical body of the Virgin) is given association and therefore, by implication, equal status with the Godhead.

As Jung welcomed the declaration of the Assumption of the Virgin as a spontaneous revelation of the unconscious, so he recognized that with the coming of the Aion of Aquarius, humanity is about to face a new task. At the beginning of the Christian era, what humanity needed most were the values embodied in the Christian revelation. These values concerned to a large extent the concept of the light side of God and of human nature itself. Only when this was done could other, equally important, but more ambiguous recognitions be allowed to surface into consciousness. The writer of Revelation became aware of the still-present dark side of God and of life, but Jung regarded him as somewhat naive, especially when compared with contemporary humanity. Today's individual has the ability to be more aware of the danger of what knowledge has been put into his hands and also of the impulses within his psyche. We do not possess any longer the purity of the ancient saints; we are, as it were, much closer to the darkness. This may enable us to withstand the onslaught of the dark powers of the soul and to become conscious of what they really are.

Purity may keep the darkness at bay and removed from the ego, but the existential life seemingly advocated by Jesus and endorsed here by Jung leads in due course to the encounter with darkness. This is not to say that we ought to renounce our Christian tradition; the kindness, goodness, and light present there may act as highly useful agents balancing the modern psyche in its attempts to deal with the dark possibilities of this age. *Answer to Job* was written in the aftermath of World War II, wherein Jung saw the eruption of the greatest mass of evil that ever appeared in human history. While observing the frightful carnage of the war and the possibly even more frightful horrors of the Nazi death camps and of the Gulag, Jung was convinced that moral power was not sufficient to keep evil at bay. Moral humanity has failed; what is needed now is wisdom, the wisdom Job sought in his own predicament.

The new savior is different from the virtuous male Messiah of old. The new redeemer is female and is called Sophia, or Wisdom. By becoming the children of Lady Wisdom, we reenter a condition where the opposites are close together. We must become aware of what is within us in its light and dark aspects. We must develop conscious resources whereby we might deal with evil possibilities. To act consciously is our greatest saving necessity. Jung reminds us of the Gnostic saying of Jesus: "If you know what you are doing, you are blessed; but if you do not know what you are doing, then you are accursed and a breaker of the Law."[3]

In Jung's day as in ours, many bewail the moral decline of the culture and the absence of values in human conduct. It is almost universally stated that humanity must attain to a higher moral level. To Jung this means that we must attain a higher level of consciousness, for morality without consciousness will inevitably go astray. Jung has given numerous indications through his teachings regarding the individuation process that contemporary humanity, rather than its happy predecessors, is chosen as the birthplace of the progressive incarnation of the Divine. We have lost our innocence, and by this very fact we have merited the descent of the Holy Spirit into our guilty, heartbroken selfhood. In the present era of history, he who regards himself as innocent has in reality not paid his debt to existence and has sheltered himself from the alchemical fire of transformation.

Jung's Gnostic myth reminds us of the imperative tasks of our lives as contemporary persons: to strive with all our might for more consciousness while not abandoning our roots in the spiritual traditions of Western culture and, most significantly, without succumbing to the perils attendant upon transformation, among which may be found the demonic pride of the inflated ego. Jung's individuated person does not "create his own reality," does not take credit for the operations of transcendence within this realm of immanence. As he states in his conclusion to *Answer to Job*: ". . . the enlightened person remains what he is, and is never more than his own limited ego before the One who dwells within him, whose form has no knowable boundaries, who encompasses him on all sides, fathomless as the abysms of the earth and vast as the sky."[4] Jung's myth with its iconoclasm, insight, and ever-fearless Gnosis must thus be reckoned as a vital contribution to insightful living in our troubled times and world.

A Personal Myth: The Tale of the Brat Prince

All human beings are creatures of myth. Joseph Campbell, who taught the value of myth to many in our culture, expressed this convincingly when he wrote: "The latest incarnation of Oedipus, the continual romance of Beauty and the Beast, stands this afternoon on the corner of 42nd Street and Fifth Avenue, waiting for the traffic light to change."[5] The outward-oriented consciousness of human beings frequently and indeed regularly loses touch with the inner realities of the mind, and myths in their own picture language tell the human ego how these realities may be recognized and integrated into its life. The dialogue with these inner realities is a function of what in olden days was called Gnosis, and it is understandable that this dialogue should take place today even as it did long ago and far away.

As noted before, Gnostic myths are a particular modality of self-understanding, not confined to any one historical period. Neither are they the sole province of prophetic figures of Jung's stature and training. It has been observed by insightful psychologists that the dreams and imaginative experiences of persons in our modern world frequently bring forth personal myths that possess distinctly Gnostic motifs. The following myth, while not the product of psychological analysis, possesses such impressive and instructive features that it appears worthy of inclusion here, particularly as an example of Gnostic mythmaking in our time.

L. V., a man between thirty and forty years of age acquainted with Gnostic myths and teachings, has developed the following personal myth as the result of repeated experiences of active imagination extending over a one-and-a-half-year period.

At first, L. V. became aware of what appeared to be himself in an earlier period and in a world very different from this one. He was a young boy living in a heavenly city of great beauty and glory, a child of divine and royal parents, whom he identified with Christ and Sophia. Although living in a beatific state of wholeness and peace, he was filled with a certain restlessness and an adventurous spirit. On the occasion of a feast in honor of his birthday or coming of a certain age he was called into the presence of his grandfather, the high God, who presented him with a magic key that would unlock any door in the city. It would appear that his elders expected him to use the key to explore various secret portions of his home city, but such was not the case.

The boy now betook himself to a portal within the wall that separated the city from the outside. Frequently, in the past, he had directed his gaze to the region outside the wall, perceiving shadowy forms there. Now he wished to find out what existed beyond the wall. He opened the door with his key, and heard a rending shriek of disturbing proportions. Through the open door there poured a veritable cloud of unsavory creatures, among them a great dark lord, whom he recognized as his own evil uncle (presumably a satanic brother of Christ) who lived in exile, having been expelled long ago from the heavenly city. The evil uncle cast a contemptuous look upon him and swiftly passed inside the city.

A gorgonlike being with huge hands and claws now seized him and, nearly piercing his chest with one great claw, hurled him into a region of black darkness. Gradually the darkness gave way to a panorama that was filled with millions of stars, some at great distance, others closer by; he was floating in starry space. After some time a light came toward him and propelled him downward until he found himself on solid ground. Primeval jungle surrounded him and before him stood a strange saurian creature gazing down at the new arrival with benevolent bemusement. It was quite apparent that the creature had come to watch over him. The frightened, lonely boy held onto the creature and cried uncontrollably. Separated from his almighty parents and torn from his home in the splendid city in the heavens, he found himself in a strange world with an alien creature as his only friend and company.

A long period ensued wherein the boy and the lizard remained in close association. After some time a symbiotic embodiment took place wherein they both inhabited a dragonlike body and roamed the earth, successfully mastering the territory and fending off potential enemies. After the passage of much time, amounting to centuries and millennia, conditions changed, and the form within which they dwelt became human. Nevertheless, the lizard remained in union with the boy, becoming a kind of guardian spirit attached to him and cohabiting his body. Many embodiments took place, but the lizard guardian was always present, supplying much needed cunning and worldly intelligence lacking in his companion.

Meanwhile, in several visions, the exile learned what drama took place in the heavenly city after his own forced departure. He saw a scene wherein his evil uncle triumphantly burst into the chamber of Sophia, intending to ravish her, thereby mingling his dark seed with the luminous substance of heaven. At first it appeared as if the terrible and sacrilegious deed would be accomplished, but soon it was evident that Sophia had freed herself from her assailant by magical means and stood laughing in a distant portion of the room. The cause of her merriment was not merely her escape. With satisfaction she pointed to the dark lord's chest where she had made appear a fiery, indelible mark: It was the encircled cross, her own symbol and emblem, which her attacker was now obliged to bear forever. With a dreadful howl of pain and humiliation, the dark one fled from the chamber and from the city.

The intrusion of the dark lord into the city and into Sophia's chamber was not without its consequences. In some mysterious fashion, and at least in part as the result of the branding of the evil one with Sophia's cross, a measure of the celestial light entered the darkness. A race of beings came into existence that bears the imprint of Sophia and yet is related to the dark lord. These beings, of somewhat vulpine appearance, are nevertheless of a rather benign dispostion and respect Sophia rather than any other divinity.

A few subsequent experiences served to elucidate the further career of the exile on earth. In one vision he saw himself in the company of an old wise man, who pointed to a particular luminary in the heavens and explained to him that he had come from beyond the stars to this world. The wise man was apparently a messenger who at long last had come to remind him of his own origins and instructed him in the wisdom that appertained to his station. The contact between himself and the homeland was thus established and strengthened.

Another development concerns the ancient saurian being incorporated into the organism of the exiled child of heaven. With the coming of greater self-knowledge on the part of its host, the lizard had grown and was able to cooperate more knowledgeably with the process of wholeness in which both were engaged. At one point the lizard said to the exiled prince: "I am your body." The gulf separating L. V.'s spirituality from his physicality had increasingly diminished, and the two sides coexisted in mutual trust.

The bringing to consciousness of this myth was accompanied by much emotion. L. V. found himself literally reeling under the impact of the story and, particularly in the earlier stages of the unfoldment of the myth, often felt despondent and weighed down by guilt and remorse over having admitted the enemy into the heavenly kingdom and having caused his own exile. As the story unfolded these feelings gradually abated, and it became clear that even the seemingly ill-advised deeds of the adventurous young prince operated within a meaningful order of supernal intent. At the same time, L. V.'s personality successfully fought off temptations of both positive and negative inflation, although not without difficulty. The realization came to him that the personal can neither take credit nor assume responsibility for the transpersonal. The issue of the exalted origins and parentage did not lead to phenomena of ego-inflation; nor did the story of the association with the lizard-being take on features of a multiple personality. After a year and a half of the unfoldment of the myth, L. V. is much more self-possessed, balanced, and functions with greater ease in life than before. The integrative effect of the myth is thus clear and evident.

We are confronted here with a personal myth that has definite Gnostic overtones and at the same time serves definite purposes of an integrative, individuational character. The story begins in a childlike condition of primitive wholeness where ego and archetypal psyche are identified. Inner and outer, above and below possess no differentiation. With his adventurousness, the "brat prince" becomes a mercurial facilitator of differentiation. His proclivity for pranks and jokes, which culminate in his opening of the gate, brings about the catastrophe of the violation of the integrity of heaven. Yet, this catastrophe does not have totally dire consequences, for the maternal wisdom (Sophia) in the fullness is not victimized. Rather, the dark intruder, though unwillingly, becomes the carrier of light into the realm of his own darkness. Satan is changed into Lucifer; the adversary becomes now a reluctant bearer of the light of wisdom.

When one contemplates one's psychic origins, one finds a double condition. On the one hand there is perceived a condition of paradisiacal wholeness, a state where one's nature is united to the essence of Divinity (being a child of Christ and Sophia); on the other hand, it is a state where creativity and growth are excluded. Children, in growing to adulthood, eventually face the problem of how to achieve union with the fullness and with the gods without succumbing to inflation attendant upon identification. In order to achieve this end, the integrity of heaven must be broken, a sin against wholeness must be committed. Without the loss of psychic innocence there can be no individuality, and without individuality, individuation in the depth-psychological sense is impossible. The brat prince must fall from heaven, so that in due time, richer in wisdom and experience, he may once more regain the glories of the celestial city.

Space does not allow us to explore the full scope of the Gnostic and psychological wealth of this myth. It is easy to discern that the ultimate reconciliation of light and dark is one of the important motifs present. It is interesting to note, for instance, that the deed that may lead to such an eventuality is brought about by Sophia. Even as in Roman Catholic lore Mary is the ultimate conqueror of the demonic serpent, so here also the final redemption is foreshadowed by Sophia's imprinting of her seal of light on the chest of Satan. The redeeming function of the divine feminine thus reveals itself clearly in this myth, even as it is present in much ancient Gnostic lore.

The issue of the body, the physical "guardian spirit" of the psyche, is another fascinating feature of this tale. The saurian creature that declares in the end "I am your body" can teach us much concerning the proper understanding of the mind-body dichotomy. Psyche (the prince) and soma (the lizard) are not one but two, yet their interaction produces an ever more harmonious relationship wherein both parties benefit and undergo a creative transformation. The cunning and resourcefulness of the lizard (and aren't humans still bearers of a "lizard brain"?) afford the psyche protection and opportunity for experience. The conjunction of the soul of the prince with the nature of the lizard ensures many useful developments on the part of both beings. One may also note that much of the neo-Gnostic lore to be found in such sources as H. P. Blavatsky's works contains references to spiritual monads from far-off realms of light who take up residence in crude animal bodies of earth and thus begin their long evolutionary journey.

As always, the question arises: What is the most profitable way to treat myths of this nature? Most frequently in the past, visionary persons were wont to present their own inner experiences by attaching to them metaphysical claims of representing revealed truth. Today's world also is filled with prophets, mediums, and "channels" who claim absolute validity for their mythic insights. It is well to take to heart Jung's wise words. "In view of this extremely uncertain situation," he wrote, "it seems to me very much more cautious and reasonable to take cognizance of the fact that there is not only a psychic but a psychoid unconscious, before presuming to pronounce metaphysical judgments. . . . There is no need to fear that the inner experience will thereby be deprived of its reality and vitality."[6]

Unknowable, transpsychic factors are ever at work behind the unconscious psyche and its mythic images. We may call them aeonic beings after the fashion of the Gnostics, or psychoid archetypes, following Jung's intimations. The basis and substance of the myths that rise to the surface of the consciousness of men and women cannot be explained by the use of concepts and words belonging to any discipline. The myth, and with it the growth and transformation of the human soul, goes on, and in it may be discovered the treasures of a Gnosis that continues to assist the illumination of the dark recesses of our lives and discloses the treasures of meaning and redemptive insight.

PART III
The Other Gospels

Gnostic Alchemical Serpent

11

The Secret Sayings of Jesus:
The Gospel of Thomas

The Gnostic scriptures discovered at Nag Hammadi make up a library of diverse religious material. When one attempts to classify them according to subject matter, one finds six separate categories. Some works deal primarily with creative and redemptive mythology, giving various accounts of the creation of the world, of the pre-fall existence of Adam and Eve, of the descent of the Saving Power as Jesus and at times under other names. The emphasis in these scriptures is strongly focused on the differences that separate these accounts from the book of Genesis. (Thus in *The Apocryphon of John* the phrase "not as Moses said" occurs several times.[1] Other books consist of observations and commentaries concerning various spiritual themes, such as the nature of reality, the nature of the soul, spiritual salvation, and the relationship of the soul to the world.[2] The third category of writings contains liturgical and initiatory texts.[3] The fourth category is primarily concerned with the feminine principle, particularly Sophia.[4] The fifth group includes writings that relate to the lives and experiences of some of the apostles.[5] Finally, the sixth category of scriptures contains sayings of Jesus as well as some incidents in his life.[6] In addition, there are a certain number of scriptures that may be regarded as unclassifiable and include writings from other traditions, such as the writings of Zarathustra, a portion of Plato's *Republic*, and others.

Only four of the Nag Hammadi scriptures bear the title "Gospel." In this connection, it is necessary to recall that this term possessed a different meaning in the early centuries A.D. from the one that is common today. The Greek term *Evangelion* (gospel) was originally accorded to pronouncements sent out by exalted personages, such as rulers and high officials, announcing important events of a happy nature. After the first century, the Church came to employ this term to characterize documents written by Christian writers, which in some manner embodied the message of the new dispensation inaugurated by Jesus. The early Christian period abounded with gospels, and apparently it was not unusual for the same author to write several alternative gospels, as the comparatively recent discovery of the secret Gospel of Mark indicates.[7]

The early Church nourished a tradition that held that there were three lost gospels, namely, that of Philip, Matthias, and Thomas. When we look to Gnostic authors, we find that they held views that sustain this tradition, for they affirmed that there were four recipients of the secrets of Jesus after the resurrection, namely, Mary Magdalene, Thomas, Philip, and Matthias. It is certainly worthy of note that the Nag Hammadi collection contains gospels named after two of these, namely, *The Gospel of Thomas* and *The Gospel of Philip*. In the present chapter, we shall concern ourselves with the first of these two gospels.

The Gospel of Thomas is not a story, but a collection of sayings. Save for an introductory sentence at the beginning and for the title of the treatise appended at the end, it contains one solid body of sayings, each of which is introduced by the words "Jesus said." Many of the sayings are identical with or bear a close resemblance to sayings of Jesus contained in the canonical scriptures. This has caused some scholars to surmise that *The Gospel of Thomas* might be in fact the fabled Q Document (named after the German word *Quelle*, meaning source, since it is said to be the source from whence the three so-called synoptic gospels of Mark, Matthew, and Luke were written).

The reader familiar with the format of the canonical gospels may wonder why Thomas or the other Gnostic gospel-writers concentrated on the sayings of Jesus in preference to the story of his life. The reason for this may be found in the Gnostic conception of Jesus. As indicated earlier (Chapters Three and Seven), the Gnostics felt that Jesus and the nature of his earthly career were a mystery that is not subject to rational analysis. They also held that whatever the meaning of this mystery may be, its focus cannot be found in the physical life of Jesus, namely, his birth, travels, healings, or even his death and resurrection.

Jesus, according to the Gnostic scriptures, practiced his ministry in two ways: First, he was a *teacher* who offered verbal instruction of a particular kind. When he taught he imparted more than concepts and precepts. Rather, it appears that his teaching was in the nature of stimulating the operation of a creative and transformative process in his disciples. Second, he was a *hierophant* who instituted mysteries into which he initiated those who were ready to receive them. *The Gospel of Thomas* represents a partial record of his activities as teacher, although indications of his hierophantic mysteries are present also. By contemplating a selection of the sayings contained in *The Gospel of Thomas*, the reader may gain an impression of the tone of these secret sayings, and may come to discern the difference between the Gnostic Jesus and the Jesus of conventional Christianity.

Sayings Concerning the Human Condition

If the flesh has come to be because of the spirit, it is a wonder, but if the spirit has come to be because of the body, that is a wonder of wonders. But I wonder how such a great wealth has come to dwell in this poverty. (29)*

---

*The number in parentheses indicates the number of the saying in the Gospel. The numbering of the sayings used here agrees with the system of numbering used in the majority of the published translations.

The spirit-body duality is regarded here in the light of Gnostic objective idealism, with some existential overtones. Spirit and body are both real in their own right, and together they constitute the process of incarnate existence. Pure materialism and pure idealism are both rejected. The existential task of legitimate inquiry is not to argue whether spirit is a function of body or whether the body is a product of spirit, but rather to recognize how limited the scope of consciousness has become in our present condition. The implications of the saying are that it is surely incumbent on us to undergo a transformational process of Gnosis, whereby the original wealth of pure consciousness may be recovered.

> His disciples said: When wilt thou appear to us and when will we behold thee? Jesus said: When you divest yourselves of your clothing without being ashamed, and take your clothes and trample them under your feet as the small children do, and step on them, then shall you behold the son of life and you shall not be frightened. (37)

The theme of spiritual nakedness, which occurs more than once in this gospel, may be interpreted in a narrower sense as the discarding of our persona, and in a wider sense as the need to shed the many illusory concepts and beliefs that make up the false cosmos of our personality. Gnosis does not consist so much in adding some miraculous external element to our consciousness; rather, it requires a subtracting from our minds and lives of much material that serves to obstruct insight. To confront the ineffable greatness, we must first shed our false selfhood without fear of consequences.

> Jesus said: Become passers by. (42)

The shortest saying in this gospel is truly eloquent in its simplicity and brevity. An Islamic adage states: "The world is a bridge; pass over it, don't build on it." The Gnostic does not regard this cosmos as the home of the human spirit. We are travelers in this world and should not regard ourselves as permanent residents.

If they say to you: "From where are your origins?" say to them, "We have come from the Light, where the Light has begun through itself."... If they say to you: "Who are you?" say: "We are his children and we are the chosen of the Living Father." If they ask you: "What is the sign of your Father in you?" say to them: "It is a movement and a quiet." (50)

This is a most important saying inasmuch as it deals with the definition of the identity of the Gnostic disciple. The Gnostic knows that he originates in the fullness, where the supreme light of primordial divinity dwells. The elect are those who know themselves as emanations of the supreme light. "Movement" stands for the principle of dynamic change as evidenced in becoming, realization, living; whereas "quiet" may be taken to signify the pleromic state of equipoise. Becoming and being, out-breathing and inbreathing when balanced and consciously realized constitute the hallmark of true Gnosis within the individual.

There was a rich man who had much wealth. He said: I will use my goods so that I may sow and reap and plant and fill my granaries with fruit so that I will not be deprived. This was what he thought in his heart. And that same night he died. Whoever has ears let him hear. (63)

The fruits of earthly labors and cares are precarious and evanescent. The Gnostic ought not to waste an over-amount of his psychic force on the personalistic pursuits of life, for his efforts ought to be employed elsewhere.

A woman from the assembly said to him: Blessed is the womb which bore thee and the breasts which fed thee. He said to her: Blessed are those who have heard the word of the Father and have kept it in truth. For there will be days when all of you will say: Blessed is the womb which has not conceived and the breasts which have not fed any child. (79)

The mere physical role of giving birth and nourishing has limited value. The biological cycles of nature are one of the great traps wherein consciousness is caught. To be human means more than to be a parent; it is more important to be a woman than to be a mother.

> The Kingdom of the Father is similar to a woman who was carrying a jar filled with meal. While she was walking on a long road, the handle of the jar broke off. The meal poured out behind her on the road.... After she came back into her dwelling, she put the jar down—she found it empty. (97)

This parable, which is not found in any other source, brings to our attention an important principle. When starting on our earthly journey we have a measure of the fullness present in our souls, but in the course of our lives we are in grave danger of losing this plenum of glory and creativity. Life in the world can imperceptibly rob us of our innate spiritual treasure. Only self-observation and conscious vigilance can prevent this unhappy state from obtaining.

> Simon Peter said to them: Let Mary depart from among us, because women cannot be worthy of the Life. Jesus said: I shall direct her, so that I will make her male, that she may be a living spirit, just like you men; for every woman that becomes male will enter the kingdom of heaven. (114)

It is easy to misunderstand the significant meaning contained in this saying. In several Gnostic scriptures the apostle Peter is represented as a male chauvinist, resentful of the high regard in which Jesus holds women. Jesus here tries to convince Peter, using a language Peter understands, that women may overcome the socially imposed handicap of their gender by undergoing a spiritual androgynation. It is interesting to note that in the writings of Clement of Alexandria we find Gnostic statements indicating that this same process may be applied also to men, who will enter the kingdom when having become female. In Jung's psychology, women need to integrate their animus, and men must do the same with their anima; the bringing to consciousness of the contrasexual image of each person permits entry into the kingdom of individuation and consequent wholeness.

Sayings Concerning Conduct

The disciples asked him, they said to him: Desirest thou that we fast, and in what manner should we pray. . . . and what diet must we observe? Jesus said: Do not lie; and do not do what you dislike, for all things are open before Heaven. For there is nothing hidden that shall not be revealed and there is nothing that is covered up that shall remain without being disclosed. (6)

An honest relationship with one's inner being is more important than the following of outer rules. As in many other sayings, so here we find the emphasis the Gnostic Jesus places on the existential attitude toward life, in contrast to the anxious, compulsive concern about the Law we find among his opponents, the Pharisees. Unconscious resentment, engendered by rigid rules of behavior, brings psychological disaster, for repressed feelings and desires will not stay in the psychic underworld to which they have been banished, but will return to haunt the individual. This is even more evident in the following saying:

If you fast, you will start a sin for yourselves and if you pray, you will be condemned and if you give alms you will do injury to your spirits. And if you go away into any country and travel in the regions if they welcome you, eat what they place before you, and heal the sick among them. For what goes into your mouth will not pollute you, but what comes out of your mouth, that is what will pollute you. (14)

The new dispensation proclaimed by Jesus abrogates the observances of the old Law. Aside from this important Gnostic teaching, one may also consider the emphasis in Jung's psychology on the need for the individual to discover his or her own internally authenticated moral code. Individuation is not possible until the assumptions and shibboleths of the collective are consciously scrutinized and replaced by informed choice.

Love thy brother as thy own soul, protect him as thou
would the apple of thine own eye. (25)

Gnosis and Gnosticism are not based on cold, impersonal principles of what ordinarily is understood as
"knowledge." The orthodox Christian has no monopoly
on love—far from it.

Why do you clean the outside of the chalice? Do you not
comprehend that the one who made the inside also made
the outside? (89)

This saying is addressed to the emphasis on purification, which was regarded as abrogated by the new
existential emphasis brought by Jesus. The inner and the
outer, Self and Ego, form an organic unity, albeit a unity
existing initially at the unconscious level. The ultimate
objective envisioned by the Gnostic is not the mere
purification of the personality, but the integration of the
dichotomy of personal versus transpersonal into an
abiding condition of wholeness.*

Whoever has discovered the world and has become wealthy,
let him abjure the world. (110)

Before we can deny anything we must have acquired
it. Those who do not own the world (in a psychological
sense) cannot renounce it. To find the world means to
come to terms with it, and to become wealthy means that
we must accumulate a wealth of experience. The Gnostic
teacher Carpocrates pointed out that without extensive
experience of the world, the world cannot be overcome
(see our Chapter Five).

Woe be to the flesh which is dependent upon the soul;
woe be to the soul which is dependent upon the flesh. (112)

The Gnostic worldview is not characterized by one-
sidedness. It is neither an extreme idealism that regards
the flesh as an illusion nor materialism that views the
soul as an epiphenomenon resulting from bodily

---

*See also Saying 22 of this gospel later in this chapter.

functions. Earlier we characterized Gnosticism as a form of objective idealism inasmuch as it recognizes the reality of material objectivity as well as the reality of ideation.

Concerning the Redeemer

Jesus said to his disciples: Speak of comparisons to me and tell me whom I am like. Simon Peter said to him: Thou art like a righteous messenger. Matthew said to him: Thou art like a sage with wisdom. Thomas said to him: Master, my mouth cannot express whom thou art like. Jesus said: I am not thy master, because thou hast drunk, thou hast become inebriated by the bubbling spring which I have measured out. And he took him, and he withdrew and uttered three words. When Thomas came back to his companions, they asked him: What did Jesus say to thee? Thomas said to them: If I tell you one thing which he said to me, you will raise up stones and throw them at me; and fire will issue from these stones and burn you up. (13)

All definitions of the mystery of the Self, even when embodied in Jesus, the paradigm of the individuated selfhood, are inadequate. Peter tries to define Jesus in purely spiritual terms, while Matthew sees him in merely human terms. Thomas, the Gnostic apostle, knows that he is faced with an inscrutable mystery. Jesus is no longer master over Thomas, for Thomas has availed himself of the direct experience of Gnosis, which Jesus made accessible to him. The three words signify initiation into the hierophantic secrets of Jesus. Divulging them would naturally excite the antagonism of those who had not received the initiation. Even one's companions in the search for Gnosis will turn against one, when a special grace that one received is denied them.

I will give you what no one's eye has seen and what no one's ear has heard and what no hand has touched and what has not arisen in the heart of human beings. (17)

The Gnosis brought about by the Redeemer is truly the knowledge of the wholly other. It is not the product of nature or of evolution or of the effort of the lesser man, who is of the earth, earthy. The difference between Gnosis and worldly knowledge is not quantitative but qualitative; the cleverness of the ego is a quality of a different order from the wisdom of the Self.

> People probably think that I have come to cast peace upon the cosmos and they do not know that I have come to bring strife upon the earth; fire, sword, war. . . . (16)

> I have cast fire upon the cosmos, and behold, I guard it until the cosmos is ablaze. (10)

The way of Gnosis is the way of creative conflict. Many seek peace and peace of mind, and what they find is merely the bovine tranquility of unconsciousness. The fire mentioned is the same fire that the alchemists employed as the agency of transformation through the conflictual interaction of the opposites. One is reminded here of Prof. Gilles Quispel's sage statement: "Alchemy was the Yoga of the Gnostics."

> His disciples said: Point out the place where thou art, because it is necessary for us to seek it. He said to them: Whoever can hear let him hear. Within a man of light there is light and he illuminates the whole world. When he does not shine, there is only darkness. (24)

The place of Christ is in every person who has attained Gnosis. Thus, the place where he is, is in reality in us. Consciousness, which is Gnosis, illumines the world. Thus, we need to cultivate the light within us and thereby contribute to the enlightenment of all the world.

> I took my position in the midst of the cosmos and in the flesh I did appear to them; I found them all drunk, I found none among them thirsty. And my soul was afflicted for the children of men, because they are blind in their hearts and do not perceive that empty they have come into the world and that empty they seek to exit from the world again. But now they are all drunk. When they have shaken off their wine, then will they turn around. (28)

The Redeemer finds those whom he desires to redeem

intoxicated with the influences of the external world. Jesus seems to be saying: "Although I have become like them, I can't communicate with them because they are still looking outside of themselves for the values of life. The *metanoia* (turning around, often called 'repentance') will come when they empty themselves of the extraverted involvements and fascinations which are like a drunkenness."

> Whosoever drinks from my mouth shall come to resemble me and I myself will become he, and the hidden things shall be revealed to such a one. (108)

The mouth is the gateway of the soul; consequently, the soul-kiss is the sign of Gnostic initiation. The initiate becomes inwardly united with the initiator and becomes the partaker of those truths that have hitherto remained concealed.

> I am the light that is above them all, I am the all, the all came forth from me, and the all became me. Cleave the wood, I am there; raise up the stone and you will find me. (77)

The Greek word for "all" is *pan*, which is also the name of the goat-footed god of nature. Jesus here states that though by virtue of his supernal consciousness he is above the cosmos and above nature, he is also one with nature. When perfected, nature and the totality of creation will attain the greatness of the celestial man (*anthropos*), of whom Jesus as the Son of Man is the manifestation. As the paradigm of the ineffable greatness, Jesus is also present in nature, and his light may be discovered in the stone and in the wood. At the same time, it is necessary to recognize that only one who is *above* the all can have a proper relationship with the all. Those who are merely contained within nature, without having emancipated themselves from nature's thralldom, are unconscious and need to differentiate themselves from nature so that they, too, might be above it. As usual, Gnosticism defies all categories: It is neither theism nor pantheism but a mystic vision that transcends and unites both.

Concerning Self-Knowledge

He who knows the all but fails to have self-knowledge
lacks everything. (67)

If you bring forth what you have within you, that which
you have will redeem you. If you do not have it within
yourselves, that which you do not have will kill you. (70)

. . . Whoever discovers his own self, of him the world is
not worthy. (111)

These are some of the sayings most closely and directly
related to modern psychological insight. The psyche contains within itself the potential for redemption or destruction. Self-knowledge is the one and only solution to the
innumerable afflictions of life; no commodity of life of
any kind can make up for its lack. Unconscious content
of a destructive potential must be brought to consciousness, lest it turn ever more malign and destroy the individual's sanity, if not his very life. In order to overcome
the world, it is necessary that one find and know oneself
first. Few persons versed in psychology would disagree
with these recognitions.

Let him who searches not cease searching until he finds,
and when he finds, he will be disturbed, and when he has
been disturbed, he will be amazed and he will have
dominion over the all. (2)

Here we have a concise description of the stages of
Gnosis, or Self-knowledge. By "searching" is meant the
awakening to the need for inner meaning; by persistence
the success of the search is assured; and "finding" signifies
the awareness of the growth of consciousness. To the
surprise of many, however, psychological development
does not bring about serenity and what is called peace
of mind. Far from it, the discovery of individuation brings
transformative conflict and much psychic turmoil. As one
approaches the archetypal psyche with all its numinous
denizens, the only appropriate reaction is a reverent
amazement; whereas the final outcome is dominion over

the natural world of the psyche, which is an accompanying sign of wholeness.

If those who lead you say to you: "Behold the kingdom is in heaven," the birds of heaven will enter therein before you. If they tell you: "It is in the sea," then the fish will enter before you. However, the kingdom is within you and it is also outside of you. If you know yourselves, then you will be known and you will know that you are the children of the living father. But if you have no knowledge of yourselves, then you are in poverty and you are poverty. (3)

The heavenly kingdom of meaning and individuation is not attained by extraverted means. The bird and fish are able to enter the realm of greater being by virtue of their natural authenticity and thus may prove superior to humans, who know not their true nature. The unconsciousness of the human mind is the most terrifying form of poverty, for to lack meaning is to lack the central core of the process of living. Self-knowledge establishes the axis that connects ego and self and leads to authentic living.

The disciples said to Jesus: Tell us how our end will be? Jesus said: Have you found the beginning so that you ask about the end? For where the beginning is, there will be the end also. Blessed is he who shall stand at the beginning and he shall comprehend the end and he shall not undergo death. (18)

The meaning of death presents one of the great haunting questions of human life. Jesus tells us here that death, the end, ought to be viewed not as an isolated phenomenon but as part of a process. The same might be said about all end-events, such as the end of civilization or the end of the cosmos. Gnostic eschatology could be called a process eschatology, for it refuses to separate the end of things from their beginnings and thereby reveals the meaning concealed not in individual events but in their connections within a process. History is conditioned by the non-historic; meaningless chronological time is awash in a timeless time of transcendental significance. At the beginning we find the fullness from whence we came, and the process of meaningful living offers us the promise that it is to this same fullness that we shall return.

> If two are reconciled with each other in this one dwelling, they then shall say to the mountain: "Move!" and it shall be moved. (48)

The reconciliation of the opposites is the key that unlocks the storehouse of limitless psychic energy. Miracles are performed by those in whom "the two have become one" (as in saying 22). It is interesting to note how the above saying, with its intrapsychic emphasis, in the canonical Gospel of Matthew is turned into one possessing an extraverted emphasis: "Blessed are the peacemakers, for they shall be called the sons of God." (18:19)

The true peacemaker, according to Thomas, is the one who has made peace within himself. A cognate theme is expressed in the following saying:

> Blessed are you who have become unified and have become the elect, for you shall find the kingdom; because you come from it, and you shall return to it again. (49)

Our present rendition of this saying is far from literal, but reflects the obvious intention of the saying. The standard translation of the key word as "solitary" is grossly misleading. The person in whom the dualities have become united is not a monk but rather *vir unus*, the human having become one whose consciousness has comprehended the soul's true origins and who is thus enabled to return to the point of origination once more. References to the unified person in this gospel are numerous; thus, in Saying 75 it is stated that the unified person will enter the bride chamber in preference to others.

Every student of Jung would agree with the following characterization of what in depth psychology are known as the archetypal images:

> When you see your image, you are glad. But when you see your images which came into being before you,

which neither die nor are made, how much will you then endure! (84)

The state of transformed, unitive consciousness wherein all opposites are reconciled and transcended is represented by the Gnostic Jesus as the true objective of the life of the spirit, which to advance he came into this world:

> Jesus saw children who were being nursed. He said to his disciples: These children who are being nursed are like those who enter the kingdom. They said to him: Should we then become children in order to enter the kingdom? Jesus said to them: When you make the two one, and when you make the inmost as the outermost and the outer as the inner and the above as the below, and when you make the male and female into a single unity, so that the male will not be only male and the female will not be only female, when you create eyes in the place of an eye, and create a hand in the place of a hand, and a foot in the place of a foot, and also an image in the place of an image, then surely will you enter the kingdom. (22)

Once again we find the image of small children, this time nursing at their mothers' breasts. The nursing babe may be taken as a metaphor for the human, who having been born from the matrix of the unmanifest is still close to the nourishing power of the archetypal psyche. Individuation (entering the kingdom) brings the human ego into a state wherein this intimate closeness with the deeper sources of spiritual nourishment is reestablished. The disciples misunderstand Jesus, interpreting his statement literally, so that a more explicit statement on his part is indicated.

The next portion of the saying demonstrates the intent of the metaphor most impressively. The union of the opposites within the psyche brings complete renewal, so that no portion of the human being remains unchanged. Introversion and extraversion, matter and spirit, good and evil, animus and anima having become welded into a new, indivisible unity; the person has become a totally new being and as such has entry into a kingdom of ultimate, numinous meaning.

It may be useful at this point to summarize the principal recognitions that are indicated by the sayings we have quoted and that, significantly, organize themselves according to a quaternary pattern in the following fashion:

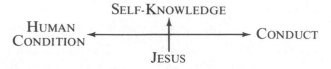

The proper understanding of the human condition leads to the kind of conduct that is conducive to Gnosis, whereas Jesus as the image of the individuated Selfhood of the human being shows the way to the unitive knowledge of the Self.

The premise of Gnosticism regarding the human condition is that the human soul and spirit do not require an external institution for their redemption, but rather they contain within themselves the capacity for spiritual direction. The Redeemer is a helper and a shower of the way, but the way must be trod by the individual himself. (Vicarious salvation and a need for a church as an "ark of salvation" consequently are negated.)

Safe rules and commandments become hindrances to those who, having spiritually outgrown them, are ready for Gnosis. Transformation within the Gnostic model brings about a creative disruption of psychological defenses and thereby facilitates the "solitary" (unitary) condition, which is the state of being of the autonomous individual. Society, family, laws, commandments, and beliefs are relativized as the individual comes to sacrifice any form of unconscious identification with them. (In the canonical scriptures, Jesus admonishes people not to call any man on earth father [Matt. 23:9] and states that those who love father and mother more than him are not worthy of him [Matt. 10:37-38]).

Ignorance, not sin, is the cause of the suffering attendant upon the human condition. Knowledge of the self, which is essentially identical with the supreme Self or transcendental being, is the goal of the Gnostic life. This goal brings with it the unification of all opposites and thus union with all life.

In the New Testament Gospel of Matthew (16:24-25) there is a sentence that has given translators frequent anguish: "Whoever cares for his own safety is lost; but if a man let his self [original: *psyche*] be lost for my sake, he will find his true self [*psyche*]." To attempt to convey more meaning, the translators have thus sometimes translated the same word, *psyche*, by two different terms. It is more than likely that if one should evaluate this statement in the light of the sayings of Jesus in *The Gospel of Thomas*, and add some modern psychological terms to boot, one could make the phrase read: ". . . if a man will lose his ego, for my sake, he will find the Self." Such is the insight that might be brought to us by the lost gospel, attributed to Thomas, found by a wandering peasant in an old jar beneath the sands of Nag Hammadi!

12

Means of Transformation:
The Gospel of Philip

Secret rites of power administered in order to facilitate the transformation of the human soul have been present in the religions of all times and cultures. Christianity was no exception. *The Secret Gospel of Mark*, quoted by the church father Clement of Alexandria, and its accompanying letter were discovered in 1958 by Prof. Morton Smith. They have brought to the attention of contemporary students the idea that Jesus himself functioned as a hierophant, conferring secret initiations, and that at least certain communities within the Christian church maintained an initiatory order of strictly graded practice and instruction. Clement thus informs his correspondent in the letter just noted that one set of public gospels was made available to lower-ranking Christians, while a second set of secret gospels was made available to more advanced members of the community, and that the "hierophantic secrets of Jesus" were imparted only verbally in a secret manner.[1]

Gnostic Christians appear to have cultivated initiatory mysteries in addition to those known to more conventional communities. None other than Plotinus remonstrated with the Gnostics, who had attracted some of his students, by saying: "They say only, 'Look to God,' but they do not tell anyone where or how to look."[2] There can be little doubt that the Gnostics employed effective methods for the cultivation of transcendental states of consciousness.

Several sources in the Nag Hammadi collection describe techniques of spiritual discipline. Such books in this collection as *Zostrianos, The Treatise of the Eighth and the Ninth,* and *Allogenes* are replete with descriptions of spiritual practices and the ecstatic conditions of mind induced by such practices. None can equal, however, in this respect, *The Gospel of Philip,* which like *The Gospel of Thomas* contains a large number of sayings attributed to Jesus, interspersed with explanatory commentaries. Philip's gospel has not attained the relative popularity enjoyed by that of Thomas, and the reason for this circumstance is to be sought in the emphasis that the former attaches to the Christian mysteries, or sacraments, as Gnostic means of transformation.

Since the Protestant Reformation, Christianity has been increasingly moving away from the mystique of the sacraments. Today, even the former bastion of sacramental faith, the Roman Catholic Church, seems to be undergoing its own belated neo-Protestant reformation, wherein the archetypal power of the seven historic sacraments is progressively waning. One may doubt whether C. G. Jung could write today as he did in 1939 when commenting on the fact that he encountered fewer neurotic Catholics than Protestants or atheists.

There must be something in the cult, in the actual religious practice, which explains the peculiar fact that there are fewer complexes, or that these complexes manifest much less in Catholics than in other people. That something besides confession is really the cult itself. It is the Mass, for instance. The heart of the Mass contains a living mystery, and that is the thing that works. . . . And the Mass is by no means the only mystery in the Catholic Church. There are other mysteries as well. . . . Now these mysteries have always been the expression of a fundamental psychological condition. Man expresses his most fundamental and most important psychological conditions in this ritual, this magic, or whatever you call it. And the ritual is the cultic performance of these basic psychological facts.[3]

With the diminishing of the mystery in our day, the hitherto valuable element of sacramental worship and its psychological effects are bound to lessen. As Jung warned us, continuing his above statement: "That explains why we should not change anything in a ritual. A ritual must be done according to tradition, and if you change one little point in it, you make a mistake. You must not allow your reason to play with it."[4] It is precisely this rational "playing with" the ancient sacramental rituals in past and present that is responsible for the lesser attention received thus far by *The Gospel of Philip*.

It is perhaps no exaggeration to say *The Gospel of Philip* is primarily a manual of Gnostic sacramental theology, in other words, an account of the Gnostic mysteries. The fountain of these mysteries, according to this gospel, is Jesus himself:

> The Lord worked all things as a mystery; a baptism and an anointing and a eucharist and a redeeming, and a bride-chamber. (68)*

Here we find a listing in Gnostic terminology of five of the seven traditional Christian sacraments. (According to the first translator of Philip, Dr. H. M. Schenke, a restored passage in Saying 60 reads: "For the mysteries are seven.") It is very likely that the two final mystery-sacraments, the redemption and the bride chamber mentioned above, have been subsequently changed by the mainstream Church into the much more mundane sacraments of penance and matrimony. In order to place these matters in perspective it may be useful to look at the Gnostic sacraments in their proper order.

Baptism was practiced by the authors of this gospel in two forms. Ordinary baptism as administered by the orthodox was known to the Gnostics as "psychic baptism," because it was designed for people whose consciousness

---

*The system of numbering the sayings here employed is the one used in the normative work, *The Gospel of Philip*, trans. R. McL. Wilson (New York: Harper Row, 1962).

was lodged in the mind-emotion complex and who were not ready to enter the realm of spirit. A higher form of baptism was known as "pneumatic baptism," indicating that when administered in this fashion, the baptismal rite no longer merely served the purpose of purifying the soul, but rather put the personality in touch with the higher, or spiritual Self. Baptism as well as all the other mysteries possessed an indelible character; their effect could never be wiped out:

> God is a dyer. As the good dyes, which are called "true," dissolve with the things dyed within them, so it is with those whom God has dyed. Inasmuch as his dyes are immortal, they are immortal by means of his colors. But God immerses what he immerses in water. (43)

Anointing (in modern times called confirmation) is the second initiatory sacrament. Water is used to wash, oil is employed to seal. Oil, when ignited, burns and is thus associated with the element of fire, whereas baptism is associated with water. These two elements have traditionally been regarded by the ancients as the primary polarity, which when conjoined produce wholeness. Thus the following saying becomes meaningful:

> The soul and the spirit entered existence from water and fire. The child of the bride-chamber came into being by these and by Light. The fire is the chrism, the light is fire, the light also is formless, we speak not of it, but of the other whose form is white, which is of the light and beautiful and bestows beauty. (66)

Having entered the stream of the living waters by way of baptism and having been tempered in the fire of the anointing, the Gnostic Christian is ready to partake of the eucharist:

> The eucharist is Jesus. For he is called in the Syrian language Pharisatha, which means "the one who is stretched out," for Jesus came in order to crucify the world. (53)

The cup of prayer contains wine and also water, and it is ordered as the kind of blood over which one gives thanks. And it is filled with the Holy Spirit, and it belongs to the wholly completed human. When we drink of this, we shall receive for ourselves the (condition) of the completed human. (100)

The mystery of the bread and wine is thus unmistakably the one whereby the living presence of the Redeemer has been made available to his followers. By way of partaking of this mystery, the Gnostic is prepared to accept the two supreme mysteries, namely, the redemption and the bride chamber. In a heroic act of renunciation and commitment called "redemption," the Gnostic initiate becomes free of the compelling attachments to this world and its rulers. *The Gospel of Philip* gives us only minor details concerning this mystery, but the anti-Gnostic church father Irenaeus repeats certain statements that were ritually uttered by those who have received this sacrament: "I am established, I am redeemed, and I redeem my soul from this aeon, and from all that comes from it, in the name of IAO, who redeemed his soul unto the redemption of Christ, the living one." And the people present respond: "Peace be with all on whom this name reposes."[5] The author then states that the initiate is subsequently anointed with the oil of the balsam tree, which is the symbol of the sweet savor that transcends all terrestrial things. Such are some of the faint echoes left behind of the mystery of the redemption, known in Greek as *apolytrosis.*

The supreme mystery of the bride chamber (sometimes called the spiritual marriage or the mystery of the syzygies) is the decisive event in the reunion of the divisions of the human being. As noted in various ways in our recounting of the Gnostic myths, one of the fundamental mythologems of the Gnostics concerns the division separating the human personality and the higher self or "twin angel." While on earth, the human being is said to possess a body, a soul, and a spirit. These three are coexisting in a state of imperfect association, which is rendered perfect by the experience of the bride chamber. Irenaeus, interpreting the teachings of the followers of Valentinus, describes this mystery as the marriage of the human spirit to an angel of the Redeemer who resides in the heaven world above this earth. In modern terms one might define this mystery as a sacred rite of individuation wherein the person becomes a true *individuum*, or indivisible unity.

No less than thirteen different sayings in *The Gospel of Philip* refer directly to the bride chamber. Here are some of the most important:

> Everyone who becomes an offspring of the bride-chamber will receive the light. . . . If anyone does not partake of it while he is in this world, he will not partake of it in the other place. One who has partaken of that light will not be seen, nor can such a one be detained; and none shall be able to afflict such a one even if he should abide in the world. And again when he departs from the world he has already received the truth in the aspect of the images. The world has become the aeon already. For the aeon is for such a one a Pleroma, and it is in this manner: it is disclosed to such a one alone, not hidden in the darkness and the night, but hidden in a perfected day and a sacred light. (127)

The marvelous effects of the mystery are further described:

> But the bride-chamber is concealed. It is the holy of holies. . . . There is a glory that is superior to glory, there is a power which is above power. Thus the perfect things are revealed to us, and so are the hidden things of the truth; and the holy things of the holy are disclosed, the bride-chamber calls unto us to enter. (125)

It is evident then, that the mystery of the bride chamber, though obtained by the individual while still in embodied existence, joins him or her with a realm of supernal bliss and transcendence. Whether still living on earth or in an after-death state, the person who has undergone the experience of the bride chamber is utterly free from the danger of being captured and afflicted by the powers of this world. The fullness of the Pleroma is no longer a longed for condition pertaining to a world beyond this one, for earth and heaven, the below and the above are now one. "Those who put on the perfect light, the powers do not see them," declares Saying 77.

Several sayings state that the bride chamber exists in order to reestablish the primordial unity that existed in the human being before the separation of the sexes, as symbolized by the dividing of Adam and Eve in the story of Genesis:

> At the time when Eve was in Adam, then there was no death; but when she was separated from him death came to exist. If completion shall occur again, and the earlier identity is attained, then death will be no more. (71)

> If the feminine had not separated from the masculine, she would not die with the masculine. This separation became the origin of death. It was because of this that Christ came, so that he might take away the separation which was there from the beginning and thus again reunite the two; and so that he might give life to those who died while separated and make them one. (78)

> Also the feminine is united to her consort in the bride-chamber. And those who have united in the bride-chamber will never be divided again. (79)

The psychologically informed reader cannot help but be reminded by these sayings of the contrasexual images of the anima and animus spoken of by Jung. The psychic androgynation envisioned by psychology as the result of the process of individuation has apparently been anticipated (and sometimes achieved) by the protopsychologists called Gnostics. The death from which this union redeems humans may be envisioned as the death of consciousness induced by the lack of integration of the psyche. (Students of both Western and Chinese alchemy have similarly interpreted the issue of immortality versus mortality in alchemical symbolism.)

Although the mystery of the bride chamber is represented as having been made available to humankind by Jesus, it appears that the mystery itself has a high divine origin, having been enacted in the supernal regions by the high divinities themselves:

> Is it permitted to even speak of this mystery? The all-Father joined with the virgin who came down, and a fire enlightened him that day. He appeared in the great bride-chamber as one who came into being from the bridegroom and the bride. So Jesus established everything in it through these mysteries. And it is right for each one of his disciples to thus enter into his rest. (82)

The transcendental bride chamber thus is said to have united God the Father with God the Mother (the Holy Spirit), and Jesus has replicated this divine example for the benefit of divided humanity. Nor is the bride chamber absent from the early history of the human race. In Saying 102, we are told that just as true humanity is remade today in the bride chamber, so the same has occurred long ago, producing a race whose members were called by such names as "the true man," the "Son of Man," and similar names. The mystery is thus clearly not a novel phenomenon, but one that was available to the spiritual flowering of the human race in every age.

While a large number of the sayings in this gospel concerns the Christian Gnostic sacraments, particularly the supreme mystery of the bride chamber, a number of others concern other themes of the spiritual life, although most of these may be related in some manner to the subject of the sacraments. Since the bride chamber is vitally concerned with the union of the masculine and the feminine, it is understandable that prominent sayings should be devoted to the feminine principle. In addition to Sayings 32 and 55 (quoted in Chapter Four), we may list one other here:

> Some said: "Mary conceived of the Holy Spirit." They do not know what they are saying. When did it ever happen that a woman conceived of a woman? Mary is the virgin whom the powers never defiled. She is a mighty anathema to the Hebrews, which denotes apostles and apostolic men.

This virgin whom no power defiled [revealed herself so
that] the powers might defile themselves. And the Lord
would never have said "My Father which is in heaven,"
unless he had another father, but he would have just
said, ["My father."] (17)

Although Mary, the mother of Jesus, is mentioned less
frequently by the Gnostics than Sophia or even Mary
Magdalene, her importance is still considered by them as
very great. The Holy Spirit in their view is none other
than God the Mother and thus cannot be the paternal
agency of Jesus' conception. Mary is a being untouched
by the dark powers who rule this world and a manifestation of the unsullied (ever virgin) feminine power of the
Divine. Many of the followers of Jesus, such as Peter,
were still deeply mired in Hebrew patriarchy and thus
were put off by the complex mystery of the divine feminine
that made its appearance in connection with Jesus. The
true father of Jesus is the highest masculine power of the
fullness and not any of the intermediate rulers, whose
force is mingled with all other beings to some extent.

As becomes clear upon contemplating the various
scriptures of the Gnosis, human nature is never regarded
as corrupt or the body as incapable of experiencing
sanctification (contrary to the teachings of St. Augustine
and other church fathers):

> When the pearl is thrown into the mud, it does not become
> therefore devalued, nor does it become more valuable if it
> is anointed with oil of balsam. Rather, it possesses the
> same worth in the esteem of its owner. It is the same with
> the children of God, wherever they may find themselves,
> for their value is known by their Father. (48)

> The holy person is holy completely, right down to his very
> body. For he makes the bread holy when it is offered, and
> also the cup, and any other thing he receives, for he
> sanctifies these. Then how could he not consecrate the
> body also? (108)

The essential dignity of the human spirit and soul are

cardinal tenets of the Gnostic worldview. The essence of
the human being is not merely created by God but *is* God,
not in the exclusive but in the inclusive sense inasmuch
as it is part and parcel of Divinity. Psychologically, this
might be seen to mean that the psyche may be subject
to unconsciousness (the mud into which the pearl falls)
but its very nature entitles it to the highest respect.
Similarly, temporary unconsciousness and ill-advised
behavior (sin) do not indicate that with the necessary
growth and development of consciousness true spiritual
greatness is precluded. Critics of the Gnostics often
accused them of deprecating the human body. The above
saying puts such accusations to shame. The body can be
sanctified by the indwelling consciousness, as can matter
and nature and all creation. To the holy all things are
holy, while to the unconscious all of life is but darkness
of darkness.

Another criticism leveled against the Gnostics (notably
by some neo-Platonists) was that they had no regard for
virtue. The following saying, however, extolls the three
chief virtues of Christianity and adds to them a fourth,
Gnosis:

> The workings of this world are made possible through four
> forms. [The goods of the world] are gathered into the
> storehouse by way of water, earth, air and light. And the
> workings of God are likewise through four; faith and
> hope and love and Gnosis. The earth is faith, in which
> we take root. The water is hope, by which we are nourished.
> The air is love, by which we grow. And the light is Gnosis
> by which we ripen. (115)

Were the Gnostics radical dualists as some have inferred? Is it true that they divided all being into two
categories, beneficent light and evil darkness, and envisioned the purpose of the true life to be simply the
liberation of the light from the darkness? No, says *The
Gospel of Philip*:

> The light and the darkness, life and death, the right and
> the left, are twin siblings of each other. It is impossible

to separate them from each other. Thus the good are not truly good, nor the evil evil, nor is life life, nor is death death. Thus each one of these will be resolved into its origin as it was in the beginning. But those who have risen above the world, these are the ones who are indissoluble and eternal. (10)

The untransformed human exists in a world where the opposites are fiercely and hopelessly entangled in each other's conflictual embrace. To attempt to disengage them from each other by intellectual analysis or absolute moral judgment is an exercise in futility. It is only by rising above the opposites that the spiritual perspective of true Gnosis arises. The intrapsychic implementation of these insights is further elucidated in Saying 40, where the author uses the metaphor of domesticated and wild animals living on the same earth. Similarly, says the gospel, one having Gnosis uses the powers that are subject to conscious control but does not cast out the dark side of the mind any more than the light side. Rather, such a person recognizes that both are necessary for the achievement of wholeness. The saying ends with the statement that this indeed represents the design of Divinity: "The Holy Spirit shepherds everyone and rules all these powers, the 'tame' ones as well as the 'wild' ones, and also those which are united. For indeed she keeps them shut up together in order not to let any of them escape, even if they wished."

Philip also reveals that, contrary to the popular view of Gnosticism, the Gnostic view of the cosmos does not imply the absence of a supernal divine design in creation. According to the following saying the creating rulers in their ignorance are not aware of the hidden design operating within the creation they wrongfully assume to be their exclusive domain:

The rulers held that it was by their unique force and will that they were performing their works, but the Holy Spirit, in secret, had organized everything through them as it intended. Truth is sown in all places, that truth which existed from the beginning. And many perceive it when it is sown. But only a few see it being harvested. (16)

The liberating mysteries of the Gnosis are designed to bring about a deification (apotheosis) of the human being. By inducing an experiential knowledge of things transcendental the knower becomes increasingly affinitized to transcendence and comes to realize the hitherto hidden divinity within himself:

> It is not possible for anyone to see anything of the things that are truly real unless he becomes like them. Such is not the way with those in the world: they see the sun without being the sun; and they see heaven and earth and all other things, but they are not these things. This is the truth of the matter. Thou, however, didst see the Spirit, and thou didst become spirit. Thou didst behold Christ, and then thou didst become Christ. Thou didst behold the Father, thou shalt become the Father. Therefore in this world thou dost see everything but dost not see thyself. But in that other place thou seest thyself. Therefore what thou seest, that thou shalt assuredly become. (44)

The experience of Gnosis, facilitated by the sacramental mysteries, transports the knower into a realm of exalted consciousness where unitive knowledge is possible. Faith, in the Gnostic sense, consists mainly in being faithful to this kind of experience. By being faithful to one's experience of transcendence one also develops the capacity of loving action, which is connected with the sharing of Gnosis with others:

> Faith receives, love gives. No one will be able to receive without faith. No one will be able to give without love. Therefore, in order to truly receive, we have faith, but this is so that we may love and give, since if one does not give in love, he has no profit from what he has given. (45)

Love is indeed far from absent in the teachings given in *The Gospel of Philip*. The great division of the psychospiritual organism of humanity into the dualities of above and below, inner and outer, male and female, and so forth is healed by love alone. The mystery of the bride chamber bears the very name of a chamber of love. Thus, the sacramental mysteries of the Gnostics appear as directed both by and towards love. The longing desire of humanity for completion by way of wholeness meets the unconditional affection of Divinity proceeding from the fullness. Yet, this divine affection needs vehicles wherein to manifest and become effective. It is here that the doctrine of the *images* as taught in this scripture becomes understandable. The naive notion, often cultivated by mainstream Christians, that declares the sanctifying grace of Divinity can reach the soul without a special vehicle is not shared by the Gnostics. A number of sayings in Philip expound a teaching concerning the images in which the supernal principles proceeding from the fullness are manifest on earth:

> Truth did not enter this world unclad, but it came in types and images. This aeon will not receive truth in any other manner. There is rebirth, and there is an image of rebirth. It is truly necessary that [human beings] should be born again through the image. What image is the resurrection? The image must rise again through the image. . . . If one does not acquire [the images] for oneself, the name also will be taken away from one. But if one receives them in the anointing of the Pleroma, of the might of the cross, which the apostles called "the right and the left," then such a person is no longer a Christian but a Christ. (67)

Those conversant with modern psychology will necessarily be reminded here of Jung's teaching regarding the archetypes and archetypal images. Such images may indeed be envisioned as conveyors or receptacles of such psychic energies as are manifest as meaning, consciousness, and transformation. Jung's statement quoted early in this chapter, that humanity's "most fundamental and most important psychological conditions" are contained in such archetypal rituals as the sacraments receives validation here from Gnostic sources. The "Christing" of the human person occurs not in a purely personal and internal fashion, but it can (perhaps even must) be facilitated by the initiatory mysteries to which this gospel is dedicated.

We are thus presented with a seeming paradox. On the one hand, it might appear that the Gnostic attitude, since it is oriented toward personal spiritual experience, would be incompatible with formal practices of mysteries and sacraments. On the other hand, we have incontrovertible evidence before us that declares the existence of a formal, graduated initiatory sacramental practice explicitly Gnostic in character and associated with the highest flowering of the Gnosis in the school of Valentinus. Whatever Gnostics might have been, they were not proto-Protestant antiritualists, for their adherence not only to sacraments but also to a doctrine of apostolic succession is attested to. Thus, Saying 95 states that "the Father anointed the Son and the Son anointed the apostles—the apostles anointed us. He who is anointed possesses the all. He possesses the resurrection, the light, the cross, the Holy Spirit. As the Father gave him this in the bride chamber, such a one received it."

According to *The Gospel of Philip* (as well as other Gnostic documents), the availability of spiritual power is supplemented by the ability of the duly initiated to pass on such spiritual power. Personal *charisma* is undoubtedly present, but so is the *charisma* that is initiatory and thus institutional, that is, passed on in an orderly, definite tradition and succession. Gnostic individualism does not imply a renunciation of sacramental grace and of the apostolic authority to administer such grace. Like C. G. Jung many centuries later, Valentinus, Marcus, and other Gnostic hierophants administered rites that acted as means of grace, means of transformation. The non-Gnostic church after Constantine continued with this practice, but it lacked the original emphasis. The greater mysteries of the redemption and of the bride chamber were lost, although they surfaced centuries later in the

Cathar rite of the *consolamentum*. Baptism was reduced to psychic baptism, and the anointing became a folk rite of passage for adolescent fledgling Christians. Still, as Jung so correctly pointed out more than fifty years ago, the sacraments of Christendom retained a certain measure of their original power and remained able to convey a certain, though subdued, Gnosis. It is to be hoped that the discovery of such lost gospels as that of Philip may stimulate informed interest in the subject of the initiatory means of transformation. Should this indeed occur, the efforts of the knowers of old may bear fruit in an age in dire need of the grace of Gnosis.

13

Redemption and Ecstasy:
The Gospel of Truth and
The Gospel of the Egyptians

Two more scriptures from the Nag Hammadi find bear the title "gospel." One of these, *The Gospel of Truth*, is contained in the well-known Jung Codex, the first of the collection to be taken out of the troubled Egypt of the 1950s and made available to scholars (see Chapter One). The other is *The Gospel of the Egyptians*, also called "The Holy Book of the Great Invisible Spirit." Both of these books appear to have attracted attention in ancient times. Writing around A.D. 180, Irenaeus mentioned a scripture authored by Valentinus called the Gospel of Truth. After the Jung Codex became available to scholars, many felt confident that the new find was indeed none other than the fabled gospel written by the greatest of the Gnostics, Valentinus. The scholar chiefly responsible for the purchase of the codex, Gilles Quispel, wrote:

> It appeared that the Gospel of Truth beyond doubt came from the school of Valentinus and was identical with the writing which was referred to by Irenaeus. A new heretical gospel, the only one of its kind which is as yet available to students, had been discovered. Our surmise has proven to have been correct.[1]

Similarly, information concerning a "Gospel According to the Egyptians" has existed for a long time. Such an apocryphal scripture was mentioned occasionally by the fathers of the Church, and though it is impossible to determine whether the two fragments bearing this name found in the Nag Hammadi collection are identical with the gospel alluded to in the early literature, it is possible that we are indeed in possession of this long-lost gospel.

The Gospel of Truth is a poetic work of Christian mysticism with powerful Gnostic overtones. Should it occur to anyone to question the compatibility of mystical Christianity with Gnosticism, this scripture might convince him or her otherwise. Not even the most carefully written, Christ-centered tract of Evangelical derivation could demonstrate greater devotion to the figure of Jesus Christ than is found in this scripture attributed to the "arch-heretic" Valentinus or one of his closest disciples. The sublime beauty of its meditative thought and the poetic flight of its language qualify it as one of the great treatises of early Christian mysticism, to be placed alongside such classics as *The Cloud of Unknowing* and the writings of Dionysius the Areopagite. The tone is evident in the opening passage:

> The Gospel of Truth is a joy for those who have received the gift of knowing the Father of truth by way of knowing him through the power of the Logos, who came forth from the fullness, the Logos who is ever present in the thought and insight of the Father, he who is addressed as the savior, such being the name he receives because of the work he is to perform for the redemption of those who do not know the Father. The name "gospel" is the proclamation of hope, and the discovery for those who search for him.

In effect, the author of this gospel says to us that though the non-Gnostic Christian believes Jesus is the Son of God who came to redeem humankind from sin, this story is still very incomplete. A much more complete tale is told here and may be summarized thus: There is a Source of all called the Father (called Depth by Ptolemy or Space by H. P. Blavatsky in our time). From this ultimate progenitor emerges Truth, the quintessential wisdom of the Father, whereby the Father can be known. To know the truth is the ultimate objective of human life; upon it depend such issues as love, authenticity, and above all, freedom. "Ye shall know the truth, and the truth will make you free," says the New Testament Gospel of John. Although she is the first emanation of the Father, Truth (Aletheia) may also be envisioned as God the Mother, the supernal and transcendental aspect of Wisdom (Sophia). From the Father of all and Truth the Mother proceed the Word (Logos), who is the revelation of consciousness and the agency that leads the human mind to truth, awareness, and wholeness. Using terms familiar to depth psychology, we might say that the Word is the archetypal image, the Truth the archetype, and the Father the psychoid archetype-as-such, and that all three are expressions of the same principle of ultimate redemptive wholeness.

In the first few passages of the gospel we literally see the plot thickening. The all, or creation, searched for its own source, and in its anguish it emanated a thick substance like fog, which prevented it from perceiving clearly. Within this fog of unconsciousness another personified principle, named Error (*Plane*), arises and waxes powerful. Not knowing the truth, this being of error now fashions its own cosmos, but it is an inauthentic world, a substitute reality, from which truth is missing. Thus, we are presented early in the text of this gospel with a psychologically meaningful description of our existential condition. Unconsciousness causes a meaningless existence within which the human psyche roams about without the authenticity it needs.

In his essay "Analytical Psychology and Weltanschauung" Jung describes this condition: "Human beings have the feeling that they are haphazard creatures without meaning, and it is this feeling that prevents them from living their lives with the intensity it demands if it is to be enjoyed to the full. Life becomes stale and is no longer the exponent of the complete human being." The gospel tells us that the nature of this existential condition is error, lack of truth; the cognate term in Indian philosophy might be *maya*, usually translated as illusion.

How is this error, this illusion, to be dispelled and authenticity regained? Through the saving agency of the Word, manifesting in the Christian mythos as Jesus:

This is the happy news of the one who is sought, the gospel that is manifest to those who are perfect through the mercy of the Father; it is the hidden mystery, called Jesus the Christ. Through this gospel he enlightened the ones who were in darkness. He rescued them by enlightenment out of oblivion, he showed them the way. This way is the truth which he taught them. . . . For this reason Error (*Plane*) grew wrathful at him, tormented him, was distressed at him, and then Error was brought to naught. He was nailed to a tree; he became the fruit of the Gnosis of the Father. . . . And he discovered them in himself, and, moreover, they discovered him in themselves; they discovered the incomprehensible, inconceivable one. They discovered the Father, the perfect one, the one who created the all, while the all remained contained within him, and the all was in need of him.

The gospel goes on extolling the virtues of the Savior, in an earlier passage described as a guide, peaceful and unhurried, whom the false wise men of this world hated, but who was beloved by those called "children" because of their guilelessness. His gospel may be likened to a book that is at once a living reality, embodying his redemptive mission:

For this reason Jesus came forth; he assumed identity with that book. He was nailed to a tree; he made public the message of the Father on the cross. O such great teaching! He descends down to death, even though life eternal encompasses him. Having divested himself of the perishable rags, he assumes imperishability, which no one can ever take away from him. He entered the empty spaces filled with terrors, he passed those by who were stripped naked by oblivion. He was knowledge and perfection, and he proclaimed the things that are in the heart of the Father, and thus he taught those who were willing to receive.

As indicated in the above passage, not everyone

responded to the message of the Redeemer in equal measure. Those who "were stripped naked by oblivion" he was obliged to pass by, but he found response from those who were chosen by their own Gnosis. These are described as follows:

> The one who has Gnosis is a being from the height. If such a one is called, he hears and he answers, and he returns to the one who calls him, and he ascends to him. And such a one knows in what manner the call comes. Having Gnosis, such a one obeys the will of the one who called him, he wishes to please his caller, and thus he receives the repose. . . . The one who thus has Gnosis knows from where he comes and whither he goes. He understands as someone who frees himself and awakes from the stupor wherein he lived and thus returns to himself.

The changes brought about in life and in the world by the redemptive action of the Logos are indicated by a parable in which some people move into a house and find a number of useless, damaged jars that the new owner of the house decides to remove from the rooms. At the same time there are other jars that, having retained their usefulness, are rehabilitated and filled by the owner. The meaning of the metaphor is revealed in the following passage:

> When the Logos came into the midst . . . a great disturbance took place among the jars because some of them had been emptied out, others were filled . . . others broken up. All the places were shaken and disturbed inasmuch as they were without true order and stability. Error (*Plane*) was perturbed, and it did not know what to do. Error was grieved, it was in mourning, it was afflicted because it knew nothing at all. When Gnosis drew near to it—for such is the downfall of Error and of all its emanations—it proved itself empty, having nothing inside of itself.

The image of jars, and even more of broken shards, is not unknown in esoteric lore. The Kabbalah speaks of shards (*Klipoth*) when describing the counterproductive, discontinuous elements of evil that afflict the sparks of light in this manifest world. Similarly, the autonomous complexes of the unconscious might be likened to broken shards that the archetype of wholeness must discard from the newly constellated internal household which comes about in the course of individuation. Yet, such psychic forces cannot be expected to yield to the new Self without opposition. The false self, Error, also arises in agitation, for its long, dark reign is at an end and its hollow, unproductive character revealed at last.

We may see here the difference between the Christianity embodied in *The Gospel of Truth*, on the one hand, and the non-Gnostic Christianity of the self-styled orthodox, on the other. It is not from sin, personal and original, that the redeeming Logos frees humankind, but rather from the confusion and illusion brought about by unconsciousness. This condition is graphically described by the gospel:

> One flees to one knows not where or one remains fixed at the same spot when one desires to move forward, while pursuing one knows not whom. One feels that one is in a battle, one dispenses and receives blows. Or one feels as if one is falling from a great height, or one seems to be flying through the air without the benefit of wings. At times it appears as if one were killed by an unseen murderer, without having noticed any pursuer before.... These things happen until the moment when those who have experienced all this wake up. Then they see nothing ... for all those dreams were ... naught. It is thus that they rid themselves of their ignorance, even as it were a dream which they esteem as naught.

The redeemed elect, i.e., "the living who stand written in the Book of Life," receive through *The Gospel of Truth*, which Christ brings them, the awakening that frees them from illusion and restores them to their true Self. The revelation of God comes about through the knowledge of Christ, who is not merely an agency external to the soul but is found to be present within the spirit of the human being ("they discovered him in themselves, they discovered the incomprehensible, inconceivable one").

It may be appropriate to conclude this summary of *The Gospel of Truth* with the beautiful injunction addressed to the redeemed:

> The day from on high has no night, and its light never wanes, for it is perfect. Proclaim, then, that you are this perfect day and that it is in you that the unfailing light dwells, you who possess the Gnosis of the heart. Utter the truth to those who seek it, and speak Gnosis to those who in their error have made mistakes. Make firm the foot of those who have stumbled and stretch out your hands to those who suffer from sickness. Feed those who are hungering and afford repose to those who are weary, and raise up those who wish to rise, and awaken those who sleep. For you are the "Gnosis of the heart" that is manifest.

The knower becomes the power of knowing, the Gnostic is the embodiment of Gnosis, and redemption changes the redeemed into a redeemer. It has been observed by some that distinctly heretical traits of other Gnostic scriptures such as the distinction between the Unknown God and the Demiurge find no place in *The Gospel of Truth*.[2] Yet, what is the role of Error (*Plane*) if not that of the Demiurge? Whether it is called Error, Yaldabaoth, or by any other name, the creator of falsehood, of illusion, is always recognized in the Gnostic gospels. The names, the personifications matter little; what remain are the existential realities of imperfection and unconsciousness to which all humans are subject and which are set off against the liberating knowledge of the heart, facilitated by the great messenger and incarnation of Gnosis, Jesus the Christ. The mysterious transgressivity joining Christ with the transcendental potential in each and every human spirit, the mystery of the "Christ in us, the hope of Glory" of whom Paul speaks, becomes also the point wherein Christian mysticism of the more orthodox variety joins hands with the presumably heretical Gnostics. This relativizing of heresy and orthodoxy by way of the revelation of the secret unity within the knowledge of the heart is perhaps one of the greatest virtues of this sensitively articulated and deeply felt message that justly deserves to be called *The Gospel of Truth.*

Of a different character, and yet of comparable worth, is the last one of our lost Gnostic gospels to which we are about to turn our attention: namely, the "Book of the Great Invisible Spirit," or *The Gospel of the Egyptians.* This scripture distinguishes itself from many other treatises of its kind by the fact that it is not only a mythological or cosmological narrative but also a liturgical text or initiatory liturgy, which undoubtedly was intended to serve as part of a ritual of admission into some profound mystery of the Gnosis. It is divided into three parts: (1) a description of the incorruptible realm of the high Fullness; (2) an account of the mythic history of Gnostic humanity, as personified by Seth and his descendants; and (3) an initiation text, which may merit being called a document of ecstasy because it appears to be based on the experience of ecstatic initiation undergone by a Gnostic visionary.

The threefold structure of this scripture raises certain issues. If the ecstatic text constituting part three of the gospel is indeed an attempt of a Gnostic initiate to document his own ecstatic experience, then we may inquire whether there is any reason why the author leads the reader toward his utterance of ecstasy by way of the lengthy descriptions of the realm of the fullness and of the story of the wise race of Seth. Would it not be more appropriate to treat the ecstatic initiation experience merely "experientially," as might be done today when experience and technique are so often considered sufficient unto themselves? The answer may be that to the Gnostic the *context of transcendence* is of equal importance with the experience of transcendence. It is certainly true that the Gnostics of the early centuries cultivated vivid, impressive ecstatic experiences. (One other outstanding document of such an experience is the *Eight Reveals the Ninth,* a treatise from Nag Hammadi mentioned in Chapter Two.) Yet, such experiences were always undergone within a specific mythology where cosmology, theogony, and spiritual history were allowed to play a vital part. The Gnostics were aware that extraordinary experiences in themselves are incomplete and are always in need of amplification, leading to assimilation. In psychological terms, only the assimilated experience of the archetypal psyche is transformative, and such assimilation is inevitably enhanced by a helpful mythological context within which the experience finds its appropriate place.

The first part of this gospel presents us with the ultimate or highest context in the image of the Incorruptible Realm. To the practicing mystic and Gnostic, questions regarding the supreme field of being are of great importance. Is there something beyond who we are, what we are, and where we are? Is there something beyond our petty lives and, moreover, even beyond the cosmos, that is, transcending the system of sun, moon, planets, and stars? The Gnostic answers that there is a *beyond*. (This Gnostic insight finds its analogues in other esoterically toned approaches to spirituality. In Hinduism we encounter the concept of Parabrahman, that which is beyond the knowable deity. Some schools of Buddhism call the same reality by the name of *Adi Buddha*, the ultimate Buddha essence, and the Kabbalah calls it *Ain Soph Aur*, limitless light.) This is the ultimate context of transcendence, that which was and is and always shall be: timeless, limitless, yet filled with the potential of all time, all space, all life, and all consciousness. *The Gospel of the Egyptians* gives a graphic description of this incorruptible realm and in typical Gnostic fashion enumerates a grouping of eternal beings who populate this supreme field of fullness. Presiding over the Pleromic region is the brooding presence of the Great Invisible Spirit, also referred to as the Parent. This ultimate Being is manifest in a trinity: the Father, the Mother, and the Son. From these transcendental centers of creativity emanate a large number of Aeons, Glories, Thrones, and other beings. Of particular importance are four pairs of powers called the Luminaries, one of whom is Abrasax (Abraxas), the Gnostic mythic figure that appears so prominently in *Seven Sermons to the Dead* by C. G. Jung.

The matter of a *context of transcendence* leads us directly to considerations of a *context of transmission*. The need for this context may be envisioned in the following manner: There is an imperishable realm that gave us life and light, but *we* find ourselves in a perishable realm where life is mingled with death, and light is combined with darkness. How are we to attain to our original estate? By way of the transmission of assistance from above, which means by way of the seeds of light proceeding from the fullness and planted in our midst. As we have noted in other myths and scriptures of the Gnosis, the supreme light has repeatedly sent its emissaries into the lower worlds of manifestation for the purpose of facilitating the enlightenment and liberation of the creatures present there. The prototype of all Gnostic messengers of light according to this gospel is Seth, third son of Adam and Eve, who unlike the imperfect, contending brothers Cain and Abel had a clear knowledge of his own nature and of his connection with the imperishable realm and its celestial denizens.

Seth is represented as the father of a race of enlightened, knowing humans who uphold the principles of Gnosis in every generation. The gospel describes them as follows: "This is the vast, imperishable race that came forth from three (earlier) worlds." (One is reminded here of the teachings of Theosophy that indicate that certain human monads/spiritual essences have come to earth after having existed in other cosmic systems.) The race of Seth may also be understood as a body of enlightened Gnostic adepts present in the world in every generation who possess a distinguished, luminous prehistory in their own right.

The illustrious company of these spiritual descendants of Seth is subject to the relentless enmity of the Demiurge and his troublesome servants:

And the flood shall come as a prefiguration for the end of
the age against the world. On account of this race the
conflagrations also will come upon the earth. . . . And grace
cometh through the agency of the prophets and the watch-
men who come from the living race. Plagues and famines
also are visited upon all because [of the enmity of the
demiurge]. All these things will come to pass on account
of this great, imperishable race.

Next we are told by the gospel that because of the perse-
cutions visited upon the illustrious company of the
children of Seth a host of guardian spirits and powerful
helpers was dispatched from the great aeons. Led by the
spirit of great Seth himself, these beings are ready to
extend their grace and assistance to the embattled members of the illustrious race. Great sacraments have been
prepared "to make the holy people be born again by the
Holy Spirit, and invisible, holy mystic symbols." The
second part of the gospel thus ends with an invitation
extended to the elect to partake of the initiation prepared
for them by their father Seth and the guardian spirits
who have come to their rescue.

The next and final portion of *The Gospel of the Egyptians*
must be understood as an ecstatic account rendered by
an initiate of the mystery experienced within the context
of the sacrament of Seth. Significantly, although the
sacrament is traced to the work of Seth, the invocations
and prayers of thanksgiving that form part of this section
of the gospel are addressed to Jesus by his particular
mystic name, Iesseus-Mazareus-Iessedekeus. There can
be little doubt that these prayers are indeed the result of
vivid ecstatic experience and that the strings of mystic
letters reproduced in the text are in the nature of glos-
solalia—that is, of ecstatic utterances expressed in sounds
that do not reflect any earthly language. (Such combina-
tions of letters, known technically as "barbarous words,"
are frequently present in Gnostic texts where direct
accounts of transcendental experiences are presented.) A
short example of such utterances will have to suffice for
our considerations here:

> O Iesseus! Ieoeuooa!
> In very truth! . . .
> O living water!
> O child of the child!
> O name of all glories!
> O eternal being! . . .
> O being, which beholds the aeons
> In very truth!
> AEEEEEIIIIYYYYYYOOOOOOOO,
>
> O existent for ever and ever! . . .
> O existent forever unto eternity!
> You are what you are! You are what you are! . . .
> Having myself become acquainted with
>   your being
> I have now mingled myself with your
>   unchanging being;
> I have surrounded myself and come to be
>   armored in loveliness and light, and I have
>   become a shining one.

After these ecstatic utterances are concluded, a descriptive postscript declares that this book was composed by the great Seth, and that he had placed it in high mountains so concealed that the sun never rises upon them. At the proper time, when the ages are complete, Seth will come forth and according to the promise of this book to the illustrious race, and accompanied by the eternal light and the divine feminine beings Sophia and Barbelo he will travel with his children into the incorruptible worlds. The association of this text with the Christian mythos is finally affirmed by the personal note of the scribe, whose spiritual name is given as Eugnostos and who concludes with the words:

> O Jesus Christ, O son of God, O Saviour!
> O fish! Holy indeed are the origins of this holy
>   book of the Great Invisible Spirit! Amen.

Different though they might appear in outward appearance, these two gospels, the Valentinian *Gospel of Truth* and the "Sethian" *Gospel of the Egyptians*, tell a common story. Whether meditating on the Gnostic saving mission of Jesus as assisting humanity to discover the divine self within[3] or presenting a context of transcendence and transmission for an initiatory experience of ecstasy, the intent is the same: to remind humankind of its high and holy origins, as well as its present predicament of incomprehension, and to assure men and women of the availability of redemption and a return to consciousness, glory, and bliss.

It is also to be remembered that informative though such gospels are, they constitute but a minuscule portion of the vast body of Gnostic teaching and initiatory experience. Much of such wisdom and spiritual discipline remained unwritten, which was due to Gnostic principle rather than to any other cause. Transcendental experience is by definition incommunicable, and the instructions of Gnostic adepts contained in sayings, myths, parables, and exhortations could not communicate Gnosis (at best, they were merely similar to the proverbial Zen Buddhist finger pointing to the moon). "The knowledge of the things that are" (as G. R. S. Mead called it) must be arrived at by the individual, although select individualized teaching and practices may assist one to approach such knowledge within a meaningful and helpful context of psychological receptivity. Such a knowledge always would appeal to relatively few. Those who would be satisfied with faith in the statements received from others, those who did not balk at having faith in the faith of someone else, would always disqualify themselves when it came to Gnosis. Many centuries after the time of the Gnostics, C. G. Jung expressed their attitude poignantly when describing his own position regarding the spiritual needs of the modern world:

> I am not . . . addressing myself to the happy possessors
> of faith, but to those many people for whom the light has
> gone out, the mystery faded, and God is dead. For most
> of them there is no going back, and one does not know
> either whether going back is the better way. To gain an

understanding of religious matters, probably all that is
left us today is the psychological approach. That is why
I take these thought-forms that have become historically
fixed, and try to melt them down again and pour them
into moulds of immediate experience.[4]

The "other gospels," long lost and now rediscovered,
appear to hold the potential of being of great assistance
to those engaged in the task of melting down the rigid
theologies and arid philosophies of this age and of
pouring their essence into molds of the immediate and
yet timeless Gnostic experience.

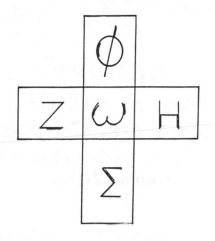

Cross of the conjunction of Light and Life

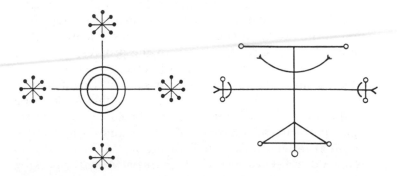

Mandala figures from the Books of Jeu

Epilogue
From Hiroshima to the Secret Gospels:
The Alternative Future of Human History

Not long before his death in 1961, C. G. Jung had a series of visions of a future great catastrophe. According to Marie-Louise von Franz, who remained the custodian of the notes and charts concerning these utterances, Jung saw a worldwide catastrophe, possibly in the nature of a fiery holocaust, occurring in about fifty years (i.e., about 2010), which according to some students coincides with the controversial date the Mayan calendar is said to come to an end.[1] Fully ten years earlier in his book *Aion*, Jung predicted the coming of the age of the Antichrist, placing its culmination within or possibly soon after the termination of the twentieth century. The cosmic synchronicities outlined by Jung in *Aion* concern the progression of the so-called Platonic months, also known as zodiacal ages. Thus, it may be regarded as a meaningful coincidence that the age of Pisces, which started roughly at the time of the birth of Christ, occurred at the same time the religion of Christianity developed and became the normative spiritual influence for much of the world. The fish also is the old, well-known symbol for Christ. After the passing of the first millennium of the Piscean age, the shadow side of Christianity could no longer be contained and repressed alternative movements (many of them of Gnostic origin) such as the Cathars, Waldensians, the Holy Spirit movement, and the followers of Joachim of Fiore arose with great might, to the discomfort of the

232

Roman church. Thus, the "kingdom of the second or dark fish" was initiated and rises toward its culmination as the end of the second millennium approaches. (The astrological sign of Pisces is often represented as two fish—one light, the other dark in color—swimming in opposite directions.) It was Jung's view that *if the dark or enshadowed side of the Christian archetype does not manage to enter* and become integrated into consciousness, a most powerful and malefic manifestation of this shadow might attain ascendancy, and that this baneful event would in all likelihood occur at a date not far removed from the year 2000. This would be the advent of the Antichrist of whom Jung wrote:

> If we see the traditional figure of Christ as parallel to the psychic manifestation of the self, then the Antichrist would correspond to the shadow of the self, namely the dark half of the human totality, which ought not to be judged too optimistically. So far as we can judge from experience, light and shadow are so evenly distributed in man's nature that his psychic totality appears, to say the least of it, in a somewhat murky light. The psychological concept of the self, in part derived from our knowledge of the whole man, but for the rest depicting itself spontaneously in the products of the unconscious as an archetypal quaternity bound together by inner antinomies, cannot omit the shadow that belongs to the light figure, for without it this figure lacks body and humanity. In the empirical self, light and shadow form a paradoxical unity. In the Christian concept, on the other hand, the archetype is hopelessly split into two halves, leading ultimately to a metaphysical dualism—the final separation of the kingdom of heaven from the fiery world of the damned.[2]

In short, the spiritual imbalances within the psychological framework of non-Gnostic Christianity are so great that if they fail to be reconciled in an abiding union of psychic fullness, the inner tension brought about by the unreconciled opposites is bound to bring the uneasy coexistence of these constituent portions to a disastrous end. The likelihood is great that Jung's vision of the fiery catastrophe concerned the breaking asunder of the psychic structure of Western culture with an accompanying physical holocaust of a natural or a thermonuclear origin.

Jung, and with him other persons of a generally Gnostic orientation, was also aware of another set of ideas that bear a relationship to the age of the Antichrist and the vision of the catastrophe communicated by Jung to Marie-Louise von Franz. These ideas were popularized by the church father Origen in the second century A.D. and are subsumed under the Greek apellation *Apokatastasis Panton* (the return of the All). At the end of time all things must return to God, the source of all, said Origen, who employed several quotations from the New Testament to authenticate his theory (Matt. 10:26; I Cor. 4:5; Luke 12:2; Matt. 17:11; Acts 3:20-21). It must also be remembered that this same Origen was once associated with the greatest Gnostic teacher, Valentinus, and thus may have absorbed some of the Gnostic teachings in this regard.

Valentinus, and with him many Gnostic and neo-Gnostic writers, held that creation is composed of several (usually three) portions or waves. The first of these is gross matter, which serves as the staging ground for the drama of cosmic life; the second is life, or the scattered sparks of divine light that fall into the relative darkness of preexisting materiality; and the third is the revelatory descent of guiding and salvific figures, Dhyani Buddhas, Avatars, Sons of the Firemist, as they are called in various traditions. The gathering back of the all to its source thus may come about in one of two ways: First, the tension of the opposites having been reduced by developing consciousness, the antagonism of the dualities disappears and, rather like envisioned in alchemy, the *coniunctio* brings into existence a wonder and mystery that is capable of freely and consciously uniting itself with its source in the divine fullness. As noted in *The Gospel of Thomas*, the facilitation of this union was in fact the supreme objective of Jesus, who as true *soter* (healer) came to "make the two into the one."* The second possibility is rather more dramatic. Here the opposites do not find a way to reconcile and consequently the cosmos remains in a permanent state of alchemical *nigredo*, manifest in unrelieved suffering, conflict, and chaos. The broken heart of the universe is not healed and the efforts of the saviors do not produce their intended result.

Thus, there is only one option open: Like Shiva in his destructive aspect, the Antichrist, the "dark fish," obtains ascendancy and breaks asunder the material framework, so that the light and life captured within it may be freed from its shackles and ascend unhampered into the fullness. Neo-Gnostic myths and pronouncements declare that minor manifestations of this apokatastatic process have occurred repeatedly in the distant history of our world, bringing about the destruction of vast continents inhabited by high cultures. Some of the legendary names associated with such events are Atlantis and Lemuria.

According to Jung, we live now in an "End Time" period: This is not only a *fin de siècle*, but it is a *fin de l'age*. As such, it is pregnant with great possibilities, both destructive and constructive. The critical and in a sense final character of our times is intuited by man, and the reactions brought forth in response to it are varied. Millenarians and Harmonic Convergers, UFO devotees and the advocates of the return of Quetzalcoatl vie for attention with Bible Fundamentalists desirous of Armageddon. End Time scenarios range from the ludicrous to the terrifying, while the essentially unspiritual and prosaic majority culture stands by bemused.

In the midst of all the excitement and confusion, one element stands out with some measure of convincing realism: the prospect of thermonuclear destruction. In many ways, one is bound to feel somewhat jaded now by the coming and going of antiwar and antinuclear

---

*For the complete passage see the concluding paragraph of the present epilogue.

movements, replete with wishful thinking, sentimentality, and unrealistic ways of regarding human nature. By this latter part of the twentieth century, people have demonstrated for peace, marched for peace, danced for peace, formed green political parties, and more recently and interestingly, called mightily to all and sundry with such slogans as "Visualize world peace!" This latter shibboleth, so appealing in its quasi-spiritual aura of meditative and positive imagery, was brilliantly analyzed by the writer Dennis Stillings in 1988:

> My interest in the antinuclear movement was awakened a short time ago . . . when I went to a local lecture on these issues. The speaker was a well-known representative of a New Age organization. . . . As the talk went on, I found myself very much interested in what was being said. The speaker began to talk of the power of imagery in accomplishing the fire walk, paranormal metal-bending, and remote viewing. . . . He emphasized that clarity and definiteness of the image was all-important, that with a clear and definite image you can change reality. Again I agreed. He then moved into a discussion of the use of imagery in preventing nuclear war, stating that if you formed an image of peace, you can bring it into reality. I became fascinated. As the lecture ended, I realized that he had not suggested any clear and definite image to work with. I was dumbfounded. The punch line to the whole talk was missing.
>
> Seriously disappointed that I had not been provided with an image, I felt it incumbent upon myself to come up with one of my own. But I could not do it. All I could get were bucolic scenes like rolling hills in the sunshine with soaring birds, and, perhaps, a farmer plowing behind an ox. Now, that may be a peaceful image, but it is not an image of peace that can "change reality." Try as I might, I could not come up with anything I regarded as satisfactory. The closest I could come to a clear and definite image of peace was the peace that followed after nuclear war. This really distressed me, because if there were anything to this imagery business, those people out there thoughtlessly "imaging peace" might, in fact, be creating disaster—the

clear, definite peace that follows the storm, the fight, the nuclear holocaust. . . . [Here the author inquires into the actual scenes occurring at Hiroshima and Nagasaki some time after the bomb and finds that they were frequently most idyllic—S.A.H.] In my opinion, there is no *clear and definite* image of peace that does not also draw into consciousness imagery of its opposite: violence and war.[3]

Not only had the writer of this passage discovered in a practical situation the coincidence of the opposites in the depths of his psyche, but more importantly he came to realize that the naive notions espoused by the well-intentioned may not only be lacking in efficacy but also could be productive of results quite contrary to those intended.

Some years ago, in the 1960s, the minstrels sang to us the words "The times, they are a-changing," and so they did. Our comfortable seat of nineteenth century manufacture, possessing the beautiful cushion of evolutionary progress and the fashionable contours supplied by technology, has begun to smolder, and nuclear power sends its acrid odor into our refined nostrils. The noted Jungian psychologist Gerhard Adler said in a lecture in April 1946:

Don't we all still remember the one morning last year when we woke up and found the world changed with one word, "Hiroshima"? Don't we all remember the shock, the giddy feeling as if the bottom had dropped out from underneath somebody's feet, and each of us was this somebody just as much as the wretched men, women and children far away on an island in the Eastern hemisphere? Tragic and strange as it may be, isn't it true to say that for the first time since endless days mankind had felt and rediscovered its common fate? Had felt and rediscovered the fact of communion, the fact of the Indian "*Tat twam asi*"— of the "This is you"? Alas! Our seat had become very hot indeed to make us jump![4]

In the same lecture Gerhard Adler went on to point out that the atom bomb was not an isolated phenomenon in time, but that it was the natural result of a movement in mind that rejected the unifying religious and spiritual valuations of life and led to a position adopted by more and more people, indicating to them the world no longer appeared as an organic and meaningful entity. The ego and the conscious mind were regarded as the whole personality; the meaning of the superpersonal selfhood had been lost. The laws that govern nature became ever more visible, but the laws that govern the role of the human being in this world became ever more blurred. The unity of life and meaning had been split. Human beings were no longer in possession of their dignity as the exponents and functions of a meaningful world. Marxism came to add the final and most pathetic expression of this attitude of meaninglessness and alienation when it reduced the significance of the human being to an "economic unit." Jung wrote of this condition:

> The twentieth century thus shows a devastating sense of frustration and futility in the image of the world of the average man. It can be defined as something like this: the world is without divine direction; it is without imminent sense or inner coherence (except the purely mechanical one); it is without intrinsic responsibility. And this means that man had no reality or function in this world beyond the one that his ego had defined for himself.[5]

A humanity that failed to acknowledge the existence of the superpersonal and nonrational forces as a factor in life was finally convinced of the reality of the irrational and the unexpected. When the community of spirit fails, the community of fear prevails. The British playwright of the 1940s, Ronald Duncan, wrote aptly in his play, *The Way to the Tomb*:

> I am treading an old path with new feet.
> I am standing in footprints already in my mind.
> Is not the test of reason to put it to a fear?
> And it was here the ferret's tooth of fear
>   struck at my bone.
> And the draught of alarm blew out my reason.[6]

The decisive question is truly: Is not the test of reason to put it to a fear? The virtue of fear has thus been restored to humanity. Two devastating world wars and the threat of nuclear weapons have brought fear back to the arrogant human ego. Gerhard Adler said it well in 1946:

I can't help feeling that there is a deep symbolic meaning in the story of the atom bomb. It is the shattering force that has come out of our human autarchy, it is the *enantiodromia* to man as the creator, it is the divine symbol of fate hidden in the human sin of reliance on rationality and reasonability. It is a tremendous and terrifying question mark to man.[7]

Today, more than forty years later, the terrifying question mark is still with us. With every year it grows somewhat larger and more puzzling. In more recent times, dark puzzlements of an ominous character have been added to this question mark. Not only the alarmist fringe but also the balanced center of the culture are increasingly aware of ecological crises that are only marginally connected with the issue of nuclear power and quite unconnected with nuclear war.

In addition, astrophysical speculation based on considerable research has increasingly brought into focus the likelihood of the presence in space of something called "dark matter," represented as a massive presence beneath the visible universe, a hitherto unknown quantity deduced only gravitationally but not visible in any way. Scientific reporter Dennis Overbye writes, quoting highly reputable sources: "The universe has a shadow, and, because of that, it may also have an end." Astronomers, he writes, "have slowly, reluctantly recognized a darker, more passive presence beneath the pale film of the visible universe." This shadow world of dark matter may be "ordinary matter that failed to achieve the grace of light. . . . And if there is enough of it, dark matter could some day cause the universe to collapse in fiery and terminal splendour."[8] These passages with expressions such as "shadow" conjure up visions of Jungian archetypal projections into the material universe and also seem to run parallel to Jung's statements in *Aion* to the effect that the shadow of our culture may herald its end. Mainstream religiosity has convinced us long ago that while all good things come from God, all calamitous and evil conditions come from ourselves. (There is even a Latin theological saying: *Omne bonum a Deo, omne malum ab homine*; all good from God, all evil from man.) Thus, we naturally assume that large-scale devastation and destruction on the planet must be caused by humanity, but it may be useful to contemplate that science assures us dark shadows from beyond the reach of our efforts may cause the earth's demise in a fiery splendor surpassing all man-made nuclear explosions. Distressing as this may prove to those ever desirous of placing guilt upon the human race, the end may come and it may not prove to be our fault at all!

It would appear that even as humanity has its psychological shadow the cosmos may possess its own great shadow and that all of these shadows are potentially perilous. The Gnostic wisdom has always held that the light will emerge from the darkness by one means or another. One interesting, relatively late Gnostic teaching within Kabbalistic Judaism has named this principle of liberation, or gathering, *tikkun*, a concept closely resembling the Gnostic and Christian concepts of *apokatastasis*. *Tikkun* is the process whereby the lost light-sparks are drawn up from their imprisonment among the dark shards that abound in the unregenerate realms of the cosmos. *Tikkun* is primarily the task of the Messiah, but all wise and righteous human beings play a vital role in it. This task of restitution is in fact the Gnostic alternative to the forcible and violent extraction of the light from darkness, such as may occur in man-made and cosmic catastrophes alike. Unconsciousness, the unwillingness to redeem the shadow within ourselves and in the world, leads to destruction; egos, cultures, and worlds are equally shattered by the pent-up force of the unmet darkness that lurks in psychic and cosmic depths. Holocausts and cataclysms, whether envisioned as the flood that submerges Atlantis or the nuclear conflagration that devastates the earth: all of these are light extractors, extreme measures for the freeing of surviving soul power when no other means are available. Astrological imagery embodied in zodiacal ages thus joins with the Gnostic myth of the trapped light in the world and is brought into the field of constructive vision by the psychological Gnosis of Jung. As we are told in *The Gospel of Philip*, if we know that which is within ourselves it will save us, if we do not know it, it will kill us or at least destroy the form within which our life has chosen to embody itself.

Prima materia, original matter, primal chaos of being, such were the expressions applied by the alchemists to that creative condition from whence after many engagements of transformative action the unitary stone of the philosophers is destined to emerge. There is much evidence available to indicate that our situation today is one where the alchemical paradigm ought to find its redeeming application. As an alternative to tragic, though perhaps life-and-light-liberating destruction, we are faced now with the need to produce the conjunction of the opposites, leading by way of their union to the *unus mundus*, the alchemically reunited world. As noted in the last chapter, the alchemist cannot subject the finished world of the four elements (symbolic of the ego world or the culture at an impasse) to a true creative change. The modern world is in many ways in a spiritual cul-de-sac, in a dead-end street coming from a glorious past but leading nowhere. To a major extent this lamentable condition has come to pass because of the wrong-headedness and spiritual aridity of the religious structures in Western society. The root and cause of these undesirable features are none other than the misunderstanding of the nature of the Gnosis and its ensuing repression in early Christendom. This Gnosis, we must remember, is not just a vague term denoting some undefined spiritual insight but a definite spiritual phenomenon with distinct and undeniable characteristics. Gnosis and Gnosticism are one, and to separate them is but

Epilogue

her sinister strategy, originating in obscurantism and obtuseness.

Gnosticism as rediscovered by way of the discovery of its most important documents; Gnosticism wedded to its immediate predecessor, the alternative Judaism of the Essenes; and last but not least, Gnosticism as amplified and brought into psychological relevance by Jung—this is the missing alchemical ingredient of Western spirituality and culture. In a very real sense, it is the *prima materia*, the creative, existential matrix, out of which the salvific transformational elements may emerge that could save the West from its decline and fall. The terrifying question mark of nuclear destruction and its related tragic destructive modalities can only be answered by going back to the kind of primal spiritual experiences that are the core of all Gnosis, while abandoning reliance on superstructures and overcompensations masquerading as dogma, commandment, and ideology of whatever stripe.

It goes without saying that in this proposed task of restoration of Gnosis and Gnosticism the teachings of C. G. Jung must play a role of singular distinction. Catholic priest and Jungian writer Fr. John P. Dourley rightly said:

> It would be a significant step toward survival if every discipline concerned with life on earth were to seriously examine, in concert, Jung's conception of a personal and historical Self intrinsic to the life of the psyche, an inner center capable of bringing the Gods and Goddesses it unleashes upon humanity into configurations of greater harmony, wealth of being and consciousness. Should such a psychic reality prove not to exist at all, or should humanity fail to bring its power to consciousness, humanity would seem destined to continue to wait for its redemption through the intervention of an extrinsic deity.
>
> Given the enmity bred between and within the traditions historically spawned by such "divine" interventions, and given humanity's current technological capacity to destroy itself, this wait may now be short.[9]

As we have seen throughout our journeyings among the myths and metaphors, the scriptures, and the mysteries of the Gnostics, the natural divinity of the individual human spirit is one of the chief themes running through the images of the alternative reality presented to us by the Gnosis. As Jung powerfully stated in his *Answer to Job*,* the human spirit (Job) is spiritually superior to the God of this world, who is in need of the Gnosis that only humanity can supply. The human spirit, said the Gnostics and affirms Jung, descends from the supreme Godhead and as such is of supreme value in this world. Self-knowledge *is* knowledge of God, and the discovery and experience of the Divine and of the individual center of essential Self are ultimately identical. Indoctrinated by the dogmas enforced for century upon century by the devotees of the monotheistic God, numerous contemporary persons resist these Gnostic and depth-psychological insights, as Jung himself recognized:

> Whoever speaks of the reality of the soul or psyche is accused of "psychologism." Psychology is spoken of as if it were "only" psychology and nothing else. The notion that there can be psychic factors which correspond to divine figures is regarded as a devaluation of the latter. It smacks of blasphemy to think that a religious experience is a psychic process. . . .
>
> Faced with this situation, we must really ask: How do we know so much about the psyche that we can say "only" psychic?[10]

The breaking down of the superstructures of culture has thrown contemporary humanity back into its own depths, and it is in these profound and mysterious regions that we must look for a new-old answer. The recovery of the wisdom of the Gnostics, especially as illuminated by modern depth psychology, fulfills two functions: On the one hand, it points to the need to return to primal experiences, and on the other, it points to the potential source of the creative answer. Gnosis leads us thus back to our roots and foundations, to the basic truths and facts of our more than merely rational and deeper than merely personal nature. In the final analysis, it is only experience

---

*See Chapter Ten of the present work.

that truly counts. Theologies, metaphysical assumptions, and philosophical categories never equal experience. In the individual and conscious experience of the super-individual and primordial images of our inner world, the union of the opposites, the synthesis of all binaries, including those of light and shadow, has become possible.

Our time is perilous and disruptive. We do not know if the instruments of destruction that have appeared in our day will leave us enough time for Gnosis, for individuation. Still, Goethe told us that all things transitory are meant for us as symbols, and the present uncertain and insecure situation may in some ways be just another attempt on the part of the human spirit to face up to the creative chaotic state of the *prima materia*. It is not impossible that as the dissolution of matter in the splitting of the atom releases its imprisoned transcendental fire, so the dissolution of the consensus reality of culture and conditioning may release a transformative alternative reality, thus leading us to the philosopher's stone in the uniting symbol of the Self that gives meaning and unity to the scattered parts. Could it be that our less than happy condition might turn out to be a heroic attempt to heal the gap between the light and the dark instead of a prelude to the doom of culture and cosmos? Could such perils as the split atom, the ecological crisis, the cosmic perils of "dark matter" be understood as symbols of terrifying potency, forcing the human spirit to either accept world destruction or to pluck wholeness out of danger and chaos?

Three seemingly unrelated events occurred within a short span of time at the end of the greatest upheaval of human making, World War II, synchronistically converging with their mysterious connection of meaning: The exploding of the first nuclear weapon at Hiroshima, the discovery of the Gnostic collection of scriptures at Nag Hammadi, and the unearthing of the Essene scrolls in the cave at Qumran. Destruction and its alternative; liberation from form and redemption within form. Those instructed by Jung's theory of synchronicity may readily recognize within this meaningful coincidence a signal from the heavens. Risen from the sleep of the centuries and emerging into the focus of consciousness, the other, alternative reality beckons to us with its vision of transformative redemption. We have nothing to fear but unconsciousness. The Antichrists, Behemoths, and Leviathans threatening us are but the creatures of our unconscious projections, which may vanish like a nightmare when the process of individuation becomes operative. The kingdom, the reconstituted world of wholeness, opens its gates to us as the words of the archetype of the individuated Self of humanity receive their final vindication:

> When you make the two one, and when you make the inmost as the outermost and the outer as the inner and the above as the below, and when you make the male and female into a single unity, so that the male will not be only male and the female will not be only female, when you create eyes in the place of an eye, and create a hand in the place of a hand, and a foot in the place of a foot, and also an image in the place of an image, then surely will you enter the kingdom.[11]

Notes

Prologue

1. C. G. Jung, *Psychology and Alchemy*, Collected Works, Vol. 12, par. 10.
2. C. G. Jung, *The Archetypes and the Collective Unconscious*, Collected Works, Vol. 9, part 1, par. 45.
3. C. G. Jung, "Psychological Commentary to W. Y. Evans-Wentz, *The Tibetan Book of the Great Liberation*" (Oxford: Oxford Univ. Press, 1954), p. xxxi.
4. C. G. Jung, *Psychology and Alchemy*, Collected Works, Vol. 12, par. 8.
5. C. G. Jung in *The Tibetan Book of the Great Liberation*, p. xli.
6. C. G. Jung, *Psychology and Religion: West and East*, Collected Works, Vol. 11, par. 17.
7. John P. Dourley, *The Illness That We Are*, (Toronto: Inner City Books, 1984), p. 94.
8. C. G. Jung, "Transformation Symbolism in the Mass," *Psychology of Religion: West and East*, par. 444.

Chapter 1

1. *Bhagavad Gita*, Chapter 4.
2. International Symposium on Jesus and the Gospels, held at the Michigan Union, Ann Arbor, Mich., April 1985.
3. C. G. Jung, "A Psychological Approach to the Dogma of the Trinity," *Psychology of Religion West and East*, par. 170.

Chapter 2

1. Joshua V, 14.
2. John M. Allegro, *The Dead Sea Scrolls and the Christian Myth*, (New York: Prometheus Books, 1984), pp. 63-64.
3. R. Bultmann, *Theologie des Neuen Testaments* (1951), p. 361.
4. *The Eighth Reveals the Ninth: A New Hermetic Initiation Discourse*/Tractate 6, Nag Hammadi Codex VI/Lewis S. Keizer,

247

trans., (Seaside, CA: Academy of Arts and Humanities, 1974), pp. 98-99.

5. *Thanksgiving Hymns*, Col. VIII.

6. Allegro, *The Dead Sea Scrolls and the Christian Myth*, pp. 12, 13.

7. Ibid., p. 16.

8. Hugh Schonfield, *The Essene Odyssey*, (Shaftsbury, England: Element Books, 1984), p. 2.

9. Bultmann, *Theologie des Neuen Testaments*, p. 361.

Chapter 3

1. *Odes of Solomon*, Ode 41.

2. See *C. G. Jung, Letters*, G. Adler and Aniela Jaffe, eds., (Princeton, NJ: Bollingen Series XCV, Princeton Univ. Press, 1973-1975), Vol. 2., especially pp. 6, 21, 89, 157, 275.

3. John M. Allegro, *The Sacred Mushroom and the Cross: A Study of the Nature and Origins of Christianity within the Fertility Cults of the Ancient Near East* (Garden City, NY: Doubleday, 1970).

4. Morton Smith, *Jesus the Magician* (San Francisco: Harper and Row, 1978).

5. (New York: Stein and Day, 1971.) Published in English as *Rabbi J.*

6. Hugh Schonfield, *The Passover Plot: New Light on the History of Jesus* (New York: Bernard Geis Assoc., 1965).

7. Josephus, *Antiquities* III, II. 3, par. 49.

8. Joshua 3:7.

9. Ibid., 10:14.

10. J. M. Allegro, *The Dead Sea Scrolls and the Christian Myth*, p. 77.

11. *Damascus Document* V. 2-4.

12. Allegro, *The Dead Sea Scrolls and the Christian Myth*, p. 79.

13. *Assumption of Moses*, I. 16 ff.

14. *The Gospel of Philip*, Logion 19.

15. *The Essene Odyssey*, p. 37.

16. *Chronicles, Ezra, Nehemiah*, also *Psalms*.

17. *The Essene Odyssey*, pp. 10-11.

18. John Allegro, *The Dead Sea Scrolls: A Reappraisal* (London and New York: Penguin Books, 1956), p. 47.

19. Allegro, *The Dead Sea Scrolls and the Christian Myth*, p. 107.

20. See *Mysterium Coiunctionis*; also *Two Essays in Analytical Psychology*.

21. C. G. Jung, *The Spirit in Man, Art and Literature*, Collected Works, Vol. 15, par. 127.

22. Ibid., par. 128.

23. C. G. Jung, *The Structure and Dynamics of the Psyche*, Collected Works, Vol. 8, par. 417.

24. *The Gospel of Philip*, Logion 67.

25. Lucindi Frances Mooney, *Storming Eastern Temples: A Psychological Exploration of Yoga* (Wheaton, IL: Theosophical Publishing House, 1976), p. 158.

26. C. G. Jung, "A Psychological Approach to the Dogma of the Trinity," *Psychology and Religion: West and East*, Collected Works, Vol. 11, par. 295.

Chapter 4

1. (Wheaton, IL: Theosophical Publishing House, 1944), p. 6.

2. See G. Quispel, "Gnosis," in *Die Orientalischen Religionen im Römerreich*, (Leiden, Holland: E. J. Brill, 1981), p. 414.

3. Ibid., p. 419.

4. *The Book of Wisdom*, 8:3 (Duay Version).

5. Ibid., 8:2.

6. Ibid., 9:10 and 9:11.

7. *Proverbs* 1;20-22.

8. Ibid., Chapters 3 and 8.

9. Recension from "The Great Announcement," Hippolytus, Refutations, VI. 18.

10. *Gnosis als Weltreligion*; die Bedeutung der Gnosis in der Antike, (Zürich: Origo Verlag, 1972), p. 69.

11. *Hymns of Thanksgiving*, Col. VII.

12. Ibid., Col. IX.

13. *Ezechiel* I.

14. Allegro, *The Dead Sea Scrolls and the Christian Myth*, p. 99.

15. Josephus, War. II, viii, II. par. 154-55.

16. *The Gospel of Philip*, Logion 32.

17. Ibid., Logion 55.

18. *Panarion*, also *The Dead Sea Scrolls and the Christian Myth*, p. 170.

19. *Les Gnostiques* (Paris: Editions Gallimard, 1973), trans. by Stephan A. Hoeller.

Chapter 5

1. G. R. S. Mead, *Fragments of a Faith Forgotten* (New Hyde Park, NY: University Books, 1960), p. 180.

2. Hippolytus, *Refutations*, as summarized by Mead, *Fragments*, pp. 256-257.

3. Trans. by Hort. See also Mead, *Fragments*, p. 396.

4. Ibid., p. 243.
5. *Myth and Today's Consciousness* (London: Coventure Ltd., 1984), p. 67.
6. *Logion* 85:1-4.
7. *Adv. Haer.* I. 21-4.
8. Elaine Pagels, *The Gnostic Gospels* (New York: Random House, 1979), pp. xviii-ix.
9. E. S. Drower, *The Mandaeans of Iraq and Iran* (Leiden: E. J. Brill, 1962). Also E. S. Drower, Trans., *The Canonical Prayerbook of the Mandaeans,* (Leiden: E. J. Brill, 1959).
10. Robert S. Ellwood, Jr., "American Theosophical Synthesis," in *The Occult in America: New Historical Perspectives,* Howard Kerr and Charles L. Crow, eds., (Urbana and Chicago: Univ. of Illinois Press, 1983), p. 124.
11. *Ancient Wisdom Revived: A History of the Theosophical Movement* (Berkeley: University of California Press, 1980), p. vii.

Chapter 6

1. G. Quispel, "Gnosticism" in *Man, Myth and Magic: An Illustrated Encyclopaedia of the Supernatural,* Richard Cavendish, ed., (New York: Marshall Cavendish Corp., 1970), p. 1115.
2. F. C. Burkitt, *Church and Gnosis* (Cambridge, England: Cambridge Univ. Press, 1932), p. 45.
3. Hans Jonas, *Gnosis und spätantiker Geist,* Erster Teil., p. 490. Also Rudolf Bultmann, "New Testament and Mythology," *Kerygma and Myth,* Hans Werner Bastsch, ed., (New York: Harper and Bros., 1961), pp. 1-16.
4. C. G. Jung and C. Kerényi, *Essays on a Science of Mythology,* (Princeton: Bollingen Foundation and Princeton Univ. Press, 1949), pp. 22-23.
5. Joseph Campbell, *The Inner Reaches of Outer Space: Metaphor as Myth and Religion* (New York: Alfred Van Der Marck Editions, 1986), pp. 56-57.
6. Ean Begg, *Myth and Today's Consciousness,* p. 71.
7. *The Archetypes of the Collective Unconscious,* Collected Works, Vol. 9, part 1, par. 56.

Chapter 7

1. *Svetasvatara Upanishad,* 6:16.
2. *Saddharmapundarikasutra,* 7:32.
3. Al Biruni (about 1000 A.D.), *Athar ul Bakiya,* English trans. by C. E. Sachau.

4. Author's recension from several texts. C.F. *The Hymn of Jesus*, Trans. with comments by G. R. S. Mead (London: John M. Watkins, 1963), pp. 21-55.

5. The myth of the Savior here recounted has been reconstructed from the following scriptures: *The Odes of Solomon; Pistis Sophia; The Gospel of the Hebrews; The Gospel According to Thomas; The Gospel of Philip; The Gospel of Truth; The Acts of John; The Apocalypse of Peter; Oxyrynchus Papyrus; The Secret Gospel of Mark; The Gospel of the Egyptians; The Gospel of Mary; Codex Vencelliensis; Codex Sangermanensis;* as well as quotations in the writings of Irenaeus, Tertullian, and Epiphanius. The author imposed his own style on these translated materials.

6. C. G. Jung, "A Psychological Approach to the Dogma of the Trinity," *The Psychology of Religion West and East,* Collected Writings, Vol. 11, par. 233.

7. Hymn from the Greek Orthodox Menaion of the Liturgy for December 25.

8. *Adv. Haer.* I. XXI, 2.

9. *Mimaut Papyrus,* Col. V. 130.

10. Fr. Schulze-Maizier, ed. *Mystische Dichtung aus sieben Jahrhunderten* (Leipzig: n.d.), p. 78.

11. *Psychology and Alchemy,* Collected Works, Vol. 12, par. 24.

Chapter 8

1. H. P. Blavatsky, *The Secret Doctrine* (Adyar, India: Theosophical Publishing House, 1938) Vol. V, pp. 213-214.

2. For an excellent detailed exposition of the relevant content of the Book of Noah and the Books of Enoch, see Neil Forsyth, *The Old Enemy: Satan and the Combat Myth* (Princeton, NJ: Princeton University Press, 1987).

3. Josephus, *Contra Apionem,* 2, 167.

4. Schonfield, *The Essene Odyssey,* p. 137.

5. Edward Edinger, *Ego and Archetype, Individuation and the Religious Function of the Psyche* (New York: Penguin Books, 1972), p. 15.

6. Joseph Campbell, *The Hero with a Thousand Faces* (Cleveland and New York: The World Publishing Co., 1970), p. 391.

7. *The Gospel According to Thomas,* Logia 54 and 79.

Chapter 9

1. Hans Jonas, *The Gnostic Religion: The Message of the Alien*

God and the Beginnings of Christianity (Boston: Beacon Press, 1963), p. 116.
2. *The Odes of Solomon*, James H. Charlesworth, ed., (Missoula Montana: Scholar's Press, 1977), p. 94/Ode 23: Stanzas 5-9.
3. Hans Jonas, *The Gnostic Religion*, p. 125.
4. Numerous translations of "Song of the Pearl" may be recommended. For an adequate abbreviated version see H. Jonas, *The Gnostic Religion*, pp. 112-129. For a very poetic and complete rendering see Edgar Hennecke and Wilhelm Schneemelcher, eds., *New Testament Apocrypha* (Philadelphia: The Westminster Press, 1963), Vol. 2, pp. 498-504.

Chapter 10

1. First published in German under the title *Antwort auf Hiob* (Zurich: 1952) and later included in *Psychology of Religion: West and East*, Collected Works, Vol. 11.
2. Apostolic Constitution "Munificentissimus Deus," promulgated by Pope Pius XII in 1950.
3. Logion of Jesus from the *Oxyrynchus Papyrus*.
4. "Answer to Job" in *Psychology of Religion: West and East* Vol. 11., par. 758.
5. Joseph Campbell, *Myths to Live By* (New York: Bantam Books, 1975), p. i.
6. C. G. Jung, *Mysterium Coniunctionis*, Collected Works, Vol. 14, par. 788.

Chapter 11

1. *The Apocryphon of John* (two versions); *The Hypostasis of the Archons; The Gospel of the Egyptians; On the Origin of the World; The Apocalypse of Adam; The Paraphrase of Shem.*
2. *The Gospel of Truth; The Treatise on the Resurrection; The Tripartite Tractate; The Tractate of Eugnostos, the Blessed* (two versions); *The Second Treatise of the Great Seth; The Teachings of Sylvanus; The Testimony of Truth.*
3. *The Treatise of the Eighth and the Ninth; The Prayer of Thanksgiving; The Valentinian Exposition; The Three Steles of Seth; The Prayer of the Apostle Paul.*
4. *Thunder the Perfect Mind; The Thought of Norea; The Sophia of Jesus Christ; The Exegesis of the Soul.*
5. *The Apocalypse of Peter; The Letter of Peter to Philip; The Acts of Peter and the Twelve Apostles; The First and Second Apocalypse of James; The Apocalypse of Paul.*

6. *The Dialogue of the Saviour; The Book of Thomas the Contender; The Apocryphon of James; The Gospel of Philip; The Gospel of Thomas.*

7. c.f. Morton Smith, *The Secret Gospel; The Discovery and Interpretation of the Secret Gospel According to Mark* (New York: Harper and Row, 1973).

Chapter 12

1. Morton Smith, *The Secret Gospel.*
2. Plotinus, "Against the Gnostics," *Enneads,* 2.9.
3. C. G. Jung, *The Symbolic Life,* a seminar talk given on April 5, 1939. (London: Guild of Pastoral Psychology, lecture No. 80, 1954), pp. 8-9.
4. Ibid.
5. Irenaeus, *Adv. Haer.* 121.5.ff.

Chapter 13

1. F. L. Cross, Ed. and trans. *The Jung Codex: A Newly Discovered Gnostic Papyrus.* Three Studies by H. C. Puech, G. Quispel, W. C. van Unnik (London: A. R. Mowbray Co., 1955), p. 43.
2. Ibid., p. 53.
3. C.f. Elaine Pagels, *The Gnostic Gospels* (New York: Random House, 1979), p. 95.
4. C. G. Jung, *Psychology and Religion: West and East,* Collected Works, Vol. 11, par. 148.

Epilogue

1. Transcript of *Matter of Heart,* biographical motion picture on Jung (Los Angeles: C. G. Jung Institute, 1983), pp. 25-26.
2. C. G. Jung, *Aion,* Collected Works, Vol. 9, Part 2, par. 76.
3. Dennis Stillings, "Invasion of the Archetypes," in *Gnosis: A Journal of the Western Inner Traditions,* No. 10. (Winter 1989), p. 33.
4. Gerhard Adler, *Psychology and the Atom Bomb* (London: The Guild of Pastoral Psychology, Guild Lecture No. 43, 1946), p. 3.
5. C. G. Jung, *Uber die Psychologie des Unbewussten* (Zurich: 1943), as translated by Gerhard Adler in *Psychology and the Atom Bomb,* p. 15.
6. (London, Faber & Faber, 1945), p. 95.
7. Gerhard Adler, *Psychology and the Atom Bomb,* p. 17.

8. Dennis Overbye, "The Shadow Universe," *Discover*, May 1985, p. 13ff.

9. John P. Dourley, *The Illness that We Are* (Toronto: Inner City Books, 1984), p. 82.

10. C. G. Jung, *Psychology and Alchemy*, Collected Works, Vol. 12, pars. 9-10.

11. *The Gospel According to Thomas*, Logion 22.

Note: The Collected Works of C. G. Jung, trans. by R. F. C. Hull, in entirety constitutes No. XX in Bollingen Series, published by Princeton University Press between 1960 and 1979.

Index

QUEST BOOKS
are published by
The Theosophical Society in America,
Wheaton, Illinois 60189-0270,
a branch of a world fellowship,
a membership organization
dedicated to the promotion of the unity of
humanity and the encouragement of the study of
religion, philosophy, and science, to the end that
we may better understand ourselves and our place in
the universe. The Society stands for complete
freedom of individual search and belief.
For further information about its activities,
write, call 1-800-669-1571, e-mail olcott@theosophia.org,
or consult its Web page: http//www.theosophical.org

The Theosophical Publishing House
is aided by the generous support of
THE KERN FOUNDATION,
a trust established by Herbert A. Kern
and dedicated to Theosophical education.